Caring for Infants and Toddlers

A Supervised, Self-Instructional Training Program

Volume I

Diane Trister Dodge

Amy Laura Dombro

Derry Gosselin Koralek

Teaching Strategies, Inc.

Washington, DC

Updates to Module 1 (Safe) and Module 2 (Healthy) © 2003

Teaching Strategies, Inc.
P.O. Box 42243
Washington, DC 20015
ISBN 1-879537-01-X
LCCN 91-65115

Printed and bound in the United States of America
Seventh Printing: 2003

Acknowledgments

This training program is based on several previous efforts. It draws from our publications and experiences in providing training and developing materials for child care and other early childhood settings. The primary basis for this publication is a training program we developed for the U.S. Navy and the U.S. Army Child Development Services Programs. Carolee Callen, Head of the Navy Child Development Services Branch, originally conceived the idea of a standardized, self-instructional training program for child care staff. In 1986, the Navy contracted with Creative Associates, International, Inc., a Washington, DC-based consulting firm where we then worked, to create a training program and train child care center directors in its implementation. M.-A. Lucas, Chief of the Child Development Services Division in the U.S. Army, funded an adaptation to support CDA training in Army Child Development Centers. We are indebted to these two individuals, their headquarters staff, and the staff at Navy and Army child development centers who reviewed all drafts of the materials developed under this contract and whose constructive suggestions greatly improved the program.

Caring for Infants and Toddlers combines both sets of materials developed for the military along with revisions and updates reflecting our experiences using them in real-life settings.

We wish to acknowledge many people for their contributions to this effort. Our first thanks go to several individuals who assisted us in developing the original materials for military child care settings. Peter Pizzolongo made substantial contributions to the content and format of the modules. We also benefitted in many ways from Dr. Jenni Klein's expert review and advice. Marilyn Goldhammer and Cynthia Prather each contributed to the original modules; Creative and Professionalism, respectively.

In preparing the new version, we were assisted by several educators whose experience and knowledge added validity and depth. Dr. Catherine New, a skilled trainer and center director in Bethel, Alaska, reviewed each module. Her content and format recommendations greatly enhanced the materials applicability to different cultural settings. Dr. Joan Lombardi reviewed the training materials from the perspective of the Child Development Associate (CDA) Competency Standards. Her guidance was particularly useful in ensuring that the materials are consistent with the profession's standards for caregiver competencies. Finally, Dr. Abbey Griffin carefully read the draft and gave additions and comments.

The production of this document required the specialized expertise of several dedicated individuals. Martha Cooley edited the manuscript, Elisabeth G. Hudgins designed the layout, Jennifer Barrett O'Connell designed the cover, and Frank Harvey coordinated production. We are indebted to each of them for their substantial contributions. We also appreciate the work of Rachel Friedlander Tickner (editing) and Terri Rue-Woods (production) on the 2003 updates.

Finally, we want to acknowledge the many caregivers and trainers from whom we have learned a great deal over the years we worked together. We have undoubtedly adapted and expanded on many of their excellent ideas; this training program is richer as a result.

We hope that *Caring for Infants and Toddlers* will support the important roles of caregivers and trainers and that its implementation in centers across the country will impact positively on the quality of child development programs and the care of young children and their families.

Contents

Orientation

Welcome to a unique and personalized training program designed to help you acquire or enhance the skills and knowledge you need to provide high-quality care for infants and toddlers. Whether you are new to the profession of early childhood or are someone with years of experience, this training program offers practical information on topics central to caring for young children.

How the Training Program Can Help You

Working with infants and toddlers is a rewarding profession, one in which you can grow and continually feel challenged. In order to help children grow and develop, you must understand child development and how to support children's learning. The more skills and knowledge you acquire, the more rewarding your work will be.

As an adult, you bring years of experience to the task of caring for children under 3 years old. As you go through the training program, you will find that you already have many skills that are addressed in the modules. *Caring for Infants and Toddlers* will enable you to extend and expand on your existing skills and knowledge. It will help you become a more competent caregiver. As a result, you will find caring for young children to be more and more rewarding.

The training program is organized around the Child Development Associate (CDA) Competency Standards of the Council for Professional Recognition (the Council). The goal of the CDA program is to promote professional development and recognition for caregivers who work with young children. Completing *Caring for Infants and Toddlers* is an important step in acquiring the skills you need to receive a CDA credential from the Council. You will be acquiring or enhancing skills and knowledge in the 13 CDA functional areas. Each of the individual modules of *Caring for Infants and Toddlers* addresses one of these areas. Definitions of the 13 CDA functional areas appear at the end of this orientation section.

After you have completed all the modules and demonstrated your competence in the classroom, your trainer can help you prepare for the assessment process leading to a CDA credential.

How Children Will Benefit

You play a very important role in the lives of the children in your program. The quality of the care you provide can benefit these children now and in the future. Good child development programs can enhance a child's ability to learn, to communicate ideas and feelings, and to get along well with others.

The infants and toddlers you care for come from many different kinds of family situations. Some come from stable homes where they have received the love and nurturing care that all children need in order to grow and develop to their full potential. Others come from less stable homes where parents are struggling to provide for their family's physical and emotional needs. The stresses on many families can be overwhelming. As a result, children do not always receive the love and care they need. These children are particularly at risk. They may be angry, hurt, or withdrawn. They doubt their own abilities and sometimes feel unloved.

You can make a real difference in these children's lives. By providing a high-quality program and developing a partnership with parents, you can help all children succeed.

What Makes the Training Program Unique

Caring for Infants and Toddlers has several features that make it unique and particularly appropriate for caregivers currently working with young children.

- Caregivers receive their own set of materials that become their personal resource and journal for working with infants and toddlers.

- The materials are appropriate for new as well as experienced caregivers.

- The training program is individualized; caregivers work independently, on their own schedule, and at their own pace.

- There is no set order to follow. Because the CDA functional areas are so closely related to one another, caregivers can begin with a module that interests them most or with one they feel will help them the most and set their own schedule.

- The information presented in the modules is practical and immediately applicable to everyday responsibilities. Caregivers using the modules apply what they learn in their daily work with young children.

How the Training Program Works

When you have completed this orientation section, your next step will be to take the self-assessment. This is not a test. It will introduce you to the major topics covered in each module and help you decide what modules you want to work on first. You will use the results of the self-assessment to help you identify the first three modules you want to complete. Together with your trainer you will review the results of the self-assessment and develop a schedule for working on the modules. You may decide that you wish to begin with Module 1, Safe, and continue through all the modules in order. You could also decide to begin with a module that particularly interests you precisely because you feel you already have acquired many of the relevant skills. Or you might prefer to begin with a module that addresses a training need you have identified in your self-assessment.

In completing each of the modules, you will follow a consistent sequence of steps. These steps are described below.

- **Complete the Overview**

  The Overview introduces and defines the topic addressed in the module. It explains why the topic is important and gives concrete examples of how caregivers demonstrate their competence in that functional area. You will read three short situations and answer questions to help you learn more about the topic. The last activity in the section gives you an opportunity to apply the topic to your own experiences as an adult.

- **Take the Pre-Training Assessment**

  The pre-training assessment is a two- to three-page list of key skills that caregivers should possess in each area. You will read each one and indicate whether you do these things regularly, sometimes, or not enough. After completing the assessment, you will identify three to five skills you wish to improve or topics you wish to learn more about. You will then discuss this assessment with your trainer.

- **Complete Each Learning Activity**

  Each module has four to seven learning activities. These activities begin with objectives—what you will learn—and several pages of information about the topic. After completing the reading, you will have an opportunity to apply the information. This may involve responding to questions, trying out suggestions you have read, and noting your observations of children. When you have completed each learning activity, you will arrange a time to meet with your trainer to discuss the activity and to receive feedback.

- **Summarize Your Progress**

  After you have completed all the learning activities in the module, you will be asked to review the pre-training assessment and write a brief summary of what you have learned and the skills you feel you have acquired. You will then meet with your trainer to review your progress and to determine whether you have successfully completed all the learning activities.

- **Complete the Assessment Process**

  Your trainer will give you the knowledge assessment and the competency assessment. On the knowledge assessment, you must achieve a score of 80 percent before going on to a new module. Your trainer will observe you working with children to assess your competence in the functional area.

Before You Begin

Take a few minutes to review the glossary of terms that follows this page. This will familiarize you with words and phrases that are used throughout the modules. The glossary is followed by a list of suggested readings on caring for infants and toddlers. These resources may be in your center library, or you may want to collect some for your own professional library. When you are ready, take the self-assessment and begin planning your own training.

Glossary

Child development

All the stages of growth of a child, including cognitive, physical, emotional, and social growth.

Child Development Associate (CDA)

A person who has been assessed by the Council for Professional Recognition and judged to be a competent early childhood professional.

CDA Credentialing Program

The process established by the Council to assess the competence of caregivers. Assessment and credentialing are based on performance in 13 functional areas. The CDA Credential is accepted by the early childhood profession nationwide.

Competencies

Those tasks, skills, attitudes, and values that are needed to provide high-quality child care for children. Competencies differ from knowledge in that competencies describe a caregiver's actions and performance.

Competency assessments

The performance-based section of the assessment process of *Caring for Infants and Toddlers*. For the competency assessments, caregivers will demonstrate their skills while working with young children.

Developmentally appropriate

Reflecting children's basic patterns of social, emotional, cognitive, and physical development; referring to an environment, daily routines, interactions, and activities that meet the needs of children at their stage of development.

Environment

The physical space, including furniture and materials, in which care is provided.

Functional Areas

The 13 CDA functional areas describe the major tasks or functions that a caregiver must complete in order to carry out a competency goal. Each module in this training program addresses a CDA functional area.

Knowledge assessment

The paper-and-pencil exercises of the assessment process of *Caring for Infants and Toddlers*, testing the caregiver's knowledge of the concepts presented in the module.

Mobile infants*

Children from 9 to 17 months old.

_____

*Age description as given by the Council for Professional Recognition (Washington, DC).

Observation	The act of systematically watching what a child says and does during everyday activities. Its purpose is to learn more about that child in order to plan activities that reflect the child's needs, strengths, and interests.
Pre-training assessment	Used at the beginning of each module by the caregiver and the trainer to identify what skills the caregiver has and where more training is needed.
Toddlers*	Children from 18 to 36 months old.
Young infants*	Children up to 8 months old.

---

*Age description as given by the Council for Professional Recognition (Washington, DC).

Functional Areas of the Child Development Associate Competency Standards*

Safe

Provide a safe environment to prevent and reduce injuries.

Healthy

Promote good health and nutrition and provide an environment that contributes to the prevention of illness.

Learning Environment

Use space, relationships, materials, and routines as resources for constructing an interesting, secure, and enjoyable environment that encourages play, exploration, and learning.

Physical

Provide a variety of equipment, activities, and opportunities to promote the physical development of children.

Cognitive

Provide activities and opportunities that encourage curiosity, exploration, and problem solving appropriate to the developmental levels and learning styles of children.

Communication

Communicate with children and provide opportunities and support for children to understand, acquire, and use verbal and nonverbal means of communicating thoughts and feelings.

Creative

Provide opportunities that stimulate children to play with sound, rhythm, language, materials, space, and ideas in individual ways to express their creative abilities.

---

*Council for Professional Recognition (Washington, DC).

Functional Areas of the Child Development Associate Competency Standards

Self

Provide physical and emotional security for each child and help each child to know, accept, and take pride in himself or herself and to develop a sense of independence.

Social

Help each child to feel accepted in the group, help children learn to communicate and get along with others, and encourage feelings of empathy and mutual respect among children and adults.

Guidance

Provide a supportive environment in which children can begin to learn and practice appropriate and acceptable behaviors as individuals and as a group.

Families

Maintain an open, friendly, and cooperative relationship with each child's family, encourage their involvement in the program, and support the child's relationship with his or her family.

Program Management

Use all available resources to ensure an effective operation.

Professionalism

Make decisions based on knowledge of early childhood theories and practices, promote quality in child care services, and take advantage of opportunities to improve competence both for personal and professional growth and for the benefit of children and families.

References

The following resources offer additional insight about developing quality programs for infants and toddlers. Write or phone for further information.

Caring for Infants & Toddlers in Groups: Developmentally Appropriate Practice
J. Ronald Lally, Abbey Griffin, Emily Fenichel, Marilyn Segal, Eleanor Szanton, and Bernice Weissbourd (1995). This book is a guide to the special knowledge and program design necessary to address the unique developmental characteristics of children in the first three years of life. (Available from Zero to Three: National Center for Infants, Toddlers and Families, 734 15th Street NW, Suite 1000, Washington, DC 20005-1013.)

The Creative Curriculum for Infants & Toddlers, Rev. ed.
Amy Laura Dombro, Laura J. Colker, and Diane Trister Dodge (1997, 1999). A comprehensive yet easy-to-use framework for planning and implementing a developmentally appropriate program. Designed for use in both center-based and family child care settings, it emphasizes that relationships between caregivers/teachers and children and families are the focus of curriculum for very young children. (Available from Teaching Strategies, Inc., PO Box 42243, Washington, DC 20015, 800-637-3652.)

Developmentally Appropriate Practice in Early Childhood Programs, Rev. ed.
Sue Bredekamp and Carol Copple (Eds.) (1997). This revised edition of the industry standard on appropriate practices devotes a chapter to exploring the needs and appropriate caregiving responses to children from birth through age three. (Available from NAEYC, 1509 16th Street NW, Washington, DC 20036-1426, 800-424-2460.)

Infants, Toddlers and Caregivers
Janet Gonzalez-Mena and Dianne Widmeyer Eyer (1997). This book gives a wonderful overview of infant-toddler development and quality infant-toddler child care. It emphasizes respect for the individual child and helps caregivers focus on the relationships they build with children. It addresses multicultural issues facing caregivers, such as bilingual communication and culturally appropriate curriculum. (Available from Mayfield Publishing Company, 1280 Villa Street, Mountain View, CA 94041.)

PrimeTimes: A Handbook for Excellence in Infant and Toddler Programs
Jim Greenman and Anne Stonehouse (1996). This book helps readers understand the needs of children under three, and their families and caregivers, and how to use this information to create a quality program. (Available from Redleaf Press, 450 N. Syndicate, Suite 5, St. Paul, MN 55104-4125, 800-423-8309.)

Setting Up for Infant/Toddler Care: Guidelines for Centers and Family Child Care Homes, Rev. ed.
San Fernando Valley Child Care Consortium, A. Godwin and L. Schrag, Co-Chairs. Starting a program for babies and toddlers? These experts describe how to work with parents, keep children safe and healthy, and promote all areas of their development. Includes job descriptions, staffing schedules, budgets, and discussion of family child care systems and satellite child care homes. Also includes new material on business aspects of setting up a program and serving children with special needs. (Available from NAEYC, 1509 16th Street NW, Washington, DC 20036-1426, 800-424-2460.)

Related References

Promoting Health and Safety

American Red Cross Child Care Course: Health and Safety Units
The American National Red Cross and the American Academy of Pediatrics (1990). This multimedia package provides in-depth training for caregivers on infant and child care first aid, as well as preventing childhood injuries. (Available from American Red Cross National Headquarters, 2025 E Street NW, Washington, DC 20006.)

Caring for Our Children: National Health and Safety Performance Standards: Guidelines for Out-of-Home Child Care (2nd ed.)
American Academy of Pediatrics, American Public Health Association, and National Resource Center for Health and Safety in Child Care (2002).
This definitive statement on safety standards can serve well as a reference in every infant and toddler program. (Available from the American Academy of Pediatrics, 888-227-1770, or the American Public Health Association, 301-893-1894.)

The Consumer Reports Guide to Baby Products (5th ed., 1997.)
This report provides ratings of thoroughly tested childproofing products and child gates. It includes warnings on products judged not acceptable. (Available from Consumer Reports Books, 101 Truman Avenue, New York, NY 10703, 515-237-4903, reference # P664.)

First Aid for Children Fast
The Johns Hopkins Children's Center (1995). This user-friendly manual gives step by step instructions that are easy to understand and follow. Color photographs illustrate each step. This book is an excellent resource for preparing emergency plans. (Available from Dorling Kindersley Publishing, 95 Madison Avenue, New York, NY 10016.) Additional information on the Johns Hopkins Children's Center may be obtained from their Office for Public Affairs at 410-955-8662.

Starting Point: How To Open Your Program (and Your Heart) to Children with Special Health Needs
Division of Maternal and Child Health, Graduate School of Public Health, San Diego State University (1993). This helpful manual provides guidance on providing services for children with health and/or physical challenges, developing culturally competent services, ensuring

confidentiality, preventing childhood injuries, preventing the spread of communicable diseases, providing play experiences, and dealing with challenging behaviors. A Spanish version, Punto de Partido, is available. (Available from National Maternal and Child Health Clearinghouse, 2070 Chain Bridge Road, Suite 450, Vienna, VA 22182-2536.)

Creating a Welcoming Environment

Caring Spaces, Learning Places: Children's Environments That Work
Jim Greenman (1988). This excellent book shows how to create environments that make use of space creatively, with attention to children's developmental needs. A separate chapter on infant and toddler environments includes wonderful ideas illustrated with photographs and diagrams of indoor and outdoor spaces. (Available from Exchange Press, Inc., PO Box 2890, Redmond, WA 98073.)

Landscapes for Learning: Designing Group Care Environments for Infants, Toddlers and Two Year Olds
Louis Torelli and Charles Durrett (1996). This excellent handbook on designing developmentally appropriate learning environments for infants and toddlers merges the principles of child development with architectural design. (Available from Torelli-Durrett, 1250 Addison Street, Suite 113, Berkeley, CA 94702.)

Play and Social Development

Anti-Bias Curriculum: Tools for Empowerment
Louise Derman-Sparks and the A.B.C. Task Force (1989). This classic on the subject of multiculturalism provides guidance on selecting materials for children that eliminate barriers based on race, culture, gender, age, or ability. (Available from NAEYC, 1509 16th Street NW, Washington, DC 20036-1426, 800-424-2460.)

Behavior Guidance for Infants and Toddlers
Alice S. Honig (1996). In simple and vivid language, this book offers caregivers and parents positive discipline techniques that are appropriate for infants and toddlers. Tips for thinking about fusses and "disobedience" will be useful for adults puzzled by such behaviors. (Available from Southern Early Childhood Association, P.O. Box 56130, Little Rock, AR 72215-6130, 501-663-0353.)

Creative Expression and Play in the Early Childhood Curriculum
Joan P. Isenberg and Mary Renck Jalongo (1993). Grounded in the authors' experiences teaching teachers, this book offers strategies and activities to stimulate readers' ideas of ways to promote the play and creativity of young children. (Available from Macmillan Publishing Company, 366 Third Avenue, New York, NY 10022.)

Play Is a Child's World: A Lekotek Resource Guide on Play for Children with Disabilities for Families, Friends, and Professionals
The National Lekotek Center (n.d.) The 51 Lekotek Centers throughout the United States provide support, resources, and toys to families of children with disabilities. This guide, and

appropriate adaptive toys for children with disabilities. (Available from National Lekotek Center, 2100 Ridge Avenue, Evanston, IL 60201, 800-366-7529.)

The Right Stuff for Children Birth to 8: Selecting Play Materials to Support Development
Martha B. Bronson (1995). This comprehensive manual is an excellent resource for selecting toys to match the developmental skills of children. Careful consideration is given to safety issues. (Available from NAEYC, 1509 16th Street NW, Washington, DC 20036-1426, 800-424-2460.)

Communication

Emerging Literacy: Linking Social Competence and Learning
Derry Koralek for Aspen Systems Corporation (1997). This excellent guide, targeted to teachers and other educators, provides background information and training ideas on making children partners in conversation, the magic world of reading, and setting the stage for literacy. (Available from the Head Start Bureau, Administration for Children and Families, U.S. Department of Health and Human Services, Washington, DC 20447.)

Much More Than the ABCs: The Early Stages of Reading and Writing
Judith A. Schickendanz (1999). This standard in the field traces the development of literacy skills which begin at birth. It describes ways to maximize the reading experience for children throughout the early childhood years. (Available from NAEYC, 1509 16th Street NW, Washington, DC 20036-1426, 800-424-2460.)

Reading Right from the Start: What Parents Can Do in the First Five Years
Toni S. Bickart and Diane Trister Dodge (2000). Washington, DC: Teaching Strategies. This easy-to-read, richly illustrated booklet shows parents how they can give their children (birth-age 5) the literacy experiences that lead to the language and literacy skills necessary to become readers and writers. The book focuses on everyday routines to demonstrate how to build vocabulary, learn about conversations, and discover meaning from the written word. (Available from Teaching Strategies, Inc. P.O. Box 42243, Washington, DC 20015, 800-637-3652.)

Talking with Your Baby: Family as the First School
Alice S. Honig and Harriet E. Brophy (1996). Caregivers and parents will appreciate the ideas for using "turn-talking-talk" to enhance their daily interactions with very young children. Many photos illustrate how tuned-in talk can enrich affectionate relationships and promote early learning. Diapering, bath time, shopping trips, and other ordinary routines become opportunities to increase language power. (Available from Syracuse University Press, 1600 Jamesville Avenue, Syracuse, NY 13244, 315-443-5541.)

Working with Families

Getting Men Involved: Strategies for Early Childhood Programs
James A. Levine, Dennis T. Murphy, and Sherill Wilson (1993). This book offers practical suggestions for ways to welcome and involve the men in the lives of the children in your program. (Available from Scholastic, Inc., 555 Broadway, New York, NY 10012.)

Sharing the Caring
Amy Laura Dombro and Patty Bryan (1991). Parents and caregivers are encouraged to be aware of their feelings about sharing the care of infants and toddlers. The authors offer practical suggestions of ways to build partnerships that will help children feel safe and secure in child care. (New York: Simon & Schuster)

Six Stages of Parenthood
Ellen Galinsky (1987). As it describes the stages of parenthood, this book reminds readers that parents are growing and developing too. (Available from Addison-Wesley Longman Publishing Company, One Jacob Way, Reading, MA 08167.)

Communities: Building a Network of Support

Community Mobilization: Strategies to Support Young Children and Their Families
Amy Laura Dombro, Nina Sazer O'Donnell, Ellen Galinsky, Sarah Gilkeson Melcher, and Abby Farber (1996). This guide includes detailed descriptions of hundreds of community collaborations throughout the country that have as their goal improving the lives of young children and their families. It takes the reader through the practical steps of creating change and offers tips and lessons learned, thus allowing communities to build on what others have done. (Available from Families and Work Institute, 330 Seventh Avenue, 14th Floor, New York, NY 10001.)

Program Management, Advocacy, and Professionalism

Advocates in Action: Making a Difference for Young Children
Adele Robinson and Deborah R. Stark (2002). This practical guide helps demystify advocacy by providing practical ideas and examples of how to influence policies for young children, families, and the early childhood profession. (Available from NAEYC, 1509 16th Street NW, Washington, DC 20036-1426, 800-424-2460.)

The What, Why, and How of High-Quality Early Childhood Education: A Guide for On-Site Supervision, Rev. ed.
Derry G. Koralek, Laura J. Colker, and Diane Trister Dodge (1995). An invaluable tool for the director/supervisor striving to identify what aspects of an early childhood program need improvement, this book gives staff feedback that *really* alters their practice. It is equally useful in helping teachers or caregivers take a thoughtful look at their own practices. Used in college courses, the book's detailed descriptions of what you should see in a quality early childhood program and why offers students a strong foundation of child development knowledge and of principles translated into practice. (Available from Teaching Strategies, Inc., PO Box 42243, Washington, DC 20015, 800-637-3652.)

Self-Assessment

SKILL	I DO THIS REGULARLY	I DO THIS SOMETIMES	I DON'T DO THIS ENOUGH
SAFE			
a. Providing safe indoor and outdoor environments.			
b. Responding to injuries and emergencies.			
c. Helping infants and toddlers begin to develop safe habits.			
HEALTHY			
a. Providing healthy indoor and outdoor environments.			
b. Helping infants and toddlers develop good health habits.			
c. Recognizing and reporting child abuse and neglect.			
LEARNING ENVIRONMENT			
a. Organizing indoor and outdoor areas that encourage play and exploration.			
b. Selecting and arranging appropriate materials and equipment that foster growth and learning.			

SKILL	I DO THIS REGULARLY	I DO THIS SOMETIMES	I DON'T DO THIS ENOUGH
c. Planning and implementing a schedule and routines that respond to the needs of children under 3.			
PHYSICAL a. Reinforcing and encouraging physical development.			
b. Providing equipment and opportunities for gross motor development.			
c. Providing equipment and opportunities for fine motor development.			
COGNITIVE a. Providing opportunities for infants and toddlers to use all their senses to explore their environment.			
b. Interacting with infants and toddlers in ways that promote their confidence and curiosity.			
c. Providing opportunities for infants and toddlers to develop new concepts and skills.			
COMMUNICATION a. Interacting with infants and toddlers in ways that encourage them to communicate their thoughts and feelings in appropriate ways.			

SKILL	I DO THIS REGULARLY	I DO THIS SOMETIMES	I DON'T DO THIS ENOUGH
b. Providing materials and activities that promote communication skills.			
c. Helping infants and toddlers develop listening and speaking skills.			
CREATIVE a. Arranging the learning environment to support creativity.			
b. Offering a variety of activities and experiences to promote creativity.			
c. Interacting with infants and toddlers in ways that encourage creative expression.			
SELF a. Developing a trusting and supportive relationship with each child.			
b. Helping infants and toddlers accept and appreciate themselves and others.			
c. Providing infants and toddlers with opportunities to feel successful and competent.			
SOCIAL a. Helping infants and toddlers learn to get along with others.			

SKILL	I DO THIS REGULARLY	I DO THIS SOMETIMES	I DON'T DO THIS ENOUGH
b. Helping infants and toddlers understand and express their feelings and respect those of others.			
c. Providing an environment and experiences that support social development.			
GUIDANCE a. Providing an environment that encourages self-discipline.			
b. Using positive methods to guide each child's behavior.			
c. Helping infants and toddlers understand and express their feelings in acceptable ways.			
FAMILIES a. Communicating with family members often to exchange information about their child at home and at the center.			
b. Providing a variety of ways for family members to participate in the child's life at the center.			
c. Providing support to families.			
PROGRAM MANAGEMENT a. Observing and recording information about each child's growth and development.			

SKILL	I DO THIS REGULARLY	I DO THIS SOMETIMES	I DON'T DO THIS ENOUGH
b. Working as a member of a team to plan an individualized program.			
c. Following administrative policies.			
PROFESSIONALISM a. Continually assessing one's own performance.			
b. Continuing to learn about caring for infants and toddlers.			
c. Applying professional ethics at all times.			

Module Completion Plan

Review your responses to the self-assessment with your trainer. What do you feel are your strengths, interests, and needs? Decide which areas you would like to work on first. Select three modules to begin with and set target dates for their completion. (Your trainer can let you know how much work is involved for each module.) Record the module titles and target completion dates below. You may also wish to determine a tentative schedule for completing *Caring for Infants and Toddlers*.

Module	Target Completion Date
1. _____	_____
2. _____	_____
3. _____	_____

Tentative schedule for completion of the *Caring for Infants and Toddlers* Training Program.

Module	Date
_____	_____
_____	_____
_____	_____
_____	_____
_____	_____
_____	_____
_____	_____
_____	_____
_____	_____
_____	_____
_____	_____
_____	_____

_____	_____		_____	_____
Caregiver	Date		Trainer	Date

Module 1
Safe

What Is Safety and Why Is It Important?

Safety is freedom from danger, and danger is minimized by reducing hazards. You feel safe when you know that:

- no great harm will come to you;

- you can do something to prevent dangerous situations; and

- those around you share your concern for safety and act cautiously.

Adults feel safe when they are in control of situations. They are in control when they prevent injuries and emergencies, and when they know what to do if injuries and emergencies occur.

Children begin to learn about safety from the time they are infants. They learn how it feels to be safe as their parents and other important adults protect them from danger. Over time they gain confidence in themselves and the world as they see that their adults know what to do when injuries occur. Eventually children will learn how to explore their world in safe ways and stay free from danger.

The infants and toddlers you care for depend on you to keep them safe. Children under 3 are too young to know about and avoid the possible dangers in their environment. Therefore, you have the responsibility of setting up a room that is free from dangers or reduces them for crawling infants and tumbling toddlers.

Through your actions you help young children develop attitudes about safety and begin learning how to keep themselves safe. As you share your concern about safety, for example, by explaining that Sharon (11 months) must stay seated in her highchair so she will be safe and won't fall, you are telling children that their safety is something you value. This helps make it important to them, too. By practicing safety measures such as taping down the edge of a carpet so no one trips, you are modeling how to live safely. This helps young children—who want to be like their important adults—begin making safety part of their lives. Your handling of emergencies in a calm manner says to children that situations can be managed even when trouble arises.

Keeping children safe involves:

- providing safe indoor and outdoor environments;

- responding to injuries and emergencies; and

- helping infants and toddlers begin to develop safe habits.

Listed below are examples of how caregivers demonstrate their competence in keeping infants and toddlers safe.

Providing Safe Indoor and Outdoor Environments

Here are some examples of what caregivers can do.

- Check indoor and outdoor areas for debris, poisonous materials, sharp objects, and any other dangerous objects. Remove any you find.

- Check the room daily to be sure all electrical outlets are covered.

- Check materials and equipment daily for broken parts or jagged edges and make sure they are repaired or replaced.

- Arrange the room to allow for clear fire exits.

- Supervise children at all times.

- Respond quickly to infants and toddlers in distress.

- Take safety precautions in a calm and reassuring manner without overprotecting children or making them fearful.

Responding to Injuries and Emergencies

Here are some examples of what caregivers can do.

- Help develop and post injury and emergency procedures.

- Know and follow established emergency procedures.

- Know where to find parents' emergency telephone numbers.

- Follow established procedures for conducting children to safety during fire and other hazard drills and in real emergencies, should they occur.

Helping Infants and Toddlers Begin to Develop Safe Habits

Here are some examples of what caregivers can do.

- Convey to children in actions and words that the center is a safe place and that they will be protected. "Johnny, I'll stand next to the slide if it will help you feel better about going down."

- Be there to remind children of safety rules. "Susan, let me help you crawl back onto the rug. If you crawl by the door, you might get hurt."

- Teach children how to observe safety rules on neighborhood walks. "Hold my hand when we cross the street."

- Use positive guidance techniques to keep children safe. "That hurts Teresa when you hit her with the spoon. Let me show you how to use your spoon to bang on the pots and pans."

Keeping Children Safe

In the following situations, caregivers are ensuring children's safety. As you read each one, think about what the caregivers are doing and why. Then answer the questions that follow.

Providing Safe Indoor and Outdoor Environments

Ms. Lewis gasps. Jill (14 months) is across the room, climbing on a box where balls are kept. It is sagging with her weight. "Ms. Gonzalez," Ms. Lewis says, alerting the caregiver on that side of the room. In a flash, Ms. Gonzalez is there. "Jill," she says in a calm voice. "I'm going to help you climb down off that box. It isn't a safe place for climbing, because it isn't strong enough to hold you." Jill looks startled as she finds her feet on the ground. "You know what?" Ms. Gonzalez explains, "I am going to put this box in the closet so children won't climb on it. Do you want to help me?" As they carry the box, Ellen (15 months) comes to help. "Thank you for helping make our room safer," says Ms. Gonzalez. The children smile proudly. "Now, would you like to climb on the climber? It's a good place for climbing."

1. How did Ms. Lewis and Ms. Gonzalez work together to make the center a safe place?

Ms Lewis alerted Ms G, who was closet to the child in a calm manner. Ms. G. that helped the child down and encouraged the child to help put the box away with an explanation.

2. What do you think Jill learned from this experience?

Climbing on things not intended to be climbed on can be dangerous.

Responding to Injuries and Emergencies

The fire alarm rings throughout the center. In the infant room Ms. Bates and Ms. Jackson stop what they are doing and begin gathering the children for the monthly fire drill. According to their established procedure, Ms. Bates picks up the mobile infants and places them in one of the two rolling cribs—the ones marked with the safety symbols. She calmly tells the children that they are going to go outside for a few minutes. Ms. Jackson picks up the younger infants and places them in the other rolling crib. One of the infants starts to cry. "I'll have to help you in a minute, Megan," she says, "as soon as we're all outside where it's safe." Each caregiver checks the attendance list to make sure they have all of the children. They push the cribs to the door. Ms. Bates holds the door open for Ms. Jackson to roll her crib through, then Ms.

Jackson does the same as Ms. Bates rolls her crib through the door and outside. When they are all outside, the two caregivers roll the cribs away from the building to a safe place on the grass. Ms. Jackson looks at her watch and says, "I think we beat our own record this time." She picks up Megan, who is still crying, and comforts her while Ms. Bates plays a game of "peek-a-boo" with the mobile infants. The caregivers and infants wait outside until the center director gives them the all-clear signal.

1. **How did Ms. Jackson and Ms. Bates know what to do when the fire bell sounded?**

   This was a monthly fire drill, practiced

2. **Why did Ms. Jackson wait to comfort the crying infant?**

   Ms. Jackson knows in a fire or fire
   timing is of the important.

Helping Infants and Toddlers Begin to Develop Safe Habits

Two-year-old Kirsten has recently learned to balance the cardboard blocks, one on top of the other until they fall down. Today she builds a tower with the blocks. "Me knock down," she says as she pushes her tower to the ground. The blocks fall and hit her and several other children in the area. They all protest. Ms. Moore walks over. "I know it's fun to knock down the blocks, Kirsten, but you have to be careful not to hurt anyone. We have to make sure that this is a safe place for all the children. Let's talk about how to knock down the tower safely," she says. She helps Kirsten build another block tower. Ms. Moore says, "We'll look around to make sure nobody is in the way. Then we will tell everyone the tower is coming down." They ask the children standing nearby to move back from the tower. Then Kirsten knocks down the tower. This time nobody gets hurt.

1. **How did Ms. Moore let Kirsten and the other children know that the center is a safe place?**

   By talking about making sure everyone is
   safely away from the table before knocking the
   blocks and demonstrating it.

2. How were the children learning to keep themselves safe?

By   moving   away   from the   table

Compare your answers with those on the answer sheet at the end of this module. If your answers are different, discuss them with your trainer. There can be more than one good answer.

Your Own Need for Safety

Safety is a basic need we all share. We particularly want to feel safe in our own environments —where we live and work. When we know that we are protected from harm, we feel more confident and able to focus fully on what we are doing. When we do not feel protected, we are fearful and anxious.

When you are in charge of your environment, you can make it a safe one. You probably have experienced times when you were doing something that was potentially dangerous, and you did things to make that activity safer. Do you remember times when you:

- climbed a ladder while someone held it to keep it stable;

- drove a car slowly on a slippery road; or

- carefully unplugged a lamp with a frayed cord and had the wiring replaced?

You have learned about safety through experience. When you were a child, the important adults in your life controlled your environment to keep it safe. They helped you develop an attitude and habits concerning safety. As you grew older, they helped you learn what you could do to minimize dangerous situations.

1. **Think of a situation where you didn't feel safe and describe it below.**

   When taking the train, I didn't feel safe on the platform close to the edge.

2. **What did you want to happen?**

   Maybe a rail or gate up until the train arrived.

3. **What can you learn from this experience that will help you keep young children safe?**

   To gate off areas that platforms or edges on them for the children

As you work through this module, you will learn how to set up and maintain a safe environment. Safety is important in all areas of child development—whether you are guiding children's learning, building their self-esteem, or promoting their self-discipline. Keeping children safe is one of your most important responsibilities.

When you have finished this overview section, you should complete the pre-training assessment. Refer to the glossary at the end of this module if you need definitions of the terms that are used.

Pre-Training Assessment

Listed below are the skills that caregivers use to make sure infants and toddlers are safe. Think about whether you do these things regularly, sometimes, or not enough. Place a check in one of the columns on the right for each skill listed. Then discuss your answers with your trainer.

SKILL	I DO THIS REGULARLY	I DO THIS SOMETIMES	I DON'T DO THIS ENOUGH
PROVIDING SAFE INDOOR AND OUTDOOR ENVIRONMENTS 1. Checking indoor and outdoor areas daily for safety hazards.	✓		
2. Conducting monthly safety checks to find out what needs to be repaired.	✓		
3. Keeping small, easy-to-swallow objects out of children's reach.	✓		
4. Organizing indoor and outdoor areas so infants and toddlers can move freely without bumping into anything.	✓		
5. Arranging the room to allow for clear exits.	✓		
RESPONDING TO INJURIES AND EMERGENCIES 6. Responding quickly to children in distress.	✓		
7. Taking safety precautions in a reassuring way, without over-protecting or scaring children.	✓		
8. Knowing the location of first-aid supplies and following accident and emergency procedures.	✓		

SKILL	I DO THIS REGULARLY	I DO THIS SOMETIMES	I DON'T DO THIS ENOUGH
RESPONDING TO INJURIES AND EMERGENCIES 9. Maintaining current emergency telephone numbers for all the parents.	✓		
10. Developing and posting emergency procedures.	✓		
HELPING CHILDREN DEVELOP SAFE HABITS 11. Showing children that their safety is important to you.	✓		
12. Showing children, by words and actions, that the center is a safe place.	✓		
13. Modeling ways to live safely and to be careful throughout the day.	✓		
14. Using positive guidance to redirect children from unsafe to safe activities.	✓		

Review your responses, then list three to five skills you would like to improve or topics you would like to learn more about. When you finish this module, you will list examples of your new or improved knowledge and skills.

_____

_____

_____

_____

_____

Now begin the learning activities for Module 1, Safe.

I. Using Your Knowledge of Infant and Toddler Development to Keep Children Safe

In this activity you will learn:

• to recognize some typical behaviors of infants and toddlers; and

• to use what you know about young children to keep them safe.

The children in your care rely on you to keep them safe. Their families depend on you to provide a safe environment, to prevent injuries, and to respond quickly in emergencies.

Infants start exploring their world as soon as they are born. They touch and taste everything they can, as soon as they can. As they begin rolling over, sitting up, creeping, crawling, and walking, they discover exciting new things to see and do. They also come across new dangers, such as electrical outlets and sharp corners. Keeping them safe requires your constant awareness. Because infants can't yet recognize dangerous situations, their safety is your responsibility.

Young children grow quickly and develop new skills almost overnight. Most injuries occur when infants do something they may have never done before. Keeping track of their rapidly developing skills will help you anticipate new dangers that may arise—when, for example, Randy (4 months), who has always stayed still when you changed him, suddenly rolls over, or Molly (7 months), a new crawler, makes a beeline for the block tower Rico (22 months) is building. All the caregivers in your room should be aware of who is doing what—and always expect the unexpected.

Toddlers are explorers on the move. They spend their days walking, climbing, running, shaking, pouring, collecting, and dumping. They live in the "here and now." They don't plan ahead about where they are going and what they are going to do next. For toddlers, walking forward and backward, pushing chairs across the room, and climbing over, around, and into boxes are activities in themselves. To keep toddlers safe, you need to know what behaviors are typical of children this age. You need to think like toddlers and constantly watch them. Teamwork between the caregivers in your room is very important. (Remember how Ms. Lewis alerted Ms. Gonzalez when she saw that Jill was in danger of hurting herself?)

Although they still need your help, toddlers are ready to begin learning about safety. They learn by watching you exhibit safe behavior—perhaps without thinking about it—as you put sharp objects up high and watch where you step while walking across the room. They also learn as they listen to your simple explanations and reminders, as you ask them to help wipe up a spill so that no one slips or to help you hammer a nail that is sticking out of a shelf. Toddlers will enjoy helping you sand the rough edge of a shelf. If they are feeling cooperative, they will gladly help you pick up toys that someone might trip over. The toddlers will be learning that they can help make their world a safer place, which is an important lesson. You can introduce clear safety rules to toddlers, but keep in mind that often they will not be able to remember or follow the rules.

By keeping children safe, you let them know that they can trust you and that the world is a safe place to explore. Children who have developed a sense of trust are eager to explore and learn about their environment.

The chart on the next page lists some typical behaviors of infants and toddlers. Included are behaviors relevant to safety. The right-hand column asks you to identify ways that caregivers can use this information about child development to keep children safe. Try to think of as many examples as you can. As you work through the module, you will learn new strategies for keeping children safe, and you can add them to the child development chart. You are not expected to think of all the examples at one time. If you need help getting started, turn to the completed chart at the end of the module. By the time you complete all the learning activities, you will find that you have learned many ways to keep children safe.

Using Your Knowledge of Infant and Toddler Development to Ensure Children's Safety

WHAT YOUNG INFANTS DO (0-8 MONTHS)	HOW CAREGIVERS CAN USE THIS INFORMATION TO KEEP CHILDREN SAFE
They put everything in their mouths.	remove small easy to swallow toys
They wiggle and squirm.	make sure flooring is padded, and no pointed furniture
They roll over.	do not leave infants unattended where they can fall.
They learn to sit.	use pillows to prop infant until infant is more stable
They learn to hold bottles.	never prop infants bottle, milk or juice can stop and settle at decay teeth

WHAT MOBILE INFANTS DO (9-17 MONTHS)	HOW CAREGIVERS CAN USE THIS INFORMATION TO KEEP CHILDREN SAFE
The learn to creep and crawl.	remove all sharp corners
They grab, throw, shake, dump, and drop objects they are exploring.	give infants boxes, bags & pots to put things in.
They understand many words but can't remember and follow rules by themselves.	regulate infant by reminders until infant can self regulate.
They pull themselves up to standing positions.	remove all dangerous objects that infant can reach
They begin walking.	remove obstacles off floor for clear path

WHAT TODDLERS DO (18-36 MONTHS)	HOW CAREGIVERS CAN USE THIS INFORMATION TO KEEP CHILDREN SAFE
They love to run but can't always stop or turn.	limit area & space where toddlers can run.
They love to climb and will climb on anything.	give toddlers climbing toys with padded surface
They show their curiosity by manipulating, poking, handling, twisting, or squeezing things.	make appropriate such toys available
They like to ride on toys.	have plenty of riding toys available
They enjoy playing with sand and water.	have sand & water area

WHAT TODDLERS DO (18-36 MONTHS)	HOW CAREGIVERS CAN USE THIS INFORMATION TO KEEP CHILDREN SAFE
They use the toilet independently.	have toddler size toilet area and make sure water does not get to hot.
They may not be able to remember rules. They break rules as a way of testing limits.	be ready to remind toddlers of rules. let peers help a remind keep in mind their short attention span.

When you have completed as much as you can do on the chart, discuss your answers with your trainer. As you proceed with the rest of the learning activities, you can refer back to the chart and add more examples of how caregivers keep children safe.

II. Creating and Maintaining a Safe Environment

In this activity you will learn:

- to create a safe learning environment for infants and toddlers; and

- to use a safety checklist to evaluate the safety of your setting and your toys and equipment.

The first step in keeping children safe is creating and maintaining a safe environment. How you arrange your space and your choices of toys and equipment can prevent dangerous situations from occurring. As you begin making decisions about your space, keep in mind the characteristics of the children who will be spending their days in it. You may want to refer back to the charts on infant and toddler development in the previous learning activity.

Because infants and toddlers can't think ahead and see the consequences of their actions, you must do it for them as you set up your space. As a first step, try to look at your environment through their eyes. To an infant or toddler, an exposed electrical outlet, a dangling wire, or a can of cleanser that someone left in the corner of the bathroom are interesting objects to poke, pull, and taste. Sitting on the floor at child-level can allow you to spot potential dangers you may never have noticed before. Give it a try. What do you see?

Where infants and toddlers are concerned, no setting can be entirely child-proof. The well-being of the children in your group depends on your alertness and attentiveness. You and the other caregivers in your room will find it helpful to work as a team to make your setting safe. Discuss your safety practices together. Throughout the day, station yourself at different locations. Be sure you can see every area of your space. You can take turns doing jobs such as sweeping up slippery sand and picking up toys that someone could trip on. You can also alert each other to potentially dangerous situations.

Once you have identified ways to make your environment safe, the next challenge is to keep it that way. Because children use indoor and outdoor materials continuously, wear and tear may create a dangerous situation. A safety checklist is a good tool for identifying hazards. It helps you step back for a few moments to focus on things you may otherwise overlook because you are so involved with the children in your group. Schedule routine times to check your indoor and outdoor areas as well as toys and equipment. Inspecting the outdoor play area for glass or other debris and observing to be sure no one has left cleaning materials or other poisons in children's reach need to be done daily. Checking blocks to see if they need sanding is an example of a task to do once a month.

In this activity you will use a safety checklist to evaluate the safety of your environment and another checklist to evaluate the safety of toys and equipment. Then you will complete a chart identifying any items that need attention, what steps you plan to take, and the date on which you addressed the problem.

Indoor Safety Checklist

SAFETY CONDITIONS	SATISFACTORY/ NOT APPLICABLE	NEEDS ATTENTION
CHECK DAILY		
1. Caregivers can easily move around and see every child at all times.		
2. Electrical outlets are covered. Electrical cords are out of children's reach.		
3. There are two well-marked exits in case of fire or other emergency.		
4. Cleaning materials and other poisons are stored out of children's areas.		
5. Objects small enough to be swallowed are kept out of children's reach.	'	
6. Children aren't given food that could cause choking, such as popcorn and nuts.		
7. Toys are stored on low, open shelves. The biggest, heaviest toys are on the lowest shelves.		
8. Pillows, mattresses, or mats are below high places where children might climb.		
9. Caregivers' scissors, knives, and other sharp objects are out of children's reach and secured against falling from above.		
10. Furniture has no sharp edges or corners at children's eye level.		

Indoor Safety Checklist (continued)

SAFETY CONDITIONS	SATISFACTORY/ NOT APPLICABLE	NEEDS ATTENTION
CHECK MONTHLY		
11. Smoke detectors and fire extinguishers are working properly.		
12. Electrical wires on record players, tape recorders, and other appliances are not frayed.		
13. Radiators and hot water pipes are covered or insulated.		
14. Heaters or furnaces are enclosed by barricades.		
15. Blocks are smooth and splinter free.		
16. The fire exit plan is posted.		
17. A fire drill is held every month.		

Outdoor Safety Checklist

SAFETY CONDITIONS	SATISFACTORY/ NOT APPLICABLE	NEEDS ATTENTION
CHECK DAILY		
1. No broken glass or debris is present in the area.		
2. The fence is in good repair to prevent children from straying from the area.		
3. The gate is secure and opened only by adults.		
4. Children are supervised at all times and proper child-adult ratios are maintained; caregivers play with the children rather than congregating with each other.		
5. There are safe spots for young infants.		
6. Play equipment surfaces are smooth and splinter free.		
7. The amount of material under climbers, slides, and swings is adequate to cushion children's falls.		
8. No objects or obstructions are under or around equipment where children might fall.		
9. Stay-clear zones around swings and slides are marked. Caregivers remind children what the marks mean.		

Outdoor Safety Checklist (continued)

SAFETY CONDITIONS	SATISFACTORY/ NOT APPLICABLE	NEEDS ATTENTION
CHECK MONTHLY 10. Screws, nuts, and bolts on climbing and other equipment are securely fastened and recessed.		
11. Strollers, child carts, and riding toys are in good repair (screws tightened, etc.).		

Checklist for Toy and Equipment Safety[1]

Evaluating the safety of toys and equipment is necessary whether you are buying them new or have received used items as donations. Use the checklist below to evaluate the safety of two toys of your choice and three pieces of equipment you use every day—a changing table, highchair, and crib.

Toy #1:_____ **Toy #2:** _____

Yes	No		Yes	No	
___	___		___	___	Is it washable?
___	___		___	___	Is it too large to be swallowed: at least 1 1/4" in diameter and 2 1/4" in length?
___	___		___	___	Is it free from detachable, small parts that could lodge in windpipes, ears, or noses?
___	___		___	___	Is it unbreakable?
___	___		___	___	Is it free of sharp edges, exposed nails, sharp wires, and straight pins?
___	___		___	___	Is it labeled *nontoxic*?
___	___		___	___	Is it free of parts that could pinch fingers or toes or catch hair?
___	___		___	___	For crib toys, are the cords less than 12" long?
___	___		___	___	For a riding toy, is it stable and well-balanced so it won't tip? Are all parts protected so that a falling child will not be injured?
___	___		___	___	Is it light enough for children to handle?
___	___		___	___	For a cloth toy, is it labeled *flame resistant, flame retardant,* or *nonflammable*?

_____

[1]Based on Audrianna Allen and Elizabeth Neterer, "A Guide to Play Materials," *Play: Children's Business* (Wheaton, MD: Association for Childhood Education International, 1974).

EQUIPMENT

Changing Table

Yes	No	
____	____	Does the table have a raised edge of at least 3"?
____	____	Does the table have a safety strap in good working condition, to prevent falls?
____	____	Does the table have or is it near drawers or shelves for diapers and other supplies that are easy for caregivers to reach?

Crib

____	____	Are slats spaced no more that 2-3/8" apart so that a child won't get stuck?
____	____	Are all slats in good repair (none missing or cracked)?
____	____	Do the drop-side latches catch securely?
____	____	Are cribs used with the drop-sides in the up position?
____	____	Are all screws and bolts in place and tight? Are there any rough edges or exposed bolts?
____	____	Is the paint nonleaded?

Highchair

____	____	Does the highchair have sturdy waist and crotch straps that are independent of the tray?
____	____	Does the tray lock securely?
____	____	Does the highchair have a wide, stable base?
____	____	Is the tray free of sharp edges, pinching latches, and loose parts?

Discuss your findings with your trainer and the other caregivers in your room. If you discover a toy or piece of equipment that is not safe, let your supervisor know so that it can be either repaired or removed.

ITEMS NEEDING ATTENTION	STEPS TO IMPROVE THE SAFETY OF THE ENVIRONMENT	DATE COMPLETED

Discuss what steps you noted with your trainer. Make these changes in your indoor and outdoor environment and check them off when they have been completed. Schedule times for daily and monthly safety checks throughout the year.

III. Knowing and Following Emergency Procedures

In this activity you will learn:

- to be prepared for injuries and other emergencies; and

- to follow the center's established procedures for dealing with emergencies.

Emergencies happen quickly, so the time to get ready for emergencies is before they occur. As the person responsible for the safety of infants and toddlers, you must know your center's emergency policies and procedures. You must also follow the procedures in a calm and clear-headed way. The greater your awareness of the procedures, the more quickly and effectively you can act when an emergency occurs.

Although you work hard to make your environment safe, some emergencies are caused by events outside your control. Infants and toddlers are curious and often move quickly and unexpectedly. Because of this, they sometimes have injuries. Your role is to assess quickly how serious an injury is and to respond correctly. Most injuries require only a hug, soothing words, and perhaps a bandage. Others require first aid at the center and perhaps taking children to the hospital.

Parents must be told about their children's injuries. For minor injuries (cuts and bruises), caregivers can inform parents when they pick up their children at the end of the day. For more serious injuries, parents should be contacted immediately.

Fires, floods, tornadoes, and other catastrophes may happen with little or no warning. If you know what to do when they happen, you can act swiftly. Participating in emergency drills helps everyone be ready. You should also post the emergency procedures so all adults can assist you in getting the infants and toddlers to safety.

The caregiver's role in emergencies is important. You must know the proper procedures to follow. You must remain calm. You must notify your supervisor that an injury has occurred and inform the child's parents, if necessary. And you must document, on the appropriate form, what has happened.

In this learning activity you will read "Emergency and First Aid Produres." Then you will review the established procedures at your center for evacuating children and staff in case of fire or other emergencies. Also review your center's injury procedures. Then answer the questions on emergency procedures that follow.

Emergency and First Aid Procedures[2]

Everyone Needs to Prepare for Emergencies

Even the most safety-conscious and well-prepared provider will face emergencies from time to time. How would you respond if a child fell from the climber on the playground, if you lost power during a rainstorm, if you saw smoke in the toaster oven, or if you suddenly became so ill that you could not continue caring for the children?

Because emergencies arise quickly, the time to get ready for them is before they happen. As the person responsible for the safety of the children, you must establish contingency and evacuation plans and follow them in a calm, clear-headed way. Your contingency plan will cover situations when another provider must take over for you, and your evacuation plan will cover emergencies when you must get the children out of the building as quickly as possible. The more familiar you are with your procedures, the more quickly and effectively you can act when an emergency occurs.

Although you work hard to make your environment safe, some emergencies are caused by events outside your control. Fires and other catastrophes may happen with little or no warning. If you live in an area where tornadoes, hurricanes, or floods occur regularly, you should have a plan for how you will respond. If you know what to do when these events happen, you can act swiftly. Participating in monthly emergency drills is one way to help everyone be ready. You should also post the evacuation plan and emergency procedures as a reminder of how to keep children safe.

Written Contingency Plans Are Essential

A written contingency plan states who will take care of the children in the event of an emergency, your illness, or a planned absence. Your contingency plan should include your evacuation route and procedures even if this information is also posted on your wall.

Following Evacuation Procedures Helps to Save Lives

When you need to evacuate the children from the building, your first priority is to save lives. Your written evacuation plan should state clearly what exits and procedures you will use to get the children out of the building and to a safe place. Your plan must take into account the type of structure in which your center is located. For example, an evacuation plan for a ground floor classroom might include procedures such as the following:

---

[2] Many of the strategies presented in this section are based on Abby Shapiro Kendrick and Roxane Kaufmann, Eds., *Healthy Young Children: A Manual for Programs* (Washington, DC: National Association for the Education of Young Children, 1995), pp. 93-102.

- I will sound the alarm so the children will know that we must get outside as quickly as possible.

- I will grab the children's files from the corner cabinet. (These files contain the information I will need to contact their parents.)

- The other caregiver and I will pick up the infants and put them into the carts. I will gather the other children at the door and get them to hold hands and help each other. I will hold the hand of the child at the head of the line to lead them all outside. The other caregiver will follow, pushing the infants. If the classroom door is cool to the touch, we will go down the hallway to the back door and out onto the playground. If we cannot use the hallway, we will open the window and—after one of the adults climbs out—hand the infants through from one adult to another, and then help the children climb through the window until we are all safely outside. Regardless of which exit we use, once we are outside we will lead the children away from the danger.

- Before and after we leave, we will count the children to make sure that we have everyone.

- Our director will use the center's cell phone to alert the fire department or other emergency service.

- We will take a few minutes to calm the children.

- I will call the children's parents to let them know what happened and that we are all safe.

At least once a month, it is a good idea to conduct an emergency drill so you and the children will be prepared if an actual emergency does take place. Document your monthly drills for licensing purposes. The fire marshal may require you to demonstrate an annual fire drill.

The drills should help children feel comfortable with the evacuation procedures. If a child does panic during an actual emergency, explain what has happened and what will happen next. Reassure the child that he or she is now safe and that the parents know what happened and will come to get the children as quickly as possible. Try to get the children involved in a game or quiet activity.

Do Not Use Your Fire Extinguisher for Fires that Spread

Knowing when and when not to use your fire extinguisher is an important part of being prepared for an emergency. Do not try to fight fires that spread beyond the spot where they start. For example, you will probably be able to put out a grease fire on your hot plate, but if it gets out of control, you and the children should get out of the building. Also, if the fire could block your exit, evacuate the building. Use your extinguisher only if these all apply:

- all the children are safely out of the building and in the care of another responsible person

- you can get out fast if your efforts aren't working

- you are nearby when the fire starts, or you discover the fire soon after it has started

- the fire is small and confined to a space such as a trash can, cushion, or small appliance

- you can fight the fire with your back to an exit

- your extinguisher is in working order, and you can:
    - stand back about 8 feet,
    - aim at the base of the fire, not the flames or smoke, and
    - squeeze or press the lever while sweeping from the sides to the middle.

If you have the slightest doubt about whether to fight the fire or get out of the building, **get out of the building and call the fire department**. Your safety is more important than the property you might save.

Responding to Children's Emergencies

Young children are very active. Because of this injuries sometimes occur. In these situations you must quickly assess how serious an injury is and respond correctly. Most injuries require only soothing words. Others require first aid or—rarely—a trip to the hospital. If you accompany a child in the ambulance, be sure to bring along the child's signed medical history and emergency authorization forms.

Ask the parent to come right away and get medical help immediately when you observe any of the following in a child[3]:

- Bleeding that does not stop when you apply direct pressure to the wound

- Unconsciousness

- Diarrhea, in an infant (watch for signs of dehydration, such as listlessness, fever, dry skin, and failure to urinate)

- Unusually confused behavior

- Stools that are black or have blood mixed through them

- Seizures occurring for the first time or lasting more than 15 minutes

- No urination in more than 8 hours, and the child's mouth and tongue look dry

- Continuous clear drainage from the nose after a hard blow to the head

- Temperature of 105° F or higher

- Uneven pupils (black centers of the eyes)

- Severe headache, stiff neck, or neck pain when the head is moved or touched

---

[3] (Based on American Academy of Pediatrics, PA Chapter, *Model Child Health Policies*, Revised (Washington, DC: National Association for the Education of Young Children, 1997).

- Breathing so fast or hard that the child cannot play, talk, cry, or drink

- Looking or acting very ill, or appearing to be getting worse quickly

- Stomachache so severe that it causes the child to double-up and scream; or a stomachache without vomiting or diarrhea after a recent injury, blow to the abdomen, or hard fall

- Rash or blood-red or purple pinhead-sized spots or bruises that are not associated with injury; or a rash of hives or welts that appear quickly

First Aid Procedures and Preparation

First aid—the immediate care you provide to a child who is injured or ill—is a way to manage the patient's situation until further medical care can occur. Cardiopulmonary Resuscitation (CPR) is used in situations such as aspiration of a foreign object, drowning, electric shock, and smoke inhalation to clear the patient's airway, help him or her breathe, and restart the heart if necessary.

You Need Personal Training to Be Fully Prepared

Your preparation for emergencies is incomplete without personal training. Necessary skills cannot be learned from written material alone. You should take proper courses and timely retraining in First Aid and in Cardiopulmonary Resuscitation (CPR) and Obstructed Airway Techniques. Local chapters of the American Red Cross and the American Heart Association offer courses regularly. Brief reminders of the current techniques are provided here, but these cannot substitute for up-to-date training in these areas. CPR Guidelines were revised in August 2000; you are advised to have retraining.

Maintain a Well-Stocked First Aid Kit

A basic first aid kit contains the following items, plus a quick reference manual (including CPR instructions) that you can consult in an emergency[4]:

- pen/pencil and note pad

- syrup of Ipecac

- cold pack

- current American Academy of Pediatrics (AAP) or American Red Cross standard first aid chart or equivalent first aid guide

- cell phone, or coins for use in pay phone

---

[4] Adapted by Karen Sokal-Gutierrez, M.D., from *Caring for our Children: National Health and Safety Performance Standards: Guidelines for Out-of-Home Child Care Programs,* 2nd ed. (Washington, DC: American Public Health Association; Elk Grove Village, IL: American Academy of Pediatrics; Aurora, CO: National Resource Center for Health and Safety in Child Care, 2002).

- poison control center phone number

- water

- small plastic or metal splints

- soap

- list of emergency phone numbers and parents' phone numbers

- disposable nonporous gloves

- scissors

- tweezers

- a non-glass thermometer to measure a child's temperature

- sterile gauze pads

- flexible roller gauze

- triangular bandages

- safety pins

- eye dressing

- any emergency medication for an infant or toddler with special needs (e.g., a bee sting kit or antihistamine for a child with severe allergy, honey or sugar for a child with diabetes, or an inhaler for a child with asthma)

Extra blankets, pillows, and ice packs are also good to keep on hand. (Packages of frozen vegetables are good substitutes for ice packs.)

Syrup of Ipecac—which induces vomiting—should be included in your first aid kit. However, using it is not always advisable. Some poisons, such as drain cleaner or lye, can do serious damage to the esophagus if vomited. **Before** administering syrup of Ipecac, check with the child's pediatrician, or a physician at the poison control center in your community. After administering syrup of Ipecac, take the child to a hospital for medical evaluation.

Use gloves when in contact with blood or body fluids to protect against the spread of bloodborne or fluidborne pathogens such as HIV/AIDS and hepatitis B.

When giving first aid, remember these important rules.

- **Do no harm.** (Harm might occur if you fail to treat the injury or if you make the injury worse.)

- **Do not move a hurt child except to save a life.** (Moving the child might cause further injury.)

- **Do not move a child with serious head, neck, or back injury except to do CPR or otherwise to save a life.** (Moving the child might cause further injury.)

Follow These Steps When Evaluating and Providing Care in an Emergency Situation

In an emergency, it is crucial to remain calm so you can think clearly and act appropriately. Remember the 3 C's: check, call, care. Check the scene, call for help, care for the injured.

- Survey the scene.
    - Is the scene safe?
    - Are the other children safe?
    - How many children are injured?
    - Are there bystanders who can help?

Follow These Steps If a Child Is Unconscious

- Check for unconsciousness or suspected heart or breathing catastrophes:
    - Is the child conscious and responsive?

- If an infant or toddler becomes unconscious, immediately do the ABC check as you have learned in a CPR class:
    - Open the **Airway.**
    - **Breathe** for the victim.
    - **Check circulation** and do chest compressions if needed. Then call 911 for help ("phone fast") or have someone else do so.

- Then call the child's parents.

Follow These Steps If a Child Is Choking

If a toddler (**NOT AN INFANT**) suddenly chokes and is unable to breathe, take these actions while you direct someone (a child, if necessary) to call 911.

- Try back blows to dislodge a foreign object.

- Try chest and abdominal ("Heimlich") thrusts as learned in a CPR class.

If an **INFANT** suddenly chokes and is unable to breathe, take these actions while you direct someone (a child, if necessary) to call 911.

- Try back blows to dislodge a foreign object.

- Try chest thrusts as learned in a CPR class. **Do NOT do ABDOMINAL thrusts with infants.**

If the infant or toddler choking victim becomes unconscious, provide CPR for 1 minute while someone (a child, if necessary) calls 911. If you can see foreign material in the mouth, remove it.

If the child is coughing, crying, or can speak, do **NOT** use these blows or thrusts. In this situation, calm the child and observe closely.

Follow These Steps If a Child Is Unconscious and Not Breathing, but There Is Circulation

A child is breathing if the chest is moving and air is coming out of the nose or mouth. If breathing is absent, begin rescue breathing. The following steps are a reminder of the procedure. Check your first aid or CPR instruction manual for a detailed description of the process.

- With the victim's head tilted back, pinch the nose shut. Give 2 slow breaths.

- Check for signs of circulation (such as movement). If present but child is still not breathing, give 1 slow breath about every 3 seconds.

- Do this for 1 minute (20 breaths).

- Recheck for signs of circulation and breathing.

- Call 911. Continue rescue breathing until help arrives.

Follow These Procedures When Responding to Burns

For minor burns, respond as follows:

- Immerse the burned area in cool water or apply cool (50° to 60° F) compresses to burns on a child's trunk or face to relieve the pain.

- Do not break blisters.

- Call an ambulance for burns of any size on a child's face, hands, feet, or genitalia.

For extensive burns, call an ambulance; then respond as follows:

- Remove clothing from the burn area if it comes off easily; if not, leave it alone.

- Keep the patient flat and warm. Cover the child with a clean sheet and blanket.

- Do not use ointments, greases, or powders.

For electrical burns, respond as follows:

- Do not use your bare hands.

- Disconnect the power source if possible or pull the child away from the source using wood or cloth (these will not conduct electricity).

- Call an ambulance.

- Apply CPR if necessary.

Survey for Specific Injuries and Treat as Necessary

Ask what happened and what hurts. Comfort the child and then check for injuries. Do a head-to-toe check: Head, scalp, face, ears, eyes, nose, mouth, neck, collar bones, chest, abdomen, arms, hands, legs (ask child to wiggle fingers and toes.)

Do first aid as needed.

- Stop bleeding.

- Immobilize injured bones, muscles, and tendons.

- Remove poisons, splinters, small objects.

- Clean and bandage wounds.

After you have performed necessary first aid, call the parent and explain what happened, what you did, and how the child is. Explain whether the child needs to be picked up at the center or met at the hospital.

Talk briefly with the other children to reassure them. Later you can answer children's questions and discuss how future injuries might be prevented. Complete the injury report form. Give a copy to the parent and keep a copy for your records.

Be Prepared to Respond to Poison Emergencies

A poison emergency can happen when someone swallows or touches a toxic substance, gets chemicals in the eyes, or breathes toxic fumes. The following common substances might be poisonous: cleaners and laundry products; hair care products; prescription and over-the-counter drugs; hobby and craft supplies; plant food and lawn care chemicals; cigarettes; liquor; paint and paint removal products; and workroom supplies. Whenever you suspect or know that a child has been poisoned, immediately call the poison control center or a medical clinic. Tell whoever answers the phone what product or chemical the child was exposed to (have the container with you when you make the call.) Tell the person how much the child took or was exposed to and how long ago the incident took place.

Syrup of Ipecac is a substance that induces vomiting. Using it is not always advisable. Some poisons, such as drain cleaner or lye, can do serious damage to the esophagus if vomited. Do **not** use Ipecac unless told to do so by the poison control center or the child's pediatrician. After administering syrup of Ipecac, take the child to a hospital for medical evaluation.

Stay Calm and Follow Proper Procedures

Your calm, quick response to an emergency is important. Proper procedures include: meeting immediate needs; notifying your supervisor that an incident has occurred; informing the child's parents (immediately for serious injuries or at the end of the day for minor ones); documenting, on the appropriate form, what happened.

Document All Injuries

Document all injuries on an injury report form. You can make up one of your own, or use the Injury Report Form provided on the following page. Keep copies of the completed forms in children's folders.

Parents need to be told about their children's injuries. For minor injuries (cuts and bruises), you can inform parents when they pick up their children at the end of the day. For more serious injuries, contact the parents immediately. If you have called an ambulance, they can meet their child at the hospital.

The provider's role in emergencies is important. You must remain calm, know and follow the proper procedures, notify the child's parents that an injury has occurred, and document what has happened.

It is also always a good idea to document any injuries or bruises you notice that were not there the last time you saw the child. These records will be critically important if you have to report that you have seen signs of child abuse.

Contingency and Evacuation Plans

1. Describe your contingency plan:

_____

_____

_____

_____

2. If you have used your contingency plan in an emergency, describe what happened.

_____

_____

_____

_____

3. Describe your evacuation plan:

_____

_____

_____

_____

4. If you have used your evacuation plan in an emergency, describe what happened.

_____

_____

_____

_____

Injury Report Form
(Example)

Complete within 24 hours of injury. Obtain the signature of parent or legal guardian. File the completed form in the child's record. Give a copy to the parent.

Name of injured _____ Age _____

Date of injury _____ Time of injury _____ AM/PM

Witness(es)_____

Where injury happened_____
_____
_____

Any equipment or products involved _____
_____
_____

Name of parent notified _____

Time Notified _____ AM/PM Notified by _____

Description of injury and how it happened _____
_____
_____
_____
_____

Who gave first aid and what they did _____
_____
_____

First aid given by medical personnel (who, what, when, and where) _____
_____
_____
_____

Follow-up plan for the injured _____
_____
_____

Injury prevention steps taken _____
_____
_____

Signature of person completing form _____

Date form completed_____ Parent's signature _____

Permission for Emergency Treatment
(Example)

In case of an emergency requiring medical treatment, I/we give permission for our child

(Child's name) _____ to receive such treatment services as are deemed in the best interest of the child at the time of the emergency. I/we accept financial responsibility for those services. If possible, I/we will be contacted prior to initiating treatment.

The child's date of birth: _____

The child has known allergies to: _____

The child's doctor is: _____Phone: _____

Preferred Hospital: _____

Address: _____Phone: _____

Medical insurance information:

Insurance Co. _____ Name: _____ Policy #: _____

Policy holder's name: _____ID Number: _____

Father/Guardian's Name: _____ Home or Cell Phone: _____

Employer: _____Work Phone: _____

Mother/Guardian's Name: _____ Home or Cell Phone: _____

Employer: _____Work Phone: _____

The undersigned state they have legal custody of the aforementioned child and request emergency services as indicated.

Signature: _____ Relationship to Child: _____ Date: _____

Signature: _____ Relationship to Child: _____ Date: _____

State of:_____

County of:_____

Sworn to before me this _____ day of _____ , 20__ by_____.

My commission expires:_____ Signature of Notary _____

(**Note**: Have parents complete two copies of this form - one to stay at the center and one to take on trips. This form should be signed by the person(s) having legal custody of the child and should be notarized. Attach a picture of the child to the form in case no one is available to identify him or her.)

Emergency Procedures

1. What is your emergency evacuation plan?

_____

_____

_____

2. What would you do if an infant or toddler slipped and cut his or her lip during outdoor play?

_____

_____

_____

3. What would you do if an infant began choking? A toddler?

_____

_____

_____

4. Who tells parents if their child has had a minor injury (a small cut or bruise)?

_____

_____

_____

5. Who calls for emergency medical assistance and contacts parents when a serious injury occurs?

_____

_____

_____

6. What hospital would the child and you go to in an emergency, and how would you get there?

_____

_____

_____

Discuss your answers with your trainer. If you have questions about what to do in an emergency, review your center's emergency procedures and discuss them with your supervisor.

IV. Ensuring Children's Safety Away from the Center

In this activity you will learn:

- to take safe walking trips with infants and toddlers; and

- to provide for young children's safety near traffic.

By taking walks around the neighborhood, you literally open up the world to the infants and toddlers you care for. There are interesting and new things to hear, see, and do. Children as well as caregivers enjoy the change of scenery. But keep in mind that taking children out of the center where you have created a child-proof environment involves an element of risk. This isn't to say you shouldn't do it; rather, you will need to take the necessary precautions so that your trip is enjoyable and safe for everyone.

Preparing for a Walk

In preparing for a neighborhood walk, you can avoid problems and unnecessary risks by taking the following steps:

- Whenever possible, divide up and take small group walks. One caregiver should be responsible for no more than three children, and at least one of those should be in a stroller or backpack.

- Recruit additional help from parents, senior citizens, or students from early childhood programs at a local college or high school. Plan your walks to coincide with times when these extra adults are present.

- Obtain signed permission slips from parents at the beginning of the year so parents will know that taking walks is part of your daily program and what kind of places you will be going.

- Be prepared for an emergency by always bringing a first-aid kit with you.

- Make a "trip bag" you always carry with you that has a list of emergency phone numbers and copies of emergency forms. Bring a cell phone and some money in case you have to take a taxi.

- Leave word with your director and a sign on the door telling where you are going in case someone needs to find you.

- Plan realistic destinations. Infants and toddlers are interested in everything. You don't have to go far; a walk to the corner can be filled with discoveries.

- Bring along bottles, diapers, snacks, and sweaters that children may need while you are away from the center.

- Make your walk an enjoyable experience. Talk about things you see, and sing songs.

Walking Safely Near Traffic

Some of the places you want to go, for example, a neighborhood park, a nearby pet store, or the local fruit market, may mean taking children near traffic. Mobile infants who are not yet steady on their feet should ride in strollers or child carts. Toddlers must be carefully supervised. They are capable of listening to a few simple rules about walking safely near traffic, but you should not expect that they will always remember and follow them. Here are some suggestions for ensuring children's safety when you are around traffic.

- Get to know children a little before you go for a walk near traffic. Although you should always be prepared for the unexpected, you will have some idea of those more likely to dart away.

- Be sure there is a space for each child in a stroller or child cart or a caregiver's hand to hold on to.

- Make a few simple and clear rules such as "stop when you get to the curb" and "hold my hand or onto the stroller when we cross the street." Reinforce them during all your walks.

- Explain the rules for crossing the street safely—look to the left, look to the right, look to the left again, and wait for the green light—even though children may not yet be able to understand exactly what you are saying. Follow the rules consistently.

- Keep strollers and child carts on the sidewalk when pausing on a curb to check for traffic. Avoid pushing a stroller or child cart out into the street in front of you until you know it is safe to cross.

- Make walks fun by taking giant steps, then tiny steps, or singing songs.

The planning you do before a walk goes a long way in making you feel relaxed and in control. Children will sense this and be reassured by your calm manner. You also set an example for children by following safety rules yourself. Here are some suggestions for taking safe walks with infants and toddlers.

- Use walking time to talk about scenes along the way and what you expect to see and do when you arrive at your destination, and to remind children of the traffic safety rules.

- If children become over-tired or unruly, stop as soon as it is safe to do so. If you feel things are getting out of hand, return to the center.

- Make sure all children are accounted for at all times.

In this learning activity, you will review your center's policies and procedures for ensuring children's safety on walks in the neighborhood. After recording them, you will compare them to the suggestions above and identify any additional safety precautions you want to add to ensure children's safety.

Protecting Children Away from the Center

1. **What does your program require you to do before taking infants and toddlers on walks away from the center?**

   sign out , time , with who , destination
   and time, return
        will

2. **What are the rules and procedures for ensuring infants' and toddlers' safety while on a walk?**

   my infants are in strollers and
   my toddlers holds hands , we discuss traffic safety.

3. **How can you improve the procedures and planning process to more effectively ensure infants' and toddlers' safety away from the center?**

Discuss your answers with your trainer, and implement ideas you feel are needed to ensure infants' and toddlers' safety on walks in the neighborhood.

V. Helping Children Begin to Learn About Keeping Themselves Safe

In this activity you will learn:

- to maintain a safe environment through supervision; and

- to develop and communicate simple safety rules with infants and toddlers.

Infants begin to learn about keeping themselves safe by watching and listening to their caregivers. Toddlers also learn through watching and listening, and they are ready to begin learning how to follow safety rules to keep themselves safe. The first step in teaching infants and toddlers safety is to show them, by your actions, how you prevent injuries. Children need to see adults acting in safe ways:

- walking, not running in the room;

- sitting, not standing on chairs;

- using the safety straps on highchairs and other equipment; and

- putting away broken things until they can be mended.

It is the job of each caregiver in the room to make sure that all areas of the room and the outdoor area are supervised. When one caregiver is busy changing an infant's diaper, another adult should keep an eye on the rest of the room. Some activities require closer supervision than others. Two caregivers who are moving around to different areas could agree to divide the room or yard between them. Caregivers must also be aware of how the children are feeling. If activities are too long, children may tire, and tired children often get injured. If an activity is too demanding, children may get frustrated, and frustrated children also tend to have injuries.

You have learned about how infants and toddlers behave in Learning Activity I. You should be aware of the possible hazards in the room and outdoors, as described in Learning Activity II of this module. When you know what to expect and look for when caring for children, you can prevent injuries.

It's not too early to begin developing safety rules with toddlers in your group—as long as you have realistic expectations of their behavior. Because toddlers don't fully understand the meaning of danger, they don't yet see and use rules the way we do. Sometimes toddlers will proudly follow a rule because it is a grown-up thing to do. At other times a toddler might use the breaking of rules as an opportunity to assert a newly developing sense of self, as when Cordell (20 months), who understands your words "remember, chairs are for sitting on," looks you straight in the eye and stands up on his seat.

As you begin communicating with toddlers about safety rules, they will start getting the idea that there are things they can do to keep themselves safe. Though they still need you to remind them of the rules again and again, you are laying the foundation they need to develop skills and sound judgment to keep themselves safe.

Here are some steps to follow as you help children learn to do things the safe way:

- Explain rules simply and repeat them often. "This is the riding toy path. You can kick your ball on the grass."

- Be consistent in what rules you enforce.

- Decide how best to intervene in a potentially dangerous situation. Sometimes all it takes is a look. Sometimes a few words suffice, such as "Jeremy, it is time to slow down a little so you don't crash and fall." At other times you may have to physically help a child stop what she or he is doing and then explain the reason why.

- Model safe ways to use materials and to play. Point out that you walk carefully when you are carrying a pair of scissors to the table.

- Reinforce children's safe behavior with a smile of approval or a comment such as this: "You did a good job remembering that balls are what we throw."

In this learning activity you will identify safety limits to set for one activity or toy and ways to communicate them to toddlers. Begin by reviewing the example.

Developing Safety Rules with Toddlers
(Example)

Setting *Water play*   **Age(s)** *24-36 months*   **Date(s)** *September 10*

1. What do you think are the potential safety hazards for this activity/toy?

Children spill water on the floor and the floor gets slippery. Children could slip and fall.

2. What safety limits did you develop for this activity/toy?

The water should stay in the water table.

3. How did you communicate these rules to the children?

I praised children for a good job of pouring water in the table.

I stopped a child who was about to pour a cup of water on the floor and explained that someone might fall if the floor is wet.

I asked children to help me wipe the floor dry to help keep everyone safe from falling.

Developing Safety Rules with Toddlers

Now develop safety limits for one activity or toy. Then answer the questions below.

Setting _____   Age(s) _____   Date(s) _____

1. **What do you think are the safety hazards for this activity/toy?**

   _____
   _____
   _____
   _____
   _____

2. **What safety limits did you develop for this activity/toy?**

   _____
   _____
   _____
   _____
   _____

3. **How did you communicate these rules to the children?**

   _____
   _____
   _____
   _____
   _____

Discuss your responses with your trainer.

Summarizing Your Progress

You have now completed all of the learning activities for this module. Whether you are an experienced caregiver or a new one, this module has probably helped you develop new skills for keeping infants and toddlers safe. Before you go on, take a few minutes to summarize what you've learned.

- Turn back to Learning Activity I, Using Your Knowledge of Infant and Toddler Development to Ensure Their Safety, and add to the chart specific examples of what you learned about keeping children safe while you were working on this module. Read the sample responses on the completed chart at the end of this module.

- Next, review your responses to the pre-training assessment for this module. Write a summary of what you learned, and list the skills you developed or improved.

_____

_____

_____

_____

_____

_____

_____

_____

_____

_____

_____

_____

_____

_____

Your final step in this module is to complete the knowledge and competency assessments. Let your trainer know when you are ready to schedule the assessments. After you have successfully completed these assessments, you will be ready to start a new module. Congratulations on your progress so far, and good luck with your next module.

Answer Sheet: Keeping Children Safe

Providing Safe Indoor and Outdoor Environments

1. **How did Ms. Lewis and Ms. Gonzalez work together to make the center a safe place?**

   a. Ms. Lewis spotted Jill climbing on the box. She calmly alerted Ms. Gonzalez, who was closer to Jill.

   b. Ms. Gonzalez responded quickly to Ms. Lewis' warning and calmly moved to keep Jill safe.

   c. Ms. Gonzalez put the box in the closet so the children wouldn't climb on it.

2. **What do you think Jill learned from this experience?**

   a. She learned that the box was not a good thing to climb on, but the climber was safe.

   b. She learned that Ms. Gonzalez would keep her safe.

   c. She learned that she could help Ms. Gonzalez do important and real work to make the room safer.

Responding to Injuries and Emergencies

1. **How did Ms. Jackson and Ms. Bates know what to do when the fire bell sounded?**

   a. They followed the center's established procedures for emergencies.

   b. The center held monthly fire drills to train all caregivers.

2. **Why did Ms. Jackson wait to comfort the crying infant?**

   a. She knew that she must get all the infants to safety as quickly as possible.

   b. She knew that she could comfort crying Megan as soon as she got outside.

Helping Infants and Toddlers Begin to Develop Safe Habits

1. **How did Ms. Moore let the children know that the center is a safe place?**

   a. She walked calmly to the block area.

   b. She helped Kirsten learn a safe way to knock down the block tower.

   c. She showed Kirsten how to ask the other children to move away from the tower before she knocked it down.

2. **How were the children learning to keep themselves safe?**

    a. They learned that there are ways to make an unsafe activity safe.

    b. They learned to give a warning before doing something that might hurt someone.

    c. They learned to consider other people's safety as well as their own.

Using Your Knowledge of Infant and Toddler Development to Ensure Their Safety

WHAT YOUNG INFANTS DO (0-8 MONTHS)	HOW CAREGIVERS CAN USE THIS INFORMATION TO KEEP CHILDREN SAFE
They put everything in their mouths.	Be sure toys do not have pieces that may break off and cause infants to choke. Keep small, easy-to-swallow objects out of infants' reach. Avoid toys with toxic paint that could poison infants.
They wiggle and squirm with no notice.	Dry your hands before picking up infants. They can move unexpectedly and slip out of your hands. Establish emergency evacuation procedures that do not require infants to be carried in caregivers' arms.
They roll over.	Always stay with infants on changing tables because it only takes a second for an infant to roll over and off the table. Protect infants from rolling into the nearby vigorous play of beginning walkers and toddlers.
They learn to sit.	Use a soft pillow to prop up an infant who is just learning to sit. Stay close by so the infant doesn't fall over and get hurt.
They learn to hold bottles.	Hold infants when feeding them. Never prop infants while they are drinking their bottles because infants might choke.

WHAT MOBILE INFANTS DO (9-17 MONTHS)	HOW CAREGIVERS CAN USE THIS INFORMATION TO KEEP CHILDREN SAFE
They learn to creep and crawl.	Provide protected areas for creepers and crawlers so they won't be trampled by new walkers. Keep potentially dangerous objects (such as plastic bags or easy-to-swallow toys) out of reach.
They grab, throw, shake, dump, and drop objects they are exploring.	Keep breakable toys and equipment out of reach. Provide soft objects such as beach balls and pillows for throwing games.
They understand many words but can't remember and follow rules by themselves.	Talk about rules with children, but know that they won't remember and follow them. Use the environment to help set limits. Be there to step in when necessary.
They pull themselves up to standing positions.	Lower crib mattresses so infants can't fall over the rail. Keep crib sides up. Cover sharp corners of tables or shelves that infants might bump. Provide stable objects that will support infants' weight and not tip over.
They begin walking.	Pick up items that could trip infants. Provide carpeted surfaces that will cushion falls. If you need to get the attention of an infant beginning to toddle, move in front of the child to speak to her or him; turning to the sound of your voice takes attention from walking, and the toddler may tumble.

WHAT TODDLERS DO (18-36 MONTHS)	HOW CAREGIVERS CAN USE THIS INFORMATION TO KEEP CHILDREN SAFE
They love to run but can't always stop or turn.	Provide open carpeted or grassy space that will cushion falls. Pick up toys that toddlers may trip on. Make sure floor coverings are secured. Remind toddlers to slow down and watch where they are going.
They love to climb and will climb on anything.	Be sure climbing toys are on soft surfaces. Assume that toddlers will climb on everything. Provide lots of safe, sturdy climbing equipment and lots of opportunities for climbing.
They show their curiosity by manipulating, poking, handling, twisting, or squeezing everything.	Cover electrical outlets and exposed radiators. Remove toys and other items with jagged edges or splinters. Keep sharp materials (knives, caregivers' scissors) out of toddlers' reach. Lock cleaning materials and medicines in cabinets. Remove very small objects that toddlers could put in their mouths, ears, or noses.
They like to ride on toys.	Let toddlers ride on hard, clear surfaces. Help children take turns. Discuss safe riding. Organize a riding area so riders will not crash into other toddlers.
They enjoy playing with sand and water.	Put towels under the water table and sweep sand off the floor to keep toddlers from slipping. Help toddlers change their clothes when they get too wet. Remind toddlers to keep the sand and water in the table or container.
They use the toilet independently.	Supervise toileting. Be sure water is hot enough for hand-washing but not so hot that it burns. Provide sturdy platforms for toilets and sinks not scaled to toddler height.
They may not be able to remember rules. They break rules as a way of testing limits.	Discuss rules with toddlers, but don't assume they will remember or follow the rules. Be there to observe and enforce rules when needed. Set up your space so it reminds toddlers of limits. Latch doors and gates in ways that prevent toddlers from leaving supervision—but be sure not to impede the use of exits in emergencies.

Glossary

Emergency   Unplanned or unexpected situation in which children or adults are harmed or may be harmed.

Precaution   Steps taken to prevent injuries or to ensure safety.

Safety   Freedom from danger.

Module 2
Healthy

What Are Good Health and Nutrition and Why Are They Important?

Good health is a state of well-being—physical, mental, and social—not simply the absence of disease. One area of development affects every other area of development. People who are healthy feel good about themselves.

- They are well-rested, energetic, and strong.

- They eat the right foods.

- They avoid, or use in moderation, alcohol, tobacco, and caffeine.

- They exercise regularly.

- They get along well with others.

- They have high self-esteem.

Infants and toddlers experience good health and a sense of well-being when their caregivers maintain environments that promote wellness and prevent the spread of illness and abuse. Creating such an environment involves paying attention to your own health as well as that of the children in your group.

Each of us has certain health and nutrition routines that are part of our daily lives. Some of these routines may be good for us, and some may not. Because most of us want to become and remain healthy, we try to increase the number of good routines and decrease the number of bad ones.

Infants and toddlers learn about good health and nutrition by following the lead of their parents and caregivers. As you wash your hands before eating and after toileting and when you serve and eat nutritious foods, you aren't just improving your own health; you are also making an investment in the children's future. When good habits are developed at an early age, they usually continue throughout a person's life.

You play a key role in keeping the children you care for healthy. Children under 3 have more illnesses related to infection than other age groups. Those who spend their day in a group setting tend to be exposed to more diseases than those cared for at home. Children and their parents depend on you to know how to prevent diseases from spreading and to take as many precautions as possible.

The emotional tone you create in your environment affects the health of everyone who spends their day in it. A positive, relaxed atmosphere encourages a sense of well-being in children and caregivers.

Keeping infants and toddlers healthy involves:

- providing healthy indoor and outdoor environments;

- helping children develop good health habits; and

- recognizing and reporting child abuse and neglect.

Listed below are examples of how caregivers demonstrate their competence in keeping infants and toddlers healthy.

Providing Healthy Indoor and Outdoor Environments

Here are some examples of what caregivers can do.

- Check the room daily for adequate ventilation and lighting, comfortable room temperature, and good sanitation.

- Open windows daily to let in fresh air.

- Provide tissues and paper towels in places mobile infants and toddlers can reach.

- Plan a daily schedule consistent with children's activity levels and their need for quiet times and rest. "We did a lot of climbing and running in the playground today! Now let's sit quietly and look through our books before we get ready for lunch."

- Take children outdoors daily for exercise and fresh air.

- Complete a daily health check on each child to discover symptoms of illness.

- Recognize symptoms of common childhood diseases and stay in regular contact with parents.

Helping Infants and Toddlers Develop Good Health Habits

Here are some examples of what caregivers can do.

- Help children develop self-help skills in toileting, handwashing, and toothbrushing.

- Talk with children about ways to stay healthy. "Your teeth sure look clean and shiny. You did a good job brushing them."

- Serve age-appropriate, nutritious meals and snacks.

- Encourage children to taste new foods by serving as models and offering verbal encouragement. "Mmm, this squash is so good! You try it, too."

- Help children learn to recognize that their bodies need rest, food, and movement. "Joey, you seem tired. Doesn't your bed feel good? Let me rub your back so you can rest better."

Recognizing and Reporting Child Abuse and Neglect

Here are some examples of what caregivers can do.

- Recognize the signs of possible physical, sexual, and emotional child abuse and neglect.

- Respond to children in caring ways while avoiding situations that might be questioned by others.

- Report suspected child abuse and neglect according to state laws and the program's procedures.

Promoting Children's Health and Nutrition

The following situations show caregivers promoting good health and nutrition for infants and toddlers. As you read, think about what the caregivers in each scene are doing and why. Then answer the questions following each episode.

Providing Healthy Indoor and Outdoor Environments

Ms. Lewis enters her room and opens several windows. It is a cool day, so she raises them only a few inches. She checks the area around the sink and notices that the soap dispenser is full but the towel supply is low. As she puts out a stack of paper towels, the children begin to arrive. She greets each child warmly, checking to see if the flu that has been running through the center has made any children in her group sick. "You have the sniffles today, David. Let's wipe your nose with a tissue from the box next to the sink," she says. "Try to blow your nose," she says to David (17 months). David puts his hands around the tissue and blows. "Good job," says Ms. Lewis. "Here's the waste can for the used tissue," she says as she gestures to it. David drops the tissue in. "Now let's both wash our hands to make sure all the germs are gone," she says.

1. **What are three things Ms. Lewis did to maintain a healthy room?**

   _____

   _____

   _____

2. **What did Ms. Lewis do to keep germs from spreading?**

   _____

   _____

   _____

Helping Infants and Toddlers Develop Good Health Habits

"Will you please pass me the apples?" Mr. Jones asks Jerry. Jerry (24 months) hands the bowl of apple slices to Mr. Jones. "I like crunchy, juicy apples," Mr. Jones says. Jerry watches Mr. Jones eat his apple. He reaches for an apple slice, too. "Eating apples is good for us," Mr. Jones says. After lunch, Mr. Jones and Ms. Moore clear the table with the children. Then Mr. Jones says, "Now it's time to brush our teeth." He helps three children at a time choose their toothbrushes from the holder. "Remember to brush up and down," says Mr. Jones. He brushes his teeth, too. Sandy (24 months) watches Mr. Jones, her toothbrush in hand. "My brush teeth," she says proudly smiling at him.

1. What three healthy things did Mr. Jones do with the children?

_____

_____

_____

2. How did Mr. Jones teach the children ways to keep themselves healthy?

_____

_____

_____

Recognizing and Reporting Child Abuse and Neglect

"You are soaked," Ms. Bates says to 8-month-old Lynn. "I'm going to pick you up and change your diaper. Ms. Bates holds her arms out to Lynn, who is playing on a blanket on the floor. Lynn coos. She holds her arms out toward Ms. Bates. When Ms. Bates removes Lynn's diaper, she notices that Lynn has an ugly bruise on the inside of her thigh. Ms. Bates realizes that this is the second unexplained bruise she has seen on Lynn. When she finishes Lynn's diaper change, handwashing, and sanitizing routines, she goes to discuss her observations with her center director, Ms. Colker. Ms. Colker sits with Ms. Bates while she calls Child Protective Services to report her suspicions.

1. Why was Ms. Bates worried about Lynn?

_____

_____

_____

2. What did Ms. Bates do when she suspected abuse?

_____

_____

_____

Compare your answers with those on the answer sheet at the end of this module. If your answers are different, discuss them with your trainer. There can be more than one good answer.

Your Own Health and Nutrition

Most of us know that good health and proper nutrition are important. The national focus on staying fit—stressed in the media, in schools, and at the workplace—has provided much useful information and has led to an increased motivation to stay healthy. We have learned that staying healthy improves the quality of our lives and can actually prolong them.

Most of us know what to do to stay healthy. We try to improve our health by doing the right things—and when we do, we tend to feel better about ourselves. Perhaps you have done some of the following things to improve your health.

- You began walking or jogging more often.

- You joined an aerobics class or exercise program.

- You quit smoking or vowed never to start.

- You increased the variety of foods in your diet to include more vegetables, fruits, and whole-grain products.

- You lost weight using a sensible diet.

- You began eating more starchy foods and less sugar, fats, and salt.

- You decreased the amount of unnecessary stress in your life.

- You discovered the positive effects of relaxation techniques.

You may have found, though, that changing too much too quickly led to failure. Have you found yourself saying these things?

- "I tried quitting smoking but I felt like I was going crazy and I couldn't stop eating!"

- "I don't have time to jog and still manage to go to work, cook for my family, and keep the lawn mowed."

- "Well, I'd like to cook healthier foods for my family, but it takes so long to plan and prepare. It's just easier to get fast foods."

Changing our health and nutrition habits can be hard. It is one thing to know what to do; it is something quite different to do it. Being judgmental and critical of ourselves only makes us feel worse.

An old proverb states, "If we don't change our direction, we will very likely end up in the place we are headed." We might as well do all we can to ensure our own success by being gentle with ourselves and appreciating each step we take in our desired direction. Because doing everything "right" is very hard, you might think in terms of more and less. You want to do more of certain good things, such as:

- exercising;
- eating foods low in fats, salt, and sugar; and
- getting enough sleep.

You want to do less of certain unhealthy things such as:

- smoking;
- eating fattening, salty foods; and
- drinking alcohol.

Keeping in mind your whole state of well-being—physical, mental, and social—take time to answer the questions below.

What healthy habits do you want to maintain or improve?

_____

_____

_____

What unhealthy habits do you want to decrease?

_____

_____

_____

How do you feel your health affects your work?

_____

_____

_____

List three concrete and specific steps you will take to maintain healthy or change unhealthy habits.

_____

_____

_____

Give yourself the positive support and appreciation you would give your best friend, and you are very likely to succeed.

As a reference, we have included a summary of the *Dietary Guidelines for Americans* from the U.S. Department of Agriculture and the U.S. Department of Health and Human Services. You will find this resource on the following pages.

When you have finished this overview section, you should complete the pre-training assessment. Refer to the glossary at the end of this module if you need definitions of the terms that are used.

Dietary Guidelines for Americans[1]

Eat a Variety of Foods

- Eat a variety of foods daily in adequate amounts, including selections of the following:

    - fruits
    - vegetables
    - milk, cheese, yogurt, and other products made from milk
    - meats, poultry, fish, eggs, and dried beans and peas
    - whole-grain and enriched breads, cereals, and other products made from grains

- Women and adolescent girls should eat calcium-rich foods, such as milk and milk products, for strong bones.

- Young children and women should eat iron-rich foods such as beans, cereals, and grain products.

Maintain Healthy Weight

- Eat a variety of foods that are low in calories and high in nutrients, as follows:

    - Eat more fruits, vegetables, and whole grains.
    - Eat less fat and fatty foods.
    - Eat less sugar and fewer sweets.
    - Drink fewer alcoholic beverages.

- Increase your physical activity.

- Eat slowly.

- Take smaller portions.

- Avoid second helpings.

- Drink lots of water.

Choose a Diet Low in Fat, Saturated Fat, and Cholesterol, and Moderate in Total Fat

- Choose lean meat, fish, poultry, and dried beans and peas as protein sources.

- Use skim or low-fat milk and milk products.

---

[1]Based on the U.S. Department of Agriculture and U.S. Department of Health and Human Services, *Dietary Guidelines for Americans*, 2000 (Washington, DC: U.S. Government Printing Office, 2000).

- Moderate your intake of egg yolks and organ meats.

- Limit your intake of fats and oils, especially those high in saturated fat, such as butter, cream, lard, heavily hydrogenated fats (some margarines), shortenings, and foods containing palm and coconut oils.

- Trim fat off meats.

- Broil, bake, or boil rather than fry.

- Moderate your intake of foods that contain fat, such as breaded and deep-fried foods.

- Read labels carefully to determine both the amount and type of fat present in foods.

Choose a Diet with Plenty of Vegetables, Fruits, and Grain Products

- Choose foods that are good sources of fiber and starch, such as whole-grain breads and cereals, fruits, vegetables, and dry beans and peas.

- Eat at least three servings of vegetables and two servings of fruits daily.

- Have six or more servings of grain products (breads, cereals, pasta, and rice) daily.

- Substitute starchy foods for those with large amounts of fats and sugars.

Use Sugar in Moderation

- Use less of all sugars and foods containing large amounts of sugars, including white sugar, brown sugar, raw sugar, honey, and syrups. Examples include soft drinks, candies, cakes, and cookies.

- Avoid eating sweets between meals. How often you eat sugar and sugar-containing food is even more important to the health of your teeth than how much sugar you eat.

- Read food labels for clues on sugar content. If the word sugar, sucrose, glucose, maltose, dextrose, lactose, fructose, or syrup appears first, then the food contains a large amount of sugar.

- Eat fresh fruits or fruits processed without syrup or with light rather than heavy syrup.

Use Salt in Moderation

- Learn to enjoy the flavors of unsalted foods.

- Cook without salt or with only small amounts of added salt.

- Try flavoring foods with herbs, spices, and lemon juice.

- Add little or no salt to food at the table.

- Limit your intake of salty foods such as potato chips, pretzels, salted nuts and popcorn, condiments (soy sauce, steak sauce, garlic salt), pickled foods, cured meats, some cheeses, and some canned vegetables and soups.

- Read food labels carefully to determine the amounts of sodium they contain. Use lower-sodium products when available.

Pre-Training Assessment

Listed below are the skills that caregivers use to promote good health and nutrition for infants and toddlers. Think about whether you do these things regularly, sometimes, or not enough. Place a check in one of the columns on the right for each skill listed. Then discuss your answers with your trainer.

SKILL	I DO THIS REGULARLY	I DO THIS SOMETIMES	I DON'T DO THIS ENOUGH
PROVIDING HEALTHY INDOOR AND OUTDOOR ENVIRONMENTS 1. Checking the room daily for adequate ventilation and lighting, comfortable room temperature, and good sanitation.			
2. Arranging the diaper changing area so it is easy to keep sanitary.			
3. Providing tissues and paper towels where mobile infants and toddlers can reach them.			
4. Completing a daily health check on each child to discover symptoms of illness.			
5. Washing and disinfecting toys daily.			
6. Washing hands upon arrival for work, before preparing and serving food, after changing a diaper or wiping a nose, and after cleaning up messes.			

SKILL	I DO THIS REGULARLY	I DO THIS SOMETIMES	I DON'T DO THIS ENOUGH
HELPING INFANTS AND TODDLERS DEVELOP GOOD HEALTH HABITS			
7. Helping children gradually learn to hold a bottle, drink from a cup, use a spoon, and feed themselves.			
8. Dressing children warmly to go outside on cold days.			
9. Washing infants' hands after diapering and before they eat. Helping toddlers learn to wash their own hands after diapering or toileting and before eating.			
10. Providing relaxing mealtimes during which infants are held or talked to and mobile infants and toddlers feed themselves.			
RECOGNIZING AND REPORTING CHILD ABUSE AND NEGLECT			
11. Recognizing the signs of possible physical, sexual, and emotional child abuse and neglect.			
12. Responding to children in caring ways while avoiding situations that might be questioned by others.			
13. Being alert to changes in children's behavior that may signal abuse or neglect.			
14. Knowing and following state laws and the program's policies for reporting suspected abuse and neglect.			

Review your responses, then list three to five skills you would like to improve or topics you would like to learn more about. When you finish this module, you will list examples of your new or improved knowledge and skills.

_____

_____

_____

_____

_____

_____

_____

_____

Now begin the learning activities for Module 2, Healthy.

I. Using Your Knowledge of Infant and Toddler Development to Promote Good Health and Nutrition

In this activity you will learn:

- to recognize some typical behaviors of infants and toddlers; and

- to use what you know about infants and toddlers to promote good health and nutrition.

Infants and toddlers depend on you to keep them and their environment healthy. Ensuring their health—especially in a child development center—is a big job. This is because infants and toddlers behave in many ways that make it easy for germs to spread. You need to know what infants and toddlers do so you can meet their health and nutrition needs.

Infants learn about objects by putting them in their mouths. Infants and many toddlers wear diapers that need to be changed several times a day, and they drink from bottles. Mouths, diapers, and bottles are all sources of germs. Regularly washing your hands and infants' hands after diapering helps prevent the spread of germs. Washing the toys and equipment used by infants and toddlers also helps prevent the spread of germs. Labeling bottles and supervising bottle drinking help ensure that infants and toddlers will use only their own bottles.

Infants have their own rhythms of eating, playing, sleeping, and eliminating, so individualizing daily routines is necessary to meet each infant's needs. In addition, infants grow rapidly. They need safe places to practice their new skills of grasping, rolling over, sitting up, creeping, and crawling. Their bodies need nutritious, safe foods to become strong and healthy. When choosing foods for an infant, be aware of any allergies infants may have. Avoid foods that can cause choking, such as peanuts, popcorn, and grapes. It is also important to provide a relaxed atmosphere for eating.

Toddlers need safe places and lots of time to practice their new skills of walking, running, climbing, and jumping. Active indoor and outdoor play gives toddlers a necessary release of their energy as well as an opportunity to exercise their developing muscles. Of course, toddlers need rest, too. A balanced program of active and quiet times, and indoor and outdoor activities, allows them to get the rest they need. Toddlers in full-day programs need afternoon naps to make it through the day.

Toddlers are beginning to learn many self-help skills. They are learning to put on their jackets, use the toilet, brush their teeth, wash their hands, and blow their noses. By encouraging these skills, you help toddlers learn to keep themselves healthy. Your participation in these activities reinforces the importance of preventing illness.

Many toddlers are interested in preparing foods because they see their parents and you do it often. It is important to include toddlers in simple food preparation activities and to provide relaxed times for eating meals and snacks.

By knowing what infants and toddlers are like and helping them be healthy, you are promoting their development. You are also taking the first steps to teach them the importance of good health.

The chart on the next page lists some typical behaviors of infants and toddlers. Included are characteristics related to promoting good health and nutrition. The right-hand column shows ways that caregivers can use this information about child development to promote good health and nutrition. Try to think of as many examples as you can. As you work through the module, you will learn new strategies for ensuring infants' and toddlers' health, and you can add them to the child development chart. You are not expected to think of all the examples at one time. If you need help getting started, turn to the completed chart at the end of the module. By the time you complete all the learning activities, you will find that you have learned many ways to promote good health and nutrition for infants and toddlers.

Using Your Knowledge of Infant and Toddler Development to Promote Good Health and Nutrition

WHAT YOUNG INFANTS DO (0-8 MONTHS)	HOW CAREGIVERS CAN USE THIS INFORMATION TO PROMOTE GOOD HEALTH AND NUTRITION
They have individual schedules for eating, sleeping, and eliminating.	
They wear diapers.	
They often soil or wet their clothes.	
They can choke easily.	
They put everything and anything in their mouths.	
They drink from bottles.	

WHAT MOBILE INFANTS DO (9-17 MONTHS)	HOW CAREGIVERS CAN USE THIS INFORMATION TO PROMOTE GOOD HEALTH AND NUTRITION
They begin to eat finger foods by themselves.	
They undress themselves.	
They can hold a cup with two hands.	
They understand simple phrases with key words and can follow simple instructions.	
WHAT TODDLERS DO (18-36 MONTHS)	
They run, jump, kick, climb, throw, and use indoor and outdoor large-muscle equipment.	
They learn to dress themselves.	

WHAT TODDLERS DO (18-36 MONTHS)	HOW CAREGIVERS CAN USE THIS INFORMATION TO PROMOTE GOOD HEALTH AND NUTRITION
They learn to blow their own noses and to dispose of tissues properly.	
They may be able to use the toilet and wash their hands.	
They pour, stir, and cut foods with assistance.	
They learn to eat healthy foods.	

When you have completed as much as you can do on the chart, discuss your answers with your trainer. As you proceed with the rest of the learning activities, you can refer back to the chart and add more examples of how caregivers promote good health and nutrition for infants and toddlers.

II. Maintaining an Environment That Promotes Wellness

In this activity you will learn:

- to provide and maintain a healthy environment; and

- to recognize symptoms of illness in infants and toddlers.

It is your job to be sure that your environment promotes wellness and minimizes the incidence of illness or disease. It's not something you can do alone. You need the assistance of your colleagues and the parents of the children you care for.

Work with other caregivers to keep your room in good condition during the day. You can do this by cleaning up spills as they occur, wiping off tables before and after eating, storing food and bottles properly, and throwing away garbage promptly. As much as possible, invite children to assist with these chores.

In addition, ensure that your room is sanitary. Bacteria, parasites, and viruses can be left by sick children on tables, toys, and equipment. Work together with your co-workers to minimize germs and keep them from spreading. Each infant and toddler should have his or her own sheet and blanket for napping. These should be laundered at least once a week. Throughout the day, pick up and wash toys that infants suck on. Store toothbrushes in sanitary receptacles such as slotted styrofoam egg cartons and allow them to air dry.

The bathroom is a major source of germs. You should check this room daily to make sure it is clean and well stocked with paper supplies. Changing tables should be covered with a washable surface. After each change, wipe off the surface with a bleach solution or commercial disinfectant. (You can make your own solution by adding 1 tablespoon of bleach per quart of water.) In addition, you should also place a clean sheet of paper under each child. Every time you finish diapering a child or helping a toddler use the toilet, wash your hands and the child's hands.

The most effective way to reduce illness and disease is to wash your hands properly throughout the day. Washing children's hands also prevents germs from spreading. Your hands should be washed:

- when you arrive for work in the morning;

- before you prepare or serve food;

- after you change a diaper or wipe a nose;

- after you care for a child who may have a contagious condition; and

- after you help a child with toileting or use the bathroom yourself.

Of course, no matter how careful you are, sometimes children will get sick. Germs are present even in an apparently spotless room. But you can take precautions to keep illness from spreading by communicating with parents about health issues throughout the year.

When a child is enrolled, you or your director need to tell parents what immunizations are required so they can be sure their children are up to date. Also, everyone needs to be clear about your program's guidelines concerning when children are contagious and should stay home. These guidelines should be written down and discussed early in the year. Suggest that parents consider arrangements for backup care before they need it.

In case a child does become sick during the day, be sure you have the phone numbers of parents at work, their family physician, hospital, and a contact person (in case parents cannot be reached) along with the child's medical history before a parent leaves the child with you.

The chart on the next page[2] summarizes the symptoms and incubation periods for common childhood illnesses. Become familiar with this information. Share it with parents and ask them to inform you if their child has been recently exposed to one of these illnesses. Together you will be taking the necessary precautions to keep illnesses from spreading.

---

[2] Based on the American Academy of Pediatrics, PA Chapter, *Model Child Health Policies*, Revised (Washington, DC: National Association for the Education of Young Children, 1997).
Adapted by Karen Sokal-Gutierrez, M.D., from *Caring for Our Children, National Health and Safety Standards: Guidelines for Out-of-Home Child Care Programs*, 2nd ed. (Washington, DC: American Public Health Association; Elk Grove Village, IL: American Academy of Pediatrics; and Aurora, CO: National Resource Center for Health and Safety in Child Care, 2002).

Contagious Diseases

Diseases spread through the intestinal tract	Symptoms	When child can return to the program
Diarrheal diseases	Increased liquid and number of stools in an 8-hour period.	The child no longer has diarrhea. If due to infection, 24 hours after treatment has begun.
Vomiting	Abdominal pain, digested/undigested stomach contents, refusal to eat, headache, fever.	When vomiting has stopped.
Hepatitis A	Fever, loss of appetite, nausea, yellowish skin and whites of the eyes, dark brown urine, light-colored stool.	One week after illness begins, if fever is gone.
Bacterial meningitis	Fever, vomiting, unusual irritability, excessive crying with inability to be comforted, high-pitched crying, poor feeding, and activity levels below normal.	After fever gone and a closely supervised program of antibiotics. Health Department may recommend preventive medicine for exposed children and staff.
Strep throat	Red and painful throat, often accompanied by fever.	Generally when fever has subsided and child has been on antibiotics for at least 24 hours.

Diseases spread by direct contact (touching)	Symptoms	When child can return to the program
Chicken pox	Fever, runny nose, cough, rash (pink/red blisters).	Six days after onset of rash or when all sores have dried and crusted.
Head lice	Whitish-gray nits attached to hair shafts.	After treatment and removal of nits, and child's clothes and bedding are washed in hot water (140° F).
Herpes (mouth and cold sore)	Sores on lips or inside mouth.	No need for exclusion if lesions are covered.
Impetigo	Red oozing erosion capped with a golden yellow crust that appears stuck on.	After treatment has begun.
Measles	Fever, runny nose, cough, and red-brown blotchy rash on the face and body.	Six days after the rash appears.
Mumps	Swelling of the glands at the jaw angle accompanied by cold-like symptoms.	Nine days after swelling begins.
Pertussis (Whooping Cough)	Cold-like symptoms that develop into severe respiratory disease with repeated attacks of violent coughing.	Three weeks after intense coughing begins or five days after antibiotic treatment has begun.
Purulent Conjunctivitis, (Pinkeye)	Eyes are pink/red, watery, itchy, lid swollen, sometimes painful, and pus is present.	24 hours after treatment is begun. (Not all pinkeye is contagious.)
Ring worm	Skin-reddish scaling, circular patches with raised edges and central clearing or light and dark patches on face and upper trunk or cracking peeling of skin between toes. Scalp-redness, scaling of scalp with broken hairs or patches of hair loss.	No need to exclude child. Advise parents about need for treatment.
Scabies	Crusty wavy ridges and tunnels in the webs of fingers, hand, wrist, and trunk.	After treatment has begun.
Shingles	Blisters in a band or patch.	

What Caregivers Need to Know About HIV

HIV (human immunodeficiency virus) is the virus that causes AIDS (acquired immunodeficiency syndrome). HIV attacks the immune system that normally protects the body from viruses and bacteria. This makes it difficult and gradually impossible for the body to fight off infection.

HIV is not transmitted through casual contact or from being around someone who is infected. It cannot be transmitted by mosquitoes or pets. The virus does not live by itself in the air. You cannot get it by:

- Being in the same room with someone
- Sharing drinks or food
- Being near when someone coughs or sneezes
- Hugging, shaking hands, or kissing as friends do
- Sharing a swimming pool, bath, or toilet

HIV is transmitted through blood, semen, and vaginal secretions. A person can become infected:

- **From mother to child (prenatal).** Most children with HIV infection under 13 years of age are infected this way. If the mother has HIV, her blood can transmit the virus to the baby during pregnancy or delivery. Because HIV has been found in breastmilk, mothers with HIV infection are discouraged from breastfeeding.

- **Through sexual intercourse** with a man or woman who has HIV. Sexually abused children are at risk for HIV infection.

- **By sharing intravenous needles** that contain infected blood from a previous user.

- **From blood and blood product transfusions prior to 1985,** before blood was tested for HIV infection. Many children were infected this way, including those with hemophilia.

Children with HIV infection can remain healthy for long periods of time. They have AIDS when the virus has severely damaged the immune system. Because children with HIV infection are more susceptible to germs, good hygiene is very important.

Health care professionals recommend that anyone who is exposed to blood—whether it is in an infant's stool, a toddler's nosebleed, a skinned knee, or under any conditions at all—adopt the Standard Precautions developed by the Centers for Disease Control (CDC) and the Occupational, Safety, and Health Administration (OSHA)[3].

---

[3] American Academy of Pediatrics, American Public Health Association, and National Resource Center for Health and Safety in Child Care, *Caring for Our Children: National Health and Safety Performance Standards: Guidelines for Out-of-Home Child Care*, 2nd ed. (Elk Grove Village, IL; Washington, DC; Aurora, CO: Author, 2002), pp. 101-103, Standard 3.026.

Originally designed for hospitals, these precautions have been modified for child care facilities. The precautions include:

- wearing gloves ("optional unless blood or blood containing body fluids may be involved" [AAP et al., p. 101])

- avoiding direct contact (via touch or splash) between contaminated fluid or materials and skin openings or mucous membranes

- cleaning and sanitizing blood-contaminated areas and non-disposable items

- observing proper handling of disposable blood-contaminated materials, including diapers

The Standards comment (AAP et al., pp. 101-102) that these precautions, originally developed to minimize contact with HIV, also apply to other blood-borne infections such as hepatitis B virus. Following these precautions will also help minimize transmission of other infections—even if not life-threatening—within the child care setting. In addition, following these procedures at all times prevents isolating or discriminating against a child with a disease.

Children with HIV infection may have special nutrition and therapy needs. Encourage parents to share pertinent medical information in order to best care for the child. If a child has HIV or any other medical condition, you should have a special care plan outlining measures to prevent and recognize illness, medications, and emergency procedures. If you are caring for a child with HIV infection, find out if specific training is available.

The following learning activity can help you maintain an environment that promotes wellness. First complete the Health Checklist. After reading the example that follows it, record your answers to the questions on the form titled "Maintaining a Healthy Environment."

Health Checklist

Look at your room and think about your routines. Use this checklist to assess your environment.

THINGS YOU CAN DO TO MAINTAIN A HEALTHY ENVIRONMENT	ROUTINE IS SATISFACTORY	ROUTINE NEEDS IMPROVEMENT
1. Let in fresh air daily by opening windows or doors.		
2. Wipe off tables after eating and messy activities. Ask mobile infants and toddlers to help you.		
3. Store foods so that they don't spoil.		
4. Refrigerate bottles upon arrival and when children are finished with them.		
5. Put garbage in lined metal or plastic pails with lids.		
6. Check the bathroom daily to make sure it is clean and well stocked with wipes, paper towels, and soap; report problems and missing items to your supervisor.		
7. Wrap and seal soiled disposable diapers before discarding them.		

THINGS YOU CAN DO TO MAINTAIN A HEALTHY ENVIRONMENT	ROUTINE IS SATISFACTORY	ROUTINE NEEDS IMPROVEMENT
8. Disinfect the changing table after each use.		
9. Wash your own hands whenever necessary.		
10. Launder your own clothing or smocks frequently. Have a clean change of clothing for yourself in case of a child's accident.		
11. Wash infants' hands before eating and after diapers are changed. Help mobile infants and toddlers learn to wash their hands before eating, after using the toilet or being changed, after blowing their noses, and after touching a child who may be sick.		
12. Store toothbrushes so the bristles can air dry.		
13. Conduct a health check each day to see if children have: • severe coughing, difficulty breathing, or sore throat; • yellowish skin or eyes; • pinkeye (tears, redness of eyelid lining, irritation, swelling, and discharge of pus); • infected skin patches; • nausea, vomiting, or diarrhea; • loss of appetite; or • unusual behavior.		

THINGS YOU CAN DO TO MAINTAIN A HEALTHY ENVIRONMENT	ROUTINE IS SATISFACTORY	ROUTINE NEEDS IMPROVEMENT
14. Separate sick children from others and ask your supervisor to see that they are cared for until taken home.		
15. Report symptoms of possible illness to your supervisor.		
16. Avoid touching body fluids when changing a diaper or helping a child use the toilet by using disposable latex gloves, and wash your hands immediately afterwards.		
17. Seal wet or soiled clothes in plastic bags so that parents can launder them at home.		
18. Send sheets and blankets home for laundering when needed (at least once a week).		
19. Disinfect supplies and equipment used often by children, such as rubber toys and infant seats.		
20. Be sure to communicate your program's health guidelines clearly to parents.		
21. Be sure children are kept up to date with their immunizations.		

Use your responses on the checklist to complete the chart on the next page. First read the example below.

Maintaining a Healthy Environment
(Example)

Setting *Indoors*   **Age(s)** *Young infants*   **Date(s)** *September 22*

ITEMS NEEDING IMPROVEMENT	WHAT I INTEND TO DO
I don't always let in fresh air in the winter.	*I will raise two windows just a little to let in fresh air.*
I don't wash my hands when I arrive at work.	*I will wash my hands before the children arrive.*
I don't always do a health check.	*I will make the health check part of my children's arrival routine.*
We don't check regularly to be sure children are up to date on their immunizations.	*I will work with my director to create a system so we can keep track of children's immunizations.*

HEALTHY

Now identify the items that need improvement in your environment.

Maintaining a Healthy Environment

Setting _____ Age(s)_____ Date(s)_____

ITEMS NEEDING IMPROVEMENT	WHAT I INTEND TO DO

Discuss your ideas with your trainer. Make the needed changes in your room, and check them off when they have been completed.

III. Introducing Good Health Habits to Infants and Toddlers

In this activity you will learn:

- to model good health habits in the course of daily life in your room so that infants, toddlers, and families can learn by your example; and

- to include health education in daily routines and activities.

The first step in helping infants and toddlers learn good health habits is to practice them daily in your room. You do many things every day—as you feed, change, dress, and play with the children—that ensure their good health. You listed some of these things in the first activity of this module. Here are some examples that your list might include:

- Storing bottles in the refrigerator.

- Serving healthy foods as snacks.

- Washing your hands after each diaper change, before preparing and serving food, and after taking children outdoors.

- Disinfecting the changing table after each use.

- Dressing children warmly to go outside on a cold day and encouraging toddlers to dress themselves.

- Disinfecting daily any toys that children have put in their mouths.

Infants and toddlers depend on you and their parents to ensure their health. When you practice good health habits, you are taking the first step in helping young children develop their own good habits. This is true for the following reasons:

- **Children who are well cared for feel they are valued;** as they grow older, they will want to take good care of themselves.

- **Older infants and toddlers learn by imitating the adults** who play important roles in their lives. Although these children can't understand what a germ is, they will happily wash their hands before eating if you do. This is the beginning of the development of good health habits.

- **Parents may learn new ways to keep their children healthy** by watching and talking with you. For example, some parents do not realize that letting a baby fall asleep with a bottle of milk causes tooth decay. Or they may not wash their hands as often as they should or recognize the importance of helping young children brush their teeth. The children in your care will be healthier as their parents learn good health habits from you.

- **Mobile infants and toddlers are beginning to develop self-help skills** such as eating, dressing, washing their hands, toileting, and toothbrushing. By giving children the chance to practice these skills throughout the day, every day, you are helping them develop permanent good health habits.

Many activities and routines that are already part of your program can be used for health education. These include the following:

- **Eating snacks and lunch.** Let young children help prepare healthy foods. Scrubbing carrots and tearing lettuce are activities that teach children about foods that are good for them.

- **Toothbrushing.** Explain simply to young children that their teeth are important and that brushing is a way to take care of them.

- **Changing diapers and using the toilet.** Wash your hands and children's hands after changing diapers. Wash your hands after toileting, and always have toddlers wash theirs. Discuss toilet learning with parents who need or want some support and direction.

- **Dramatic play.** Use props such as a cot, stethoscope, bandages, and a white jacket to let toddlers pretend to go to the doctor.

- **Water play.** Bathe dolls and rubber animals. Talk about parts of the body.

- **Dressing to go outside.** Let children participate in their own dressing as much as possible.

- **Children's books.** You may want to read to your toddlers *Morris Has a Cold* by Bernard Wiseman, or *How Do I Put It On?* by Shigeo Watanabe. Or you may want to write a simple book about such topics as eating fruit for snacks or making fruit salad.

In this learning activity you will observe a caregiver and one or two children during one of the daily activities or routines listed above. Then you will fill in an observation form that will help you identify the health habits that caregivers integrate into their daily routine and understand how caregivers help young children develop good habits. Begin by reading the examples on the following pages. Then answer the questions that follow.

Health Activity Observation
(Infant Example)

Child(ren) ___*Paul*___ **Age(s)** *11 months* **Date(s)** *March 31*

Setting *Diaper-changing*

Briefly describe what you observe:

Ms. Miller is changing Paul's diaper. She drops the used wipes into a garbage pail with a lid. It opens with a foot pedal. She puts Paul's wet pants in a plastic bag. When she is finished, she disinfects the table and washes her hands. She helps Paul wash his hands.

What health habits or information did the caregiver integrate into the daily routine?

She used a garbage pail with a lid and a foot pedal. She put Paul's wet clothes in a plastic bag. She disinfected the table, washed her hands, and helped Paul wash his hands.

How did the caregiver's interactions help the child(ren) develop good health habits?

Because Ms. Miller takes good care of Paul, he is learning that he is special. He will want to take good care of himself. She is beginning to teach Paul to wash his hands when he finishes in the bathroom.

Health Activity Observation
(Toddler Example)

Child(ren) *Andrea/Tim*   **Age(s)** *26 months/22 months*   **Date(s)**   *April 2*

Setting *Water play and doll-washing*

Briefly describe what you observe:

> *Ms. Wylie is sitting with Andrea and Tim, who are washing dolls. She asks if they have cleaned the doll's knuckles. Tim doesn't know what a knuckle is. Ms. Wylie and Andrea show him. They talk about the dolls' hands, noses, and legs. Ms. Wylie gives the children towels to dry their dolls so they don't catch colds.*

What health habits or information did the caregiver integrate into the daily routine?

> *Ms. Wylie talked about body parts and drying the dolls so they don't catch colds.*

How did the caregiver's interactions help the child(ren) develop good health habits?

> *The toddlers learned a little more about the parts of their body. Ms. Wylie showed them a new way to take good care of their dolls—drying them off after a bath. Being around an adult who takes good care of them will encourage the toddlers to learn to take good care of themselves.*

Health Activity Observation

Child(ren) _____ Age(s)_____ Date(s) _____

Setting _____

Briefly describe what you observe:

_____

_____

_____

_____

What health habits or information did the caregiver integrate into the daily routine?

_____

_____

_____

_____

How did the caregiver's interactions help the child(ren) develop good health habits?

_____

_____

_____

_____

Discuss your answers with your trainer. Also discuss them with the caregiver you observed.

IV. Introducing Good Nutrition Habits to Infants and Toddlers

In this activity you will learn:

- to provide relaxed, pleasant mealtimes for infants and toddlers; and

- to help infants and toddlers take part in the preparation of healthy snacks and meals.

Some adults make the mistake of using food to reward or punish young children. This is not a good practice because it may promote poor eating habits when the children grow up. When an adult tells a child, "You can't have dessert because you didn't eat your peas," the child learns that desserts are more desirable than peas. The child should be learning that it is best to eat a variety of nutritious foods.

By preparing and serving food with care and pleasure, you help the children in your room feel loved and nurtured. By providing relaxed mealtimes where you sit and talk with infants and toddlers, you show that eating together is a special time for people to share and socialize.

Many of our attitudes about food and nutrition are based on our early experiences. Therefore, it is important that we help young children develop good nutrition habits so that these habits will stay with them throughout their lives. Helping infants and toddlers enjoy mealtimes is a first step in teaching them about good nutrition.

Feeding Infants

When you feed very young infants, you can help them develop healthy attitudes toward eating by holding them as they drink from their bottles. You can talk soothingly or sing to them. In this way they will learn that mealtimes can be relaxed, enjoyable experiences.

When infants are able to sit by themselves, you can continue to help them enjoy their meals. Discuss the introduction of solid foods with a child's parents. Cereal is commonly the first food introduced. After an infant accepts this, try one or two new foods per week. Introduce new foods to infants gradually. Because infants have many more taste buds than adults do, foods often taste strong or even bitter to them. As each food is introduced, you should watch for allergic reactions such as a rash, diarrhea, coughing, or vomiting.

At around 6 months of age, infants begin to take more active roles at mealtimes. A 6-month-old can reach out and grab a bottle, the spoon you are holding, or a handful of applesauce. By offering Jessica (8 months) finger foods such as a cracker or slice of peach and her own spoon, you are helping her develop new skills and feel good about herself. Though she may insist on feeding herself, she still needs you to be sure she is eating enough food.

Eating Family-Style Meals with Toddlers

It can be a challenge to make mealtimes with a group of toddlers enjoyable. But if you enjoy yourself—at least a little!—and are relaxed, the children will sense it. Accept the fact that there will be spills. Keep a clean sponge and plenty of paper towels within reach. Share responsibilities with your co-workers; that way you won't have to watch everyone at once, and you'll have more opportunities to focus on and enjoy individual children.

One way to make mealtimes more relaxed is to serve and eat meals family-style. This means that each caregiver sits with a group of children at small tables. Everyone eats the same foods and enjoys pleasant conversation. Children are encouraged to serve easy-to-manage foods themselves. They are more likely to try new foods when they can make choices and see what other people are eating. Children who bring their own snacks and lunches will also enjoy and benefit from the experience of eating together.

Before the Meal

- Provide or encourage food service staff and parents to provide nutritious foods, including dessert. Desserts could include fresh fruit, blueberry muffins, applesauce, fruit juice, gelatin, or cornbread.

- Use very short chairs that allow a toddler's feet to rest flat on the floor while the child sits solidly in the chair seat, using the backrest.

- Seat three to four children and one caregiver at each table. If you have one large table, divide up and sit among the children.

- Encourage children to help set the tables.

- Provide toddler-sized utensils, cups, plates, and pitchers.

- Leave the salt and sugar off the table.

- Invite everyone to sit down after the tables are set.

During the Meal

- Allow toddlers to pour their own drinks using small covered pitchers.

- Maintain a leisurely mealtime pace, encouraging conversation.

- Allow children to refuse food, but encourage them to taste a little of everything.

- Show children how to use utensils if they need help.

- Model good hygiene, safety practices, and manners.

- Encourage children to help you clean up spills.

- Encourage conversation. You can talk about the foods served, but also talk about the events of the day, families, or other topics of interest to the children.

After the Meal

- Remain relaxed.

- Allow children to leave the table when they are finished. Encourage them to clean up their dishes, then go to a quiet activity.

- Have small groups of children wash their hands and brush their teeth. Caregivers should wash their hands and brush their teeth with the children.

- Ask helpers to clean and wash the tables.

Food Preparation Activities

Including children in food preparation activities is a wonderful way to introduce them to nutrition. Although they don't know what vitamins or saturated fats are, spreading cottage cheese on whole wheat bread and peeling bananas gives them a much healthier message than watching you open a package of chocolate cookies or a bag of potato chips.

Whenever possible, invite children to "cook" with you. They will feel proud to help with the real work of cutting pears, washing and tearing lettuce leaves, scrubbing carrots, and stirring fruit into yogurt.

Here are some suggestions to keep in mind as you plan food preparation activities:

- **Keep your recipes simple.** Shelling peas, scrubbing potatoes with a vegetable brush, and stirring raisins into cottage cheese to make a dip may not sound like much to you, but they are great activities for children under 3.

- **You don't need a kitchen to "cook" with children.** You can prepare plenty of foods that don't need to be heated at all. Or if you choose, you can use a hotplate or toaster oven, being sure to keep them out of children's reach.

- **Work with small groups of children.** Rather than make an announcement that it is time to cook, just begin. Children who are interested will join you.

- **Plan ahead of time.** Be sure you have all of the necessary ingredients and equipment. There is no better way to turn a cooking activity into chaos than by having to go look for a spoon.

- **Cut down on waiting time.** Have several vegetable brushes and trays of water for scrubbing potatoes and carrots. Give children small bowls to make individual portions of foods.

- **Talk about what you are doing.** Take time to experience the smells, tastes, and names of ingredients, such as cinnamon and broccoli.

Here are some food preparation activities you might want to try:

- **Mashed potatoes.** Children will enjoy scrubbing the potatoes, dropping them into the cooking pot, and mashing them after they cool. For variety, make white potatoes one day and sweet potatoes another.

- **Shelling peas.** With a little practice, older toddlers can open pea shells.

- **Broccoli.** Children will enjoy breaking the flowerets off the stalk of broccoli before you cook them.

- **Banana smoothies.** Let children peel and break bananas into pieces. Put them in the blender. Add a little milk and blend.

- **French toast.** Toddlers can help stir the mixture of egg and milk. They will enjoy adding a sprinkling of cinnamon. After cooking, cut into small pieces and serve, allowing children to choose their own piece of the French toast they helped to make.

- **Orange juice.** Invite children to roll oranges on the table and help you twist them over the juicer. Pour into cups and serve.

- **Pizzas.** Have children spoon tomato sauce on an English muffin half and then add a slice of mozzarella cheese. Broil in a toaster oven until the cheese melts.

Think beyond graham crackers and milk. There are plenty of healthy foods you can prepare with young children. Enjoy!

If you work with infants, read "Observations of Caregivers Feeding Infants Applesauce" and answer the questions that follow. If you work with toddlers, select one of the food preparation activities you just read about and try it out with the children. Then answer the questions that will help you evaluate the activity. First read the example we have included.

Observation of Caregivers Feeding Infants Applesauce[3]

Take a look now at an example of a good relationship in one of the primary caregiving tasks—feeding an infant. Imagine yourself in a small body being held lovingly on a warm lap.

Hear a familiar voice say to you, "Here's some applesauce for you." Look around and see a spoon, a hand, and beyond it a small dish of applesauce. Take time to really perceive all this. Feel the coziness as well as the anticipation. Hear the same voice say, "Are you ready?" See the spoon come up to your face. There is plenty of time for you to open your mouth for the bite. You feel the applesauce in your mouth. You taste it. You notice the texture and the temperature. You thoroughly explore this bite before you swallow. Some goes down your throat, some runs down your chin. You look up to find the familiar face. Seeing the face adds to your pleasure. You open your mouth again. You feel a scraping on your chin. The next bite comes into your mouth. You explore it. You compare it to the first bite. You take your time and get the most out of this bite before you swallow it. When you swallow you get an excited feeling—an anticipation of the next bite. You look at the face again. You reach out and your fingers touch something soft and smooth. All of these feelings are present as you open your mouth for the next bite.

Come back now from your imagining. Reflect on this experience for a moment. Now compare that imaginary experience with this one.

You find yourself high up in the air. The ground looks very far away. You feel something hard and cold at your back and a strap pushing in your middle. You are barely able to take in these feelings when suddenly there is a spoon in between your lips forcing them open. You taste applesauce. You wiggle your tongue around, swallowing the bite. The spoon again comes between your lips, and your teeth are forced open. You take another mouthful. You enjoy it a great deal—pushing it around in your mouth and out between your teeth—down your chin. You feel metal scraping your chin. More applesauce comes into your mouth. You are about to swallow this mouthful when the spoon arrives again. You take a second mouthful into the first, which you haven't swallowed yet. You work on swallowing while you feel scrape, scrape on your chin, as the spoon gathers up what is running down. More applesauce arrives in your mouth. You swallow a little of the big load and you get ready to swallow more, but before you can, the spoon finds its way in between your teeth again. Now your mouth is fuller than before. You sense a bit of urgency to get this down before the next load. You try to hurry, which only slows you down. More applesauce squishes out and runs down your chin. You feel the spoon—scrape, scrape, scrape, and more applesauce comes in to your mouth. Hold on to that feeling now and stop imagining.

---

[3]Reprinted with permission from Janet Gonzalez-Mena and Dianne Widmeyer Eyer, *Infancy and Caregiving* (Palo Alto, CA: Mayfield, 1980), pp. 30-31.

Think about the two descriptions of a caregiver feeding an infant applesauce as you answer the questions below.

Imagine you are the infant in the first example. Did you enjoy eating? Why?

_____

_____

_____

_____

_____

_____

Imagine you are the infant in the second example. Did you enjoy eating? Why?

_____

_____

_____

_____

_____

_____

What can you do to help infants relax and enjoy mealtimes in your room?

_____

_____

_____

_____

_____

_____

_____

_____

Discuss your answers with your trainer. Talk with other caregivers about ways you can help infants relax and enjoy their mealtimes more.

Plan and conduct a food preparation activity, then answer the questions on the next page about what happened. Read the example below first.

Food Preparation Activity for Toddlers

Child(ren) _Simon, Carrie, Darnell_   **Age(s)** _26-32 months_   **Date(s)** _March 12_

Setting _Kitchen area_

What you made: _Banana smoothies_

Describe the activity:

I worked with three children. At first things were confusing because I didn't have everything ready. I let the toddlers break up the fruit and put it in the blender. They liked tasting the bananas. Darnell was afraid of the blender.

What do you think the child(ren) learned about healthy food and good nutrition?

They felt good about themselves because they helped. They saw the foods we used, which are all good for them.

What would you do differently next time you prepare food with toddlers? Why?

I will warn them about the blender in case someone is afraid. I will have all the supplies I need before I begin so the activity will go more smoothly.

Food Preparation Activity for Toddlers

Child(ren) _____ Age(s)_____ Date(s) _____

Setting _____

What you made _____

Describe the activity:

_____

_____

_____

_____

_____

What do you think the child(ren) learned about healthy food and good nutrition?

_____

_____

_____

_____

_____

What would you do differently next time you prepare food with toddlers? Why?

_____

_____

_____

_____

_____

Discuss your activity with your trainer.

V. Recognizing Child Abuse and Neglect[5]

In this activity you will learn:

- to identify the four types of child abuse and neglect; and

- to recognize the signs of child abuse and neglect.

Child abuse and neglect cases are often first identified in a child development program. Caregivers who have ongoing, daily contact with children are often able to detect and report suspected child maltreatment that otherwise might go unnoticed. Caregivers are responsible for knowing how to identify signs of possible child abuse or neglect and to report their suspicions to the appropriate authorities. The first step is to know the definitions of child abuse and neglect. Each state in the United States has its own legal definitions, most of which include the elements listed below.

Child abuse and neglect includes physical abuse, neglect, sexual abuse, and emotional abuse of a child under the age of 18 by a parent, guardian, or any other person who is responsible for the child's welfare.

- **Physical abuse** includes burning, kicking, biting, punching, or hitting a child.

- **Neglect** includes failing to provide a child with food, clothing, medical attention, or supervision.

- **Sexual abuse** includes using a child for another's (can be a child or an adult) sexual gratification through such actions as fondling, rape, sodomy, and using a child in pornographic pictures or films.

- **Emotional** abuse or maltreatment includes blaming, belittling, ridiculing, and constantly ignoring a child's needs.

Children who are being abused or neglected may exhibit physical and/or behavioral signs of their maltreatment. Physical signs are those you can actually see. Whether mild or severe, they involve the child's physical condition. Frequently physical signs are skin or bone injuries, or evidence of lack of care and attention manifested in conditions such as malnutrition. Behavioral clues may exist alone or may accompany physical indicators. They range from subtle changes in a child's behavior to graphic statements by children describing physical or sexual abuse.

---

[5]Based on materials included in *A Guide for Early Childhood Professionals on Preventing and Responding to Child Maltreatment* (Washington, DC: National Center on Child Abuse and Neglect, In Press, 1991).

Caregivers play an important role in preventing or stopping child maltreatment by identifying and reporting signs of possible abuse or neglect. It is your responsibility to report your suspicions to the director of your center and to the agency designated by your state's law as the recipient of these reports. To fulfill this duty, you must be able to recognize the relevant signs.

Clues to abuse and neglect may be found in how a child looks and acts, what the parent says, how the parent relates to the child, and how the parent and child behave when they are together. No single sign or clue proves abuse or neglect, but repeated signs or several signs together should alert you to the *possibility* that a child is being abused or neglected.

Signs of Possible Physical Abuse

Physical abuse of children includes any nonaccidental physical injury caused by the child's caretaker in single or repeated episodes. Although the injury is not accidental, the adult may not intend to hurt the child. The injury might be the result of overdiscipline or inappropriate physical punishment. This usually happens when an adult is angry or frustrated and strikes, shakes, or throws a child. Occasionally physical abuse is intentional, such as when an adult burns, bites, pokes, cuts, twists limbs, or otherwise harms a child.

Young children frequently fall down and bump into things. This may result in injuries to their elbows, chins, noses, foreheads, and other bony areas. Bruises and marks on the soft tissue of the face, back, neck, buttocks, upper arms, thighs, ankles, backs of legs, or genitals, however, are more likely to be caused by physical abuse. The same may be true of repeated injuries, cigarette burns, bruises in patterns from a belt or rope, or any injury for which the explanation doesn't make sense to you.

When you are changing diapers or helping a toddler go to the bathroom you might see bruises or burns that are covered by clothing. Often abusive parents are consciously or unconsciously aware that the signs of their abuse should be concealed. They may dress their children in long sleeves or long pants even in warm weather. Another sign to look for is bruises that are at various stages of healing, as if they are the result of more than one incident.

Injuries to the abdomen or head, which are two particularly vulnerable spots, often go undetected until there are internal injuries. Injuries to the abdomen can cause swelling, tenderness, and vomiting. Injuries to the head may cause swelling, dizziness, blackouts, retinal detachment, and even death. Shaken baby syndrome is a form of child abuse that can cause hemorrhaging of the brain and eyes and can lead to mental retardation, blindness, deafness, and even death.

In addition to the physical signs that a child has been physically abused, the child might also exhibit behavioral signs. Here are some examples:

- Jackie (30 months) runs to her cubbie to get her blanket whenever she hears another child crying. She clutches her blanket and rocks back and forth, saying, "No hitting. No hitting."

- Ramon (28 months) is usually picked up by his mother. When his father comes to get him, he screams and hides behind his caregiver's legs. Earlier that day his caregiver overheard him playing with the dolls. He said, "I told you no wet pants. Now I'll beat your butt."

- Six-month-old Daniel lies quietly in his crib when he wakes up, looking around the room but not crying or trying to get his caregiver's attention.

Signs of Possible Neglect

Child neglect is characterized by a failure to provide for a child's basic needs. Neglect can be physical (for example, refusal to seek health care when a child clearly needs medical attention), educational (for example, failure to enroll a child of mandatory school age), or emotional (for example, chronic or extreme spouse abuse in the child's presence). Neglect results in death as frequently as abuse. While physical abuse tends to be episodic, neglect tends to be chronic. Neglectful families often appear to have many problems that they cannot handle.

When considering the possibility of neglect, it is important to look for consistencies. Do the signs of neglect occur rarely or frequently? Are they chronic (present almost every day), periodic (happening after weekends, vacations, or absences), or episodic (for example, seen twice during a period when the child's mother was in the hospital)?

Some examples of signs that might indicate that a child is being neglected include the following:

- Sara (20 months) falls down outside and badly scrapes her knee. The center's nurse cleans and bandages it and prepares an accident report for Sara's parents, including information on how to care for the wound. Four days later Sara complains to her caregiver that her knee hurts. The caregiver takes her to the nurse who notices that the bandage has not been changed and the wound is becoming infected.

- David (4 months) arrives at the center with a severe diaper rash. The caregiver tells his mother and asks for permission to use some ointment that will heal David's skin and protect it from further irritations. The mother says, "If you've got the time to put that greasy stuff on, go ahead." The caregiver uses the ointment all week, and the rash goes away. She gives the mother the tube to take home and use over the weekend. On Monday morning David arrives with the rash again. This pattern is repeated over a four-week period.

Signs of Possible Sexual Abuse

Sexual abuse includes a wide range of behavior: fondling a child's genitals, intercourse, rape, sodomy, exhibitionism, and commercial exploitation through prostitution or pornography. These behaviors are contacts or interactions between a child or adult(s) in which the child is being used for the sexual stimulation of the perpetrator(s). Sexual abuse may be committed by a person under the age of 18 when that person is either significantly older than the victim or when the perpetrator is in a position of power or control over another child. For example, if a 14-year-old volunteer touches the genitals of a 2-year-old who is in his or her care, this would be considered sexual abuse.

The physical signs of sexual abuse include some that a caregiver would notice while routinely caring for young children. For example, you might notice a child's torn, stained, or bloody underclothing while helping the child use the bathroom. At these same times you might notice bruises or bleeding in the child's external genitalia, vaginal, or anal areas. If a child says that it hurts to walk or sit, or if he or she complains of pain or itching in the genital area, you should take note and watch to see if this is a recurring condition.

Young children who have been sexually abused may also exhibit behavioral signs of their abuse. They might act out their abuse using dolls, or you might overhear them talking with other children about sexual acts. Their premature sexual knowledge is a sign that they have been exposed to sexual activity. They might show excessive curiosity about sexual activities or touch adults in the breast or genitals. Some children who have been sexually abused are very afraid of specific places, such as the bathroom or a bed.

Some examples of behavioral signs that might indicate that a child is being sexually abused include the following:

- A caregiver is helping Jason (34 months) get to sleep at nap time. For several weeks Jason has been having a hard time settling down. When he does fall asleep, he sometimes wakes up crying about monsters. Today he turns to his caregiver and says, "I've got a secret, but I can't tell you what it is."

- The children in the toddler room are sitting at the table with their caregivers eating lunch. Nancy (30 months) is wiggling around in her seat a lot. Her caregiver asks her if she needs to go to the bathroom. Nancy says, "No, it's not that. My bottom hurts where Gary poked me." Gary is her 12-year-old brother.

- The children and caregivers are outside on the playground. Simone (32 months) needs to go inside to the bathroom. Ms. Fox says, "I'll take her." The other caregiver, Ms. Young, says, "But it's my turn." Ms. Fox insists that she will take the child. Simone says, "I don't have to go any more." Ten minutes later Simone comes up to Ms. Young and says, "I want you to take me. You don't hurt me."

Signs of Possible Emotional Maltreatment

Emotional maltreatment includes blaming, belittling, or rejecting a child; constantly treating siblings unequally; or exhibiting a persistent lack of concern for the child's welfare. This type of abuse is the most difficult form of child maltreatment to identify, as the signs are rarely physical. The effects of mental injury, such as lags in physical development or speech disorders, are not as obvious as bruises and lacerations. Some effects might not show up for many years. Also, the behaviors of emotionally abused and emotionally disturbed children are often similar.

Although emotional maltreatment does occur alone, it often accompanies physical abuse and sexual abuse. Emotionally maltreated children are not always physically abused, but physically abused children are almost always emotionally maltreated.

Some examples of signs that might indicate a child is being emotionally maltreated include the following:

- Each time he comes to pick up Nathan (29 months), Mr. Wheeler makes fun of his son's efforts. Typical comments include: "Can't you zip that coat right? You look like an idiot." "What's that a picture of? Is that the only color you know how to use?" "Can't you climb to the top of the climber yet? All those other kids climbed to the top. What's the matter with you, are your legs too short?"

- A caregiver is making her first home visit to the Peterson family: Mrs. Peterson and her three young children. She rings the door bell and waits a long time for Mrs. Peterson to come to the door. She can hear lots of noise inside the home: loud music, adults arguing, and children crying. She rings the bell again, thinking that perhaps they did not hear her. Finally the door opens and a man pushes his way past her. She looks inside and sees Mrs. Peterson bent over, holding her stomach. The three children are standing in the kitchen doorway holding onto each other. They look very scared, but they are not crying.

Recognizing Child Abuse and Neglect Through Conversations and Interviews

Early childhood programs are generally family oriented, encouraging a great deal of formal and informal communication between program staff and families of the children in the program. You may gather important information about families from routine conversations with parents and children. During daily drop-off and pick-up times and at scheduled conferences, parents provide details of family life, discuss discipline methods, or ask for help with problems. Young children enjoy talking about their families, so they too may provide information about the family's interactions and home life.

Conversations with parents can provide clues to how the parent feels about the child. The presence of child abuse and neglect may be indicated if the parent constantly:

- blames or belittles the child ("I told you not to drop that. Why weren't you paying attention?");

- sees the child as very different from his or her siblings ("His big sister Terry never caused me these problems. She always did exactly what she was told to do.");

- sees the child as "bad," "evil," or a "monster" ("She really seems to be out to get me. She's just like her father, and he was really an evil man.");

- finds nothing good or attractive in the child ("Oh well. Some kids are just a pain in the neck. You can see this one doesn't have anything going for her.");

- seems unconcerned about the child ("She was probably just having a bad day. I really don't have time to talk today.");

- fails to keep appointments or refuses to discuss problems the child is having in the program ("That's what I pay you for. If she's getting into trouble, it's your job to make her behave."); or

- misuses alcohol or other drugs. ("I'm sorry I'm late. You know how it is. I stopped for a few drinks on my way over here.")

When you know a family well, you are in a better position to assess whether a problem may be child abuse and neglect or something else; a chronic condition or a temporary situation; a typical early childhood problem that the program can readily handle or a problem that requires outside intervention. Family circumstances may also provide clues regarding the possible presence of abuse or neglect. The risk of abuse or neglect increases when families are isolated from friends, neighbors, and other family members, or if there is no apparent "lifeline" to which a family can turn in times of crisis. Marital, economic, emotional, or social crises are some causes of family stress that can lead to child abuse or neglect.

This activity will help you learn more about how an abused or neglected infant or toddler might look and behave and about the importance of knowing what is typical behavior for the children in your care. Changes in an individual child's behavior can be a sign of abuse or neglect. In addition, children who are abused or neglected may express their emotions in a variety of ways.

Select two children in your group who you think have different ways of showing when they are happy, sad, or afraid. Observe them for two to three days. Have handy a pencil and something small to write on (index cards work well). Jot down how these children show that they are happy, sad, or afraid. Read the example that follows, and use your notes to answer the questions on the blank form.

Observation Summary
(Example)

Dates: _March 27-29_

	Name _Jay_ **Age** _8 months_	**Name** _Julie_ **Age** _20 months_
How does this child look and act when happy?	_He smiles and hums._	_She giggles and dances around._
What makes him or her happy?	_Playing with water, seeing his father at the end of the day._	_Going outside, singing songs._
How does this child look and act when sad?	_He sits by himself and holds his blanket._	_She sits by herself and rocks while she holds her blanket._
What makes him or her sad?	_Saying goodbye to his father._	_Saying goodbye to her parents._
How does this child look and act when frightened?	_Gets very quiet and puts a corner of his blanket in his mouth._	_Sucks her finger or runs to an adult._
What frightens this child?	_Loud noises._	_Thunder and lightening._

Observation Summary

Dates_____

	Name _____ Age _____	Name _____ Age _____
How does this child look and act when happy?		
What makes him or her happy?		
How does this child look and act when sad?		
What makes him or her sad?		
How does this child look and act when frightened?		
What frightens this child?		

Discuss your answers with your trainer.

VI. Reporting Suspected Cases of Child Abuse and Neglect[6]

In this activity you will learn:

- to identify your state requirements for reporting suspected cases of child abuse and neglect; and

- to overcome emotional and other barriers to reporting.

If you suspect or have reason to believe that a child might have been abused or neglected, you are ethically and legally required to report that information so that action can be taken to help the child and the family. As a caregiver you have a professional responsibility to know and understand your program's reporting requirements and those of your state or local government. You must also follow your program's procedures for reporting suspected cases of abuse and neglect. In most instances you will report your suspicions to your supervisor. She or he will then advise you about the appropriate actions to be taken.

Each state law specifies one (or more) agencies that receive reports of suspected child abuse and neglect. Usually reports are made to the Department of Social Services, the Department of Human Resources, the Division of Family and Children's Services, or Child Protective Services of the local city, county, or state government. In some states the police department may also receive reports of child maltreatment. It is important to know who receives reports of suspected child abuse and neglect in your jurisdiction. The state reporting statute includes this information.

Some states require that either a written or an oral report be made to the responsible agency. In other states an oral report is required immediately, and a written report must follow in 24 to 48 hours. You or your program will need to check your state law for the specific requirements.

Usually the state requires reporters to provide the following information:

- Child's name, age, and address

- Child's present location (for example, at the child care center)

- Parent's name and address

- Nature and extent of the injury or condition observed

- Reporter's name and location (sometimes not required, but extremely useful for the agency conducting the investigation)

Many programs have established policies defining the duties and responsibilities of all staff in reporting child abuse and neglect. Your orientation training probably includes this information. If you don't have a copy of your center's child abuse and neglect reporting procedures, ask your supervisor for one. Use it to complete the following chart.

---

[6]Based on materials included in Derry G. Koralek, *Caregivers of Young Children: Preventing and Responding to Child Maltreatment* (Washington, DC: National Center on Child Abuse and Neglect, 1992).

Program Policy on Child Abuse and Neglect

I report suspected child abuse and neglect to:

_____

_____

_____

I must give the following information:

_____

_____

_____

My report must be:

Oral: _____

Written: _____

Both: _____

Getting Ready to Report

Once you suspect that a child is being maltreated, you must waste no time in reporting. Taking this action will probably make you feel at risk, confused, and generally uncomfortable. It is not a pleasant task. To alleviate at least some of your discomfort, you can use the following checklist to prepare for the report.

- Have you documented your suspicions and reviewed your observation notes and anecdotal records? _____

- Have you analyzed your information to define what causes you to suspect abuse/neglect? Have you made a list of the physical and behavioral signs you have observed? _____

- Have you described the parent and child interactions you observed? Have you noted instances when the parent indicated that he or she finds the child difficult, worthless, or impossible to handle? Do you have examples of the parent's lack of interest in the child? _____

- Have you spoken to any of your colleagues concerning the physical and behavioral signs you have documented? If they have reason to suspect abuse or neglect, have you discussed these reasons? _____

- Have you talked with your supervisor about the support he or she will provide once you file the report and the steps the program will take if the parents try to remove the child from the program? Will you have the program's support? _____

- Have you set up a support system for yourself? (After the report is made, you may feel vulnerable and need to talk with others about your feelings and concerns.) _____

- Have you reviewed the program's reporting policy? _____

- Do you have the information needed to file the initial report? _____

- Do you have the exact telephone number and address of the agency to which you should report? _____

- If a written report is required, do you have reporting forms, or will you use a piece of paper? _____

You might not be able to wait until your answers to these questions are all in the affirmative. Instead, you must report your suspicions immediately. This checklist can help you organize your thoughts and secure the support you will need once the report is filed.

Overcoming Barriers to Reporting

When you suspect that a child in your care is being abused or neglected, you may feel very reluctant to report your suspicions. It helps to remember that a report of child abuse or neglect not an accusation; rather, it is a request to begin the helping process. But the reporting process does not always go smoothly. You may encounter difficulties that will discourage you from making future reports. If you are aware of these difficulties beforehand and plan ways to overcome them, you will be better able to fulfill your legal and ethical responsibilities to the children in your care. If you are aware of an abusive situation and do not report your suspicions, you could be fined, or even go to jail.

Some caregivers find that their personal feelings are a barrier to reporting child abuse or neglect. They simply prefer not to get involved. They are afraid that they have made a mistake and that there is a perfectly good explanation for the child's injuries or behavior. They may fear that other parents will think them incompetent or an alarmist. It is important for caregivers to remember that while they wait for positive proof of a child's maltreatment, the child is vulnerable to continued incidences of maltreatment.

Another potential barrier to reporting is the special relationship that parents and a caregiver develop over months or years, which may hinder caregivers from reporting suspected cases of child maltreatment. At times, when caregivers observe signs of abuse or neglect, they may give parents the benefit of the doubt. Even when they do suspect child maltreatment, caregivers may fear that confronting the parents would result in a hostile, indignant, or distressed reaction or retaliation. It may help to remember that as an early childhood professional, your primary responsibilities are to protect the children in your care and to support their families. By reporting your suspicions to the appropriate authorities, you are protecting children as well as helping their families get the assistance they need to change their behavior.

This activity will help you understand your responsibilities for reporting child abuse and neglect. Answer the following questions, then meet with your trainer to review the answers provided at the end of the module. There can be more than one good answer to each question.

Caregiver Responsibilities for Reporting Child Abuse and Neglect

1. Why do child maltreatment laws exist?

_____
_____
_____

2. How do maltreated children get assistance?

_____
_____
_____

3. What happens to children if nobody reports child maltreatment?

_____
_____
_____

4. Under what circumstances do I have to file a report?

_____
_____
_____

5. What will happen to me if I don't report?

_____
_____
_____

6. What if I'm wrong and the parents sue me?

_____
_____
_____

Compare your answers to those at the end of the module and discuss them with your trainer.

Summarizing Your Progress

You have now completed all of the learning activities for this module. Whether you are an experienced caregiver or a new one, this module has probably helped you develop new skills for promoting good health and nutrition for infants and toddlers. Before you go on, take a few minutes to summarize what you've learned.

- Turn back to Learning Activity I, Using Your Knowledge of Infant and Toddler Development to Promote Good Health and Nutrition, and add to the chart specific examples of what you learned about promoting good health and nutrition during the time you were working on this module. Read the sample responses on the completed chart at the end of the module.

- Next, review your responses to the pre-training assessment for this module. Write a summary of what you learned, and list the skills you developed or improved.

Your final step in this module is to complete the knowledge and competency assessments. Let your trainer know when you are ready to schedule the assessments. After you have successfully completed these assessments, you will be ready to start a new module. Congratulations on your progress so far, and good luck with your next module.

Answer Sheet: Promoting Children's Health and Nutrition

Providing Healthy Indoor and Outdoor Environments

1. **What are three things Ms. Lewis did to maintain a healthy room?**

   a. She opened the windows to let in fresh air.

   b. She opened the windows only a few inches so that the room would stay warm.

   c. She checked the paper towel and soap supply.

   d. She put out more paper towels.

   e. She conducted a health check on the children.

   f. She placed the tissues where the children could reach them.

2. **What did Ms. Lewis do to keep germs from spreading?**

   a. She helped a child blow his nose and throw away the used tissue.

   b. She washed her hands and helped the child wash his.

Helping Infants and Toddlers Develop Good Health Habits

1. **What three healthy things did Mr. Jones do with the children?**

   a. He ate apples, a healthy food.

   b. He let the children help him clear off the table.

   c. He helped the children brush their teeth after lunch.

2. **How did Mr. Jones teach the children ways to keep themselves healthy?**

   a. He talked to them about their health routines.

   b. He ate apples, helped clear the table, and brushed his teeth. By doing the things he wanted to teach, he was a model for the children.

Recognizing and Reporting Child Abuse and Neglect

1. **Why was Ms. Bates worried about Lynn?**

   She has seen unexplained bruises twice.

2. **What did Ms. Bates do when she suspected abuse?**

   She discussed the unexplained bruises with her center director.

Using Your Knowledge of Infant and Toddler Development to Promote Good Health and Nutrition

WHAT YOUNG INFANTS DO (0-8 MONTHS)	HOW CAREGIVERS CAN USE THIS INFORMATION TO PROMOTE GOOD HEALTH AND NUTRITION
They have individual schedules for eating, sleeping, and eliminating.	Individualize daily schedules to meet each infant's need for play, rest, eating, and being diapered.
They wear diapers.	Change diapers frequently. Wash your hands and the infant's hands when you are finished. Disinfect the changing table after each change to prevent the spread of germs. Set up the changing area in a separate place from the eating area to prevent contamination of food.
They often soil or wet their clothes.	Seal wet or soiled clothes in plastic bags and send them home to be washed.
They can choke easily.	Teach crawlers and toddlers to seat themselves while eating. Avoid foods that cause choking, such as grapes, peanuts, and popcorn, even though they may be nutritious.
They put everything and anything in their mouths.	Wash and disinfect toys and equipment daily to prevent germs from spreading.
They drink from bottles.	Label bottles so that infants drink from their own bottles. Be sure to refrigerate bottles promptly when each infant is finished so that milk or juice doesn't spoil. If an infant falls asleep with a bottle, be sure it contains water, not juice or milk, to prevent tooth decay.

WHAT MOBILE INFANTS DO (9-17 MONTHS)	HOW CAREGIVERS CAN USE THIS INFORMATION TO PROMOTE GOOD HEALTH AND NUTRITION
They begin to eat finger foods by themselves.	Offer infants nutritious finger foods such as pieces of banana and breadsticks so they can practice feeding themselves.
They undress themselves.	Supervise infants closely to keep them from tearing off their diapers. Help them to wash their hands if they have touched wet or soiled clothing.
They can hold a cup with two hands.	Allow infants to drink juice and milk from half-filled plastic cups so they can practice drinking.
They understand simple phrases with key words and can follow simple instructions.	Coach older infants to get a tissue or paper towel for cleaning spills to help them develop good health habits.
WHAT TODDLERS DO (18-36 MONTHS)	
They run, jump, kick, climb, throw, and use indoor and outdoor large-muscle equipment.	At all times of day, provide opportunities for toddlers to use large muscles so they receive plenty of exercise.
They learn to dress themselves.	Provide opportunities for toddlers to dress themselves. Remind them to wear jackets outdoors when it is cold so that they stay healthy.
They learn to blow their own noses and to dispose of tissues properly.	Place tissue boxes where toddlers can reach them. Remind them to throw away used tissues so that germs are not transmitted by toddlers touching themselves and others. Avoid putting used tissues in your own pockets, as the pocket is then contaminated with germs and needs to be laundered.

WHAT TODDLERS DO (18-36 MONTHS)	HOW CAREGIVERS CAN USE THIS INFORMATION TO PROMOTE GOOD HEALTH AND NUTRITION
They may be able to use the toilet and wash their hands.	Remind toddlers to use the toilet as needed. Be sure there is always a supply of soap, paper towels, and toilet paper in the bathroom so they can take care of their own physical needs.
They pour, stir, and cut foods with assistance.	Plan and conduct simple food-preparation activities with toddlers so that they can learn about foods, food preparation, and good eating habits.
They learn to eat healthy foods.	Serve family-style meals, encouraging toddlers to serve themselves and taste all foods, so they can learn how to select proper foods for themselves and begin to judge how much food will satisfy their hunger.

Answer Sheet: Reporting Child Abuse and Neglect

1. Why do child maltreatment laws exist?

   To provide protection for children who cannot protect themselves.

2. Why do child maltreatment laws exist?

   These laws exist to protect children. If a child is a victim of maltreatment, the only way that the child and family will receive help is if a report is filed.

3. What happens to children if nobody reports child maltreatment?

   If the maltreatment goes unnoticed and unreported, it is likely that it will continue and perhaps escalate.

4. Under what circumstances do I have to file a report?

   If your knowledge of the child and his or her family and your professional training and experience lead you to suspect child maltreatment, then you must file a report.

5. What will happen to me if I don't report?

   If you fail to report, under your state's laws you might be subject to fines or even a jail sentence.

6. What if I'm wrong and the parents sue me?

   When you make a report in good faith, the law protects you. You cannot be sued for reporting child maltreatment because as an early childhood professional, you are mandated to do so.

Glossary

Abstract	Existing in someone's mind—ideas or thoughts rather than real items.
Body fluids	Liquids and semi-liquids eliminated by or present in the body, such as feces, urine, mucus, and saliva.
Concrete	Relating to real objects or pictures.
Diet	The kind and amount of food and drink regularly consumed.
Disinfectant	A cleaning solution that destroys the causes of infection.
Emotional abuse	Acts of commission or omission on a child by a parent or parent substitute that result in emotional harm to the child.
Hygiene	Practices that preserve good health and eliminate disease-producing germs.
Infection	Invasion of the body by tiny organisms that cause disease.
Neglect	Failure to provide a child with food, clothing, medical attention, or supervision.
Nurturance	Behavior that is warm and caring and that leads to a feeling of comfort and love.
Nutrient	A component of food that offers nourishment to the body.
Nutritious	Having large amounts of vitamins, minerals, complex carbohydrates, or protein, and being low in fats, salt, and sugar.
Physical abuse	Bodily injury that is inflicted or is allowed to be inflicted, other than by accident.
Sexual abuse	Any form of sexual activity between a child and an adult for the sexual pleasure or profit of the adult, including fondling, intercourse, and sexual exploitation (prostitution, pornography).
Sodium	A mineral normally found in seafood, poultry, and some vegetables; one of the components of table salt.
Starch	A carbohydrate food such as cereal, potatoes, pasta, and bread.

Module 3
Learning Environment

What Is the Learning Environment and Why Is It Important?

The learning environment is the place where you care for infants and toddlers. It includes both outdoor and indoor play spaces. Features such as the size of the room, its colors, the type of flooring, the amount of light, and the number of windows all influence the quality of the indoor environment. Outdoors, a good environment has soft and hard surfaces, shady and sunny areas, and safe places to crawl, walk, run, and play.

Although you may not have much control over some of the physical aspects of your environment, there are many things you can do to make your environment a good one for the children who live there many hours a week.

Perhaps the most important factor in creating a learning environment is the quality of the interactions between adults and the infants and toddlers in their care. When caregivers create an atmosphere of caring and trust, children develop and experience positive feelings about themselves. They feel safe and secure, which frees them to explore and learn about the people and objects around them.

The furniture in the room and how you arrange it are also part of the learning environment. Materials and equipment you select and how you organize them convey important messages to children. The schedule and routines you follow each day also add to the learning environment.

In addition to being a good place for children, the environment must also be a good place for you. An environment that takes care of you will help you take better care of children. It is important that you do things to help you feel at home and comfortable, such as hanging pictures you enjoy or keeping a vase filled with fresh flowers.

Your storage areas contribute strongly to the comfort level of your environment. Being able to find what you need when you need it cuts down on frustration for you and the children and can make your job easier. Another element of a good environment is an appropriate schedule. When you create a schedule and daily routines that work well for the children in your care, each day will probably go more smoothly.

A good learning environment gives you more time to spend with children and to enjoy your job. It meets the needs of both the children and the adults who care for them.

Establishing and maintaining a learning environment involves:

- organizing indoor and outdoor areas that encourage play and exploration;

- selecting and arranging appropriate materials and equipment that foster growth and learning; and

- planning and implementing a schedule and routines that respond to the needs of children under 3.

Listed below are examples of how caregivers demonstrate their competence in establishing a learning environment.

Organizing Indoor and Outdoor Areas That Encourage Play and Exploration

Here are some examples of what caregivers can do.

- Organize the room with clearly defined spaces for sleeping, playing, eating, and diapering/toileting.

- Organize the indoor area with space for crawling, walking, tumbling, rolling, jumping, climbing, and other large-muscle activities.

- Provide soft, cozy areas where infants and toddlers can explore, play with materials, or sit back and watch.

- Organize the outdoor areas so mobile infants and toddlers can safely crawl, walk, climb, run, use wheeled toys, push wagons, and play with balls.

- Provide separate spaces outdoors for active and quiet play.

Selecting and Arranging Appropriate Materials and Equipment That Foster Growth and Learning

Here are some examples of what caregivers can do.

- Hang mobiles where infants can easily see them.

- Select toys that infants and toddlers can safely put in their mouths and that cannot be swallowed.

- Select puzzles and other manipulatives so children are challenged but not frustrated.

- Display materials on low, open shelves so children can find what they want to play with.

- Provide dolls, picture books, and toys that reflect different ethnic backgrounds and children with disabilities.

- Provide private spaces where children can be alone or spend time with a favorite caregiver or friends.

Planning and Implementing a Schedule and Routines That Respond to the Needs of Children Under Three

Here are some examples of what caregivers can do.

- Offer a good balance between active times (such as outdoor play) and quieter activities (such as reading a story).

- Allow plenty of time for daily routines such as changing diapers and dressing.

- Take infants and toddlers outside every day so they can get fresh air, experience a natural environment, and release pent-up energy.

- Adapt daily routines to meet the individual needs of each child. For example, feed an infant more often than usual when she or he seems to be especially hungry.

- Take time to talk and play with each child alone as well as to work with small groups of children.

Creating and Using an Environment for Learning

The following situations show caregivers setting up and using learning environments for infants and toddlers. As you read them, think about what the caregivers in each scene are doing and why. Then answer the questions following each episode.

Organizing Indoor and Outdoor Areas That Encourage Play and Exploration

Mr. Jones looks around the play yard. He sees lots of frustrated children. Sarah (29 months) is in the shed, pulling on a tire that is under a tangle of boards, riding toys, and rakes. Benjamin (33 months) struggles to pull the Big Wheels out of the shed. Andy (30 months) drops the watering can when a child chasing a ball races by the tomato plants he is watering. "This place needs some organizing," Mr. Jones thinks. Over the next week, he makes changes to encourage children's play and exploration. First, he arranges the tires and boards so that children can get them easily. He hangs their gardening tools within easy reach on the door of the storage shed. He moves the Big Wheels to the path and the balls to the grass away from the garden. He tells the children about the different areas and reminds them where to ride their Big Wheels and throw balls.

1. **What did Mr. Jones know about the toddlers in his group?**

_____

_____

_____

_____

2. **What are examples of quiet and active materials that toddlers might want to play with and explore in this yard?**

_____

_____

_____

_____

3. **How did Mr. Jones use this information about children and different activities to organize an outdoor area that would encourage play and exploration?**

_____

_____

_____

_____

Selecting and Arranging Appropriate Materials and Equipment That Foster Growth and Learning

"I think we need to replace one of our toys," Ms. Gonzalez says to Ms. Lewis. "Yesterday I saw Mike (19 months) turn the stacking toy upside down, causing all the plastic donut-shaped pieces to fall off. He laughed as he picked up a large blue one and slid it down the center post. Then he picked up a red, smaller piece. Because the toy is designed so that the rings must be stacked in order, he could push the red one only partway down no matter how hard he pushed. He looked frustrated and tossed the toy aside." "You're right," Ms. Lewis replies. "Let's get one with a straight post so the pieces can go in any order. And let's keep our eye out for other toys that set up children for failure."

1. **What did Ms. Gonzalez observe to make her think that the stacking toy needed to be replaced?**

   _____

   _____

   _____

   _____

2. **Why would a stacking toy with a straight post be better?**

   _____

   _____

   _____

   _____

Planning and Implementing a Schedule and Routines That Respond to the Needs of Children Under Three

Each morning at about 10:30, Ms. Bates and Ms. Jackson take the infants for a walk. Today, as they begin putting on the children's sweaters, Randy (5 months) starts rubbing his eyes and crying. Pam (8 months), usually a very happy child, whines and tugs on her ear. "I know what Randy rubbing his eyes and Pam tugging on her ear means. These two are tired," Ms. Bates says. "We should have known. Both their mothers said they were up several times last night." "I have an idea," says Ms. Jackson. "What if we divide up? You can stay here with these two while they sleep and with the three who are playing. I'll take the others outside in the big carriage." "That's a good idea," says Ms. Kim. "Then when you come back I'll take a few children outside."

1. How did Ms. Bates and Ms. Moore know that Randy and Pam were tired?

_____

_____

_____

_____

2. How did the caregivers change their daily routine to meet the needs of the young children in their care?

_____

_____

_____

_____

Compare your answers with those on the answer sheet at the end of this module. If your answers are different, discuss them with your trainer. There can be more than one good answer.

How Your Environment Affects You

We are all affected by our environment. Whether sitting in the living room, shopping in a store, climbing a mountain, or sitting in a staff lounge, we react to the environment. Our surroundings affect:

- how we feel;
- how comfortable we are;
- how we behave; and
- how effectively we can accomplish what we need to do.

Think for a moment about how you feel and behave in the following situations.

- Standing in a hot, crowded bus or subway where you are sandwiched among strangers. (Perhaps you pull in your shoulders, try to avoid any contact with others, and count the minutes until you get off.)

- Eating in a special restaurant with a favorite friend. The lights are low, and the noise level is muffled. The smells are delicious, and attractive pictures hang on the walls. (You are probably relaxed, enjoying a delightful dinner, feeling special and unhurried.)

- Preparing a meal in a strange kitchen when the owner is not there to help you. (This can be very frustrating, especially if you can't figure out how the kitchen is organized. You spend lots of time looking for the things you need. It's inefficient, and you may not cook as well as you usually do.)

It's easy to see in these examples how our environment can affect our actions and our feelings. But the influence of our surroundings is not always so clear. Sometimes we are not aware of how the environment is making us feel and act.

To identify some less obvious factors in the environment that support you or work against you, take time to answer the following questions. Think about a store where you enjoy shopping. It can be a grocery store, clothing store, hardware store, or any other store. As you imagine yourself in this store, think of what makes it a good experience. What makes it easy to find and purchase the things you need?

Type of store: _____

Why do you enjoy shopping there?

_____

_____

_____

_____

_____

Now think about a store you dislike going to. When you are there, you feel frustrated and angry. You may decide never to return again. What's different about this store?

Type of store:_____

Why do you dislike shopping there?

_____

_____

_____

_____

Look over your answers to these two questions. Many of the factors you identified that make shopping enjoyable or difficult apply to the caregiving environment as well. Your work environment should support you and work for you. It should be organized and planned to support the goals you have for children and to make your job easier and more enjoyable.

Now think of your favorite place to be; it can be indoors or outdoors. Close your eyes for a moment and imagine yourself in that space. How does it feel? Smell? Look? What do you hear? What are you doing? Are you alone, or are other people with you? Describe your favorite place below.

_____

_____

_____

_____

Many times when people describe their favorite space, they identify features such as the following:

- a quiet place to be alone,
- a soft and comfortable place to stretch out,
- a place where music is playing,
- a bright and sunny place, or
- a colorful and attractive place.

There may be many other features that describe your favorite place. Because you like this type of environment, you feel comfortable and relaxed. Keep these features in mind as you examine the caregiving environment. A comfortable environment for young children and for you makes caregiving more satisfying.

When you have finished this overview section, complete the pre-training assessment. Refer to the glossary at the end of this module if you need definitions of the terms that are used.

Pre-Training Assessment

Listed below are the skills that caregivers use to create an environment for learning. Think about whether you do these things regularly, sometimes, or not enough. Place a check in one of the columns on the right for each skill listed. Then discuss your answers with your trainer.

SKILL	I DO THIS REGULARLY	I DO THIS SOMETIMES	I DON'T DO THIS ENOUGH
ORGANIZING INDOOR AND OUTDOOR AREAS THAT ENCOURAGE PLAY AND EXPLORATION 1. Setting up a welcoming, homelike environment with spaces for sleeping, eating, playing, diapering, and toileting.			
2. Creating private, soft, and cozy areas in the indoor and outdoor space where infants and toddlers can be by themselves.			
3. Setting up the environment so infants and toddlers can practice self-help skills.			
4. Providing open areas with a variety of surfaces for infants and toddlers to explore.			
5. Having platforms, ramps, and low furniture in the room so infants and toddlers can explore and pull themselves up.			
6. Setting up the room so you can see all the children all the time.			

SKILL	I DO THIS REGULARLY	I DO THIS SOMETIMES	I DON'T DO THIS ENOUGH
SELECTING AND ARRANGING APPROPRIATE MATERIALS AND EQUIPMENT THAT FOSTER GROWTH AND LEARNING 7. Selecting materials and equipment that are challenging and allow infants and toddlers to experience success.			
8. Arranging materials to offer clear choices and promote independence.			
9. Selecting materials that are appropriate for the interests and abilities of the children in the room.			
10. Conveying positive messages through the arrangement of the environment (e.g., "This is a safe place; you can find what you need").			
11. Making sure that toys and decorations reflect the family backgrounds of the infants and toddlers in the room.			
12. Selecting and displaying simple materials for dramatic play.			

SKILL	I DO THIS REGULARLY	I DO THIS SOMETIMES	I DON'T DO THIS ENOUGH
PLANNING AND IMPLEMENTING A SCHEDULE AND ROUTINES APPROPRIATE TO THE AGE OF THE CHILDREN 13. Planning a consistent schedule and adapting it to meet individual needs.			
14. Planning for naptime to help infants and toddlers relax and feel comfortable.			
15. Allowing ample time for daily routines and using them as opportunities for learning.			
16. Planning different kinds of outdoor experiences every day.			

Review your responses, then list three to five skills you would like to improve or topics you would like to learn more about. When you finish this module, you will list examples of your new or improved knowledge and skills.

_____

_____

_____

_____

_____

_____

_____

_____

Now begin the learning activities for Module 3, Learning Environment.

I. Using Your Knowledge of Infant and Toddler Development to Create a Learning Environment

In this activity you will learn:

- to recognize some typical behaviors of infants and toddlers; and

- to use what you know about infants and toddlers to create an environment for learning.

A good learning environment for infants and toddlers responds to children's needs according to their stage of development. Young infants depend on their adults to move them to different places in the environment. Yet even so, they are active explorers. They experience their environment by looking at and listening to what is happening around them. They also learn about their world by putting into their mouths everything they can grab. They experiment to see what effect they can have on the people and things around them as they smile at a caregiver, make different sounds, and kick at a mobile.

Among other things, young infants do the following:[1]

see	mouth	tear	creep around, in, and under
watch	eat	clap together	swing
look	reach out	put in	rock
inspect	reach for	take out	coo, babble
hear	knock away	find	imitate sounds
listen	grasp	look for	react to others
smell	hold	kick	accommodate to others
taste	squeeze	turn	solicit from others
feel	pinch	roll	experiment endlessly
touch	drop	lift their heads	
	transfer hand to hand	sit up	
	shake	pull up	
	bang	crawl to, in, out, over	
		rock	

Mobile infants can move around on all fours and may be learning to walk and climb. They explore and investigate everything they can reach. They pull themselves up and hold onto furniture or railings as they move around the room. They pull things off shelves and tables. They need safe spaces in which to explore.

---

[1]Reprinted with permission from Jim Greenman, *Caring Spaces, Learning Places* (Redmond, WA: Exchange Press, PO Box 2890, Redmond, Washington 98073 (206) 883-9394), 1988), p. 49.

Young toddlers (from 18 to 24 months) are by far the most active children. Toddlers are everywhere in their environment. They move very quickly from one place to the next. They get into all areas of their environment—by climbing, touching, and moving things around.

Between 30 and 36 months, children slow down a bit. They are likely to stop for a while in their travels around their environment—perhaps to play with toys or look briefly at books.

Among other things, mobile infants and toddlers do the following:[2]

walk in, out, up, down, over, under around, through	smear	select	discover
	draw	sort	investigate by trial and error
	mix	match	
	separate	splash	explore with each sense
	pour	make sounds and words	imitate
climb in, up, over, on top	sift		try adult behavior
	stack	label	
slide	pile	read symbols	hug
swing	nest	converse	kiss
hang	set up	follow directions	test others
jump	knock over	cuddle	accommodate to others
tumble	collect	order	
take apart	gather	carry	help themselves wash, eat, and dress
put together	fill	rearrange	
doll play	dump	put in	
paint	inspect	take out	
	examine	hide	

Often when people think of a learning environment for young children, they envision a preschool room. But infants and toddlers have very different needs than children even one year older. A good learning environment for them will look very different from one planned for preschoolers. Knowing what infants and toddlers are like at each stage of development will help you create an environment to meet their unique needs.

The chart on the next page lists some typical behaviors of infants and toddlers. Included are behaviors relevant to creating and using an appropriate learning environment. The right-hand column asks you to identify ways that caregivers can use this information about child development to create a learning environment. As you work through the module, you will learn new strategies for creating and using a learning environment, and you can add them to the chart. You are not expected to think of all the examples at one time. If you need help getting started, turn to the completed chart at the end of the module. By the time you complete all the learning activities, you will find that you have learned many ways to create a good learning environment for young children.

[2]Reprinted with permission from Jim Greenman, *Caring Spaces, Learning Places* (Redmond, WA: Exchange Press, PO Box 2890, Redmond, Washington 98073 (206) 883-9394), 1988), p. 49.

Using Your Knowledge of Infant and Toddler Development to Create a Learning Environment

WHAT YOUNG INFANTS DO (0-8 MONTHS)	HOW CAREGIVERS CAN USE THIS INFORMATION TO CREATE A LEARNING ENVIRONMENT
They feel most secure at home with their parents.	
They begin to reach for objects.	
They like being held and looking at faces.	
They listen to noises around them and are interested in sounds. They look to see where sounds come from.	
They begin creeping and crawling.	

WHAT MOBILE INFANTS DO (9-17 MONTHS)	HOW CAREGIVERS CAN USE THIS INFORMATION TO CREATE A LEARNING ENVIRONMENT
They grow and change in their abilities and interests quickly from one week to the next.	
They sometimes need to get away from the group and be alone or with a special caregiver.	
They begin pulling themselves up to stand and then begin walking.	
WHAT TODDLERS DO (18-36 MONTHS)	
They copy the behavior of adults.	
They talk, run, and climb—they are very active.	
They like to do things themselves.	

WHAT TODDLERS DO (18-36 MONTHS)	HOW CAREGIVERS CAN USE THIS INFORMATION TO CREATE A LEARNING ENVIRONMENT
They may have trouble sharing. They can be very possessive.	
They may have trouble sharing. They can be very possessive.	
They can make simple decisions.	
They are becoming toilet-trained.	
They like to play with toys.	

When you have completed as much as you can do on the chart, discuss your responses with your trainer. As you proceed with the rest of the learning activities, you can refer back to the chart and add more examples of how caregivers create a learning environment for infants and toddlers.

II. Creating a Homelike Environment

In this activity you will learn:

- to locate and define each area of the room; and

- to create a homelike environment where infants and toddlers can feel secure and learn.

Like all of us, children learn best when they feel comfortable and secure. They feel this way at home, surrounded by familiar objects and by people who love them. By creating a homelike environment, you are saying to children that they can feel secure and comfortable at child care, too. You are setting the stage for them to explore and learn.

Look at your space from a child's point of view:

- Are there interesting things to look at and touch?

- Are there private spaces where children can be alone or spend time with a favorite caregiver or friends?

- Are there different levels and textures that children can explore?

- Are there handholds or low furniture for infants to grab onto when they are just learning to walk?

- Are there things to climb on and places to hide?

- Are toys and materials arranged so that children can find what they want to play with?

- Are there open areas for running, pushing chairs, pulling carts, jumping on pillows, or throwing bean bags?

- Are there small, defined areas that accommodate social activities such as painting or playing with sand?

General Tips in Planning an Environment for Infants and Toddlers

These tips may help you set up an environment designed to encourage infants and toddlers to explore.

- Set up the indoor and outdoor environment so you can easily see all children at all times.

156

- Divide the room into areas that make it clear where different activities take place.

- Use low dividers (shelves, pillows) to define areas of the room, keep crawling infants where they are safe, and protect noncrawlers from being run over.

- Make sure there are clear pathways so children and caregivers can get to and around areas. When children are crying or in distress, and during emergencies, caregivers need to be able to reach all areas of the room quickly.

- Hang decorations at different heights where the infants can easily see them when they wake up in their cribs, have their diapers changed, play on the floor, or get carried around the room by a caregiver.

- Provide slight variations in levels for children to explore. These might include carpeted platforms, steps or ramps, or cushions and hassocks. You might create a raised level beside a window so infants can climb up and see outside.

- If fire regulations permit, lower the ceiling by securely suspending a colorful cloth or a fish net. This can make a space feel cozy and special.

Special Considerations in Planning an Environment for Toddlers

Follow these suggestions when setting up an environment that meets toddlers' needs.

- **Provide at least three types of play areas** for toddlers: large open areas where they can move freely; partially enclosed areas where up to three toddlers can play with table toys, puzzles, dress-up clothes, and so on; and small areas for getting away and watching.

- **Use movable low dividers** (such as shelves, storage units on wheels, curtains, lightweight boxes) to change the size and shape of indoor and outdoor areas to better accommodate different kinds of activities.

- **Include movable objects** such as planks, sawhorses, hollow blocks, and boxes. Set aside spaces indoors and outdoors to use these items. Toddlers can move these things around to create their own play units. They can change the size or shape of areas or build their own private spaces.

- **Surprise toddlers** by making small changes in the environment. Once in a while, do something different: tie colorful streamers around the play area on a windy day, make a tunnel out of cardboard boxes taped together, or cover one of the tables with a sheet so the children can pretend it is a house, fort, tent, or whatever they choose.

- **Build a two-level play house** or a loft with stairs or a ramp leading to the top. When toddlers are in the play house or loft, they will feel powerful to be so high up. Actually, they will be only as high as an adult's eye level.

- **Set up clear pathways** that lead toddlers from one interesting area to another.

Creating a Cheerful and Calm Environment

You can help infants and toddlers feel more secure by adding special touches to your environment. Here are some suggestions for making your room a cheerful and calm place for young children.

- **Include places to hold young children.** A large rocking chair is ideal for feeding and rocking infants and cuddling and reading a story to toddlers. An overstuffed chair is relaxing for you as well.

- **Let in natural light.** Sunlight is much more restful than fluorescent lights. The shadows that play across the walls, floors, and ceiling are interesting to follow. Prisms hanging in a sunny window create dancing rainbows.

- **Hang curtains on the windows** to add color, softness, and a way to control the amount of sunlight in the room.

- **Use color wisely.** Light, neutral colors are best on walls and for shelves. Use bright colors for decorations and toys so children will notice them more.

- **Include softness in the environment.** Furnishings and materials might include carpeting; pillows or mattresses covered with pretty fabrics; bean bag chairs; playdough; sand and water; and, of course, a soft lap to sit in.

- **Add pleasant sounds,** but not all the time. If you play music all day, children will tune it out. Choose appropriate selections of music for different times of the day—jazz or pop for an active period, soft and restful music when it's naptime. More "occasional" sounds can be added by hanging wind chimes in the room.

- **Include living things in the room.** Hanging or potted plants add a special touch to any room. An aquarium will attract the attention of infants and toddlers. Watching fish swim lazily or dart around in the water can be a calming as well as fascinating activity for a curious child.

- **Create private spaces.** At times, each of us needs to get away and be alone for a while. You can create private spaces for children by making carpeted platforms, arranging large pillows in different areas of the room, and putting out cardboard boxes.

Making Adults Feel Comfortable

One of the best ways to help children feel at home in your setting is to help their parents feel at ease. Offering a cup of tea, providing comfortable adult seating, and posting notes about their children's day on a bulletin board tells parents they are welcome. Young children sense their parents' feelings. If parents feel good about your setting, it will help their children feel that "this is an all-right place."

Children also will benefit when you feel at home in your setting. If you are content and comfortable, you will have more of yourself to give. And you—your encouragement, hugs, and smiles—are the most important part of the environment for infants and toddlers.

Like any home, your environment should reflect the people who live there and use it—the children, their families, and their caregivers. By hanging family pictures on the wall, talking about the bookshelf that Jimmy's father built, and donating your old hat to the dress-up corner, you are saying that "this space is ours."

In this activity you will use a checklist to identify ways in which you already make your room feel like a home. Then you will think of new ways to make your room more homelike.

Checklist for Creating a Homelike Learning Environment

The checklist below identifies materials you might find in different areas of your environment. Read the list and put a check beside each item you now have that makes an area homelike. There are spaces for you to add other items to the list.

Entrance or Receiving Area: This is where caregivers and parents can talk during drop-off and pick-up times. If parents feel comfortable and at home in this area, their children will sense this and feel more comfortable, too. To help infants, toddlers, and their parents feel at home, this area should contain the following items:

____ An adult-height counter to make dressing and undressing easier

____ Cubbies labeled with each child's name and picture

____ Interesting pictures on the wall

____ Bulletin boards where parents and caregivers can share information and news

____ A clock

____ _____

____ _____

Kitchen Area: In this area, children can help prepare food and eat. Here they can help you stir, peel, pour, and mix as you make snacks and meals. As they learn to feed themselves, infants can squish pieces of banana and taste them while toddlers practice holding cups. This area will probably have a refrigerator and a stove or hotplate. It should also contain items such as the following:

____ Child-size tables and chairs

____ Highchairs

____ A comfortable place for you to sit with infants and toddlers

____ Pots and pans, plastic containers, spoons, pots, and measuring cups (stored in a low cupboard where young children can get them easily)

____ Sponges, mops, and paper towels for children and adults to use when wiping up spills

____ Pictures on the wall (of food or people eating together)

____ _____

____ _____

Sleeping Area or Bedroom: When caring for infants, cribs must be available all the time because each baby has his or her own schedule. For toddlers you can bring out cots or mats at nap time, using the same space available for active play earlier in the day. This is a place where you rock sleepy children and rub their tired backs. The area might include the following equipment:

_____ A crib for each infant and cots or mats for toddlers (must meet health and safety regulations)

_____ A storage place for linens and special blankets and stuffed animals from home

_____ A rocking chair

_____ Mirrors, pictures, or mobiles in cribs

_____ Pictures on the walls

_____ _____

_____ _____

Changing Area or Bathroom: This is a place where you and the children spend a lot of one-on-one time together. Here you can get to know each other better as you sing songs and play games of "I'm going to tickle your toes." This is where infants learn that they are respected as you tell them what you are going to do and let them take part in being changed. It is where toddlers learn to use the potty. Here children will feel respected rather than shamed when you treat accidents matter-of-factly. They will feel competent and proud as you let them dress and undress themselves and wash their hands. In this area, you might find:

_____ A large, sturdy changing table

_____ Pictures or mobiles hanging on the walls or above the changing table

_____ A shelf so your supplies are organized and easy to reach

_____ Low toilets and sinks

_____ Boxes, bins, or bags marked with each child's name for storing diapers and extra sets of dry clothes

_____ _____

_____ _____

Play Area or Living Room: Children spend most of their time in the play area when they are awake. It should be cheerful and welcoming. There should be interesting things for children to see and do, and open spaces to move around in and explore. Check the things you have that encourage children to explore and learn.

_____ Sofa, overstuffed chair, pillows, and laps where infants and toddlers can cuddle with adults or listen to a story

_____ A large rocking chair for feeding and rocking infants

_____ Places where infants and toddlers can play alone or in small groups

_____ Books about babies, mommies, daddies, toys, and familiar objects

_____ Pictures of children and their families (covered with clear Contact paper and hung at the children's level)

_____ Plants, flowers (out of children's reach)

_____ Slightly different levels for children to explore

_____ Surfaces and toys with different textures

_____ Dolls (reflecting different ethnic backgrounds)

_____ Open spaces for active play (for example, a large mat for tumbling or indoor climbing equipment)

_____ Record or CD player or tape recorder; simple instruments for making different sounds

_____ A quiet space for using playdough or toys

_____ _____

_____ _____

Outdoor Area or Backyard: Going outdoors offers a change of scene and fresh air. It is where children can be free to move, make noise, climb, and use their large muscles. To help children feel comfortable and encourage exploring and learning, this area should contain the following items:

_____ Different levels and textures to touch, crawl, and climb on

_____ Ways to separate noncrawlers from crawling and walking children

_____ Trees or shelters for shading children from the sun

162

_____ Smaller, defined areas for activities such as playing in the sand, gardening, and water play (in warm weather)

_____ A safe hard surface for riding toys, wheelbarrows, wagons, doll carriages, and so on.

_____ _____

_____ _____

Based on what you have learned in completing this checklist, what changes do you want to make in your environment? Write down what you want to do and why this will help create a good environment for infants and toddlers.

WHAT YOU WANT TO DO	WHY

Discuss your ideas with your trainer and other caregivers in the room. Decide what changes you will make.

III. Shaping the Messages in Your Learning Environment

In this activity you will learn:

- to identify messages in the environment; and

- to create an environment that gives positive messages to infants and toddlers.

All environments convey messages. Every room in your house says something different. Your living room probably has soft furniture, low tables with magazines, lamps, and perhaps a soft carpet. The message is: "Come sit down. Read. Talk. Relax."

A fast-food restaurant is designed to get you in and out quickly. It is set up so you can select your food, get it immediately, pay, and be seated in a matter of minutes. The message is: "Hurry up."

Many schools have individual desks lined up facing the front of the room. Sometimes the desks are bolted to the floor. The message is: "No talking to other children. Listen to the teacher. The teacher conveys all information."

Your indoor and outdoor environments also convey messages to children. If the environment is attractive, cheerful, orderly, and filled with interesting objects, the message is: "This is a good and interesting place. We care about you. You can have fun here."

When a caregiver takes an infant out of her crib and rocks her in the rocking chair, the message is: "I am here. This is a comfortable place. I will take good care of you."

A mobile swings when an infant kicks it. A ball rolls when an infant pushes it. A rattle makes noise when an infant shakes it. The message is: "You did it. You made something happen. You can do many things."

When a toddler walks in your room and sees a picture of his or her family on the wall, the rocking chair where a caregiver can sit and read a story, and flowers on the counter, the message is: "Welcome. You can feel at home here. We will take good care of you."

A low, sturdy wooden box surrounded by large pillows says: "Come here. This is a good place to practice your jumping. Have fun."

What messages do you want young children to receive when they come into your room? The way you organize your environment and what you put into each area can convey messages such as the following:

- "This is a place like your home."

- "You belong here, and we like you."

- "This is a place you can trust."

- "This is a safe and interesting place to explore."

- "You can do many things."

Here are some examples of how you can build these messages for children into your learning environment.

"This is a place like your home."

- Children are encouraged to bring special blankets or stuffed animals from home to use for comfort during the day and at nap time.

- Pots and pans and plastic containers for collecting and dumping are stored on low shelves.

- Household objects are available as play materials: cooking utensils such as plastic measuring spoons, measuring cups, and pots hang on pegboards in the kitchen area; brooms and dustpans are in the closet.

- The room has homelike touches such as plants and flowers, pretty fabric-covered pillows, or a well-lit fish tank.

- Some toys are made from everyday things (for example, a mobile made of spoons and a car made from a cardboard box).

- Infants have individual daily routines for changing, eating, and sleeping, according to each infant's home schedules.

- There is a rocking chair or sofa for parents and caregivers to sit with children and read books, talk, or cuddle.

"You belong here, and we like you."

- Pictures on the walls, in books, and in learning materials show people of different ethnic backgrounds and different kinds of families.

- Pictures of children and their families are covered with clear Contact paper and hung where the children can easily see them.

- There are special places to store each child's belongings: a place in the receiving area for coats and a place in the changing area for dry clothes.

- Picture labels on shelves and drawers show where toys and objects belong.

- Information about the day's activities is hung on the bulletin boards for parents to read.

- Caregivers arrange their schedules and cooperate so that at least one is free to greet each child and parent warmly when they arrive.

"This is a place you can trust."

- Daily routines of eating, sleeping, and toileting are set on an individual basis to meet each child's special needs.

- There is a consistent schedule so toddlers learn the order of events during the day and know what to expect.

- The indoor and outdoor environments are safe.

- Materials are always stored in the same place so children can find them.

- Caregivers respond quickly to crying and learn to recognize when it means that an infant or toddler is hungry, needs company, or needs some time to settle into sleep.

"This is a safe and interesting place to explore."

- Part of the floor is bare and part is covered with a rug, so infants can crawl and walk on different textures.

- There are places—a crib, a caregiver's arms, a house made from a refrigerator box—where infants and toddlers can be alone, play close to each other, or play in small groups.

- There are indoor and outdoor spaces for tumbling, climbing, rolling, and other large-muscle activities.

- On the walls are interesting things to look at and touch, including pictures as well as cloth of different textures.

- Attractive displays of materials invite children to use them.

- Some toys are rotated each week so there are new and interesting things to explore.

"You can do many things."

- Children have toys that respond to their actions: mobiles that move when they are kicked or rattles that make noise when shaken.

- Materials are stored on low shelves so older infants and toddlers can make choices and take the toys they want.

- Coats are kept at the children's level so those who are old enough can get their own.

- There are safe indoor and outdoor places to practice sitting, crawling, walking, and climbing.

- Materials are logically organized: drawing paper is near the markers, and smocks are near the water table.

- Toilets and sinks are child-sized so toddlers can go to the bathroom and wash their hands independently.

In this activity you will look at what messages your learning environment conveys to infants and toddlers. First read the example below; then use the blank chart beginning on the next page to list the ways in which your indoor and outdoor environments convey each message and the changes you would like to make.

Messages in the Learning Environment
(Example)

"This is a place like your home."	
How the Environment Says This Now	**New Ideas to Try**
Each child has a special blanket and stuffed animal for nap time.	*Add pots, pans, and wooden spoons.*
We have plants and flowers and stuffed pillows.	*Put curtains on the windows.*
We have a rocking chair.	*Hang pictures of children's families in the room.*

Messages in the Learning Environment

"This is a place like your home."	
How the Environment Says This Now	New Ideas to Try

"You belong here, and we like you."	
How the Environment Says This Now	New Ideas to Try

"This is a place you can trust."	
How the Environment Says This Now	New Ideas to Try

"This is a safe and interesting place to explore."	
How the Environment Says This Now	New Ideas to Try

"You can do many things."	
How the Environment Says This Now	**New Ideas to Try**

After you complete this chart, discuss your ideas with your trainer and colleagues. Agree on the changes you will make. Use the space below to note what changes you have made.

_____

_____

_____

_____

_____

_____

_____

Discuss the changes you have made with your trainer.

IV. Selecting and Organizing Toys and Materials

In this activity you will learn:

- to select toys and materials that are developmentally and culturally appropriate; and

- to organize and display these materials in ways that invite infants and toddlers to explore and play with them.

The young children you care for probably cover a wide range of ages and developmental stages. As a result, your room needs to include materials that can meet a variety of abilities and interests. It is best to select toys and other materials that can be used in many different ways and with little adult assistance. For example, mobile infants might carry or push the large cardboard blocks around the room, while toddlers might be ready to build a tower with them. Be sure to include toys that promote all kinds of development—social, emotional, cognitive, and physical—and that allow children to practice their new skills.

In selecting or making toys and materials, ask yourself the following questions:

- Will they interest infants and toddlers? Your daily observations will help you identify children's special interests.

- Do the children have the skills to handle a given toy? For example, are they ready for five-piece puzzles, or are they still mastering the shape sorting box?

- Do the toys or materials reflect the cultural backgrounds of the children or show people with disabilities engaged in meaningful tasks? Dolls, pictures in books, and wooden figures for the block area should reflect the diversity of our society and help children understand and respect these differences.

- Is the toy in question in good condition? This means no broken parts, no missing pieces, and no chipping paint. Materials should be clean and free of splinters and jagged edges.

- Is the toy safe—does it have any parts that a child could swallow?

- Does the toy promote growth and development? For example, will it help infants and toddlers learn to think? Develop language skills? Develop small and large muscle control?

This last question can be answered best after you have completed Modules 4 through 10. In these modules you will find many ideas for selecting materials that will promote children's physical, cognitive, social, and language development.

Periodically, you will have to reassess the materials in your environment to make sure they are still appropriate. Young children develop and change very quickly. A toy that was challenging last month might seem boring this month. A piece of equipment that was safe in the past can become unsafe as crawlers, walkers, and climbers become more skilled at moving around the room.

When you notice that toys are being ignored, experiment with rotating them. Put them away for a few weeks. Chances are they will be treated like new when you introduce them again. Although infants and toddlers need a large degree of consistency, they enjoy and need occasional changes in their environment.

Like most caregivers, you are probably working with a limited budget. Think creatively when you select new toys and materials. Although expensive new toys may seem appealing to you, they are not always necessary when you look at them through the eyes of children. How many times have you heard about children ignoring a new toy and playing with the box it came in instead?

Many good materials for infants and toddlers can be collected by you or the children's parents. For example, young children will enjoy dress-up clothes and dramatic play props; household items such as plastic bottles, measuring cups, plastic dishes, and silverware; cardboard boxes to push and crawl through; and scraps of paper, ribbons, and fabrics for making collages.

You can make toys from materials you collect. An oatmeal box covered with Contact paper and small blocks makes a wonderful "drop-in and dump-out" toy. Magazine pictures can be mounted on cardboard and cut into three pieces to make simple puzzles. A coffee can makes a good drum, and spools of thread are great for stringing.

Listed on the next page are suggestions for what to include in rooms for infants and toddlers. The purpose of the list isn't to say you need to have every item. Rather, the list is to be used as a resource. Share it with your colleagues and trainer to help you think about what you have and to develop priorities of things to make or buy based on the needs of children in your room.

Suggested Materials and Equipment for Infants and Toddlers[3]

Language Development

These items will encourage children to communicate with adults and each other:

- Cloth or cardboard picture books (homemade or purchased)
- Dishpan full of pictures (familiar objects and family members) mounted on cardboard
- Rocking chair, soft chair, mattress, and/or pillows
- Cloth puppets
- Pictures (familiar objects, animals, and people)

Sensory Stimulation

These items will encourage children to use their senses:

- Mobiles (homemade or purchased)
- Mirrors (unbreakable)
- Wall hangings (textured and touchable)
- Adult rocking chairs
- "Peek-a-boo" toys
- Jack-in-the-box
- Clutch balls
- Rattles (homemade or purchased)
- Squeeze toys
- Washable toys for sucking, chewing, and teething
- Bell bracelets
- Hand mitts made from baby socks
- Bean bags
- Washable soft toys, animals, and dolls
- Push, pull, and squeeze toys
- Music boxes (to wind up or to pull)
- Record player and records or tape recorder and tapes
- Texture balls
- Texture glove made from a variety of materials (to be worn by a caregiver)
- Sand and water play table or plastic bathtub or basins
- Plastic containers, cups, bowls, bottles, pitchers, and so on for sand and water play

---

[3]From Derry Gosselin Koralek, Diane Trister Dodge, Laura J. Colker, and Cynthia Prather *A Handbook for Army Education Program Specialists* (Washington, DC: Army Child Development Services, 1989), pp. IV-9-10 and IV-26-28.

Manipulative Toys

These toys foster small muscle development:

- Shape sorting box
- Pop-up toys
- Large snap beads
- Nesting cups
- Large soft blocks
- Large cardboard blocks
- Containers in graduated sizes (such as plastic bowls or cups)
- Containers and things to put in and take out of them
- Mirrors (unbreakable)
- Pegboards with large holes and large, colored pegs
- Large wooden stringing beads and short, thick strings or shoelaces
- Cardboard boxes with lids
- Busy boxes
- Stacking ring (with a straight post so pieces can be stacked in any order)

Motor Development

Large muscle development is promoted by these materials:

- Soft balls of various sizes
- Large cardboard boxes to crawl in and out of
- Soft pillows to climb on
- Small, wheeled riding toys that are propelled by feet
- Small climber with slide attached
- Tunnel made from boxes taped together or purchased
- Small cars and trucks
- Wagons to push while walking

Art

These materials can be used in a variety of art activities:

- Large nontoxic crayons and paper
- Playdough and blunt wooden dowels to use as tools
- Box of small pieces of ribbons and fabrics of varied textures and colors
- Fingerpaints and paper or shallow trays
- Smocks or old shirts
- Old tablecloth or plastic for floor covering

Dramatic Play

These materials will help children make sense of their world as they play out scenes from their daily lives:

- Pots and pans
- Large wooden or plastic spoons
- Toy telephones
- Hats
- Unbreakable cups and dishes
- Dolls (soft, unbreakable, and multi-ethnic)
- Doll bed and blankets

Music

These items will encourage singing, dancing, and the enjoyment of music:

- Record player and records, tape recorder and tapes, or CD player and disks
- A few simple rhythm instruments (with no sharp edges)

Blocks

These items will encourage children to explore shapes, sizes, and balance as they build various structures:

- Large soft blocks
- Large cardboard blocks
- Hollow blocks
- Small cars and trucks
- Animal props (farm or zoo animals)
- People props (multi-ethnic wooden family sets and community helpers)

Organizing and Displaying Materials

Your environment will promote learning most effectively if the toys and materials are properly displayed. Some suggestions follow:

- Display toys clearly on low, open, sturdy shelves so children can select what they want to play with on their own.

- Consider storing some toys with many pieces on higher shelves. Label them clearly for older toddlers, and explain that you will get them down upon request. Although this might feel restrictive, it gives children—and caregivers—freedom from the chaos and frustrations of Legos and popbeads constantly being dumped all over the room.

- Label shelves and containers with pictures and words for children to refer to when they are putting toys away.

- Provide more than one of favorite items to avoid disputes. Sharing is difficult for toddlers who are just developing a sense of self.

In this learning activity you will complete an inventory of the equipment and materials used by infants and toddlers. You will describe how items in various categories are stored and displayed. After completing your inventory, use the chart that follows to list what materials you want to add to your environment and how you plan to organize and display these materials so that children can use them without adult assistance.

Infant/Toddler Equipment and Materials Inventory

LANGUAGE DEVELOPMENT

_____   _____

_____   _____

_____   _____

_____   _____

How these items are stored and displayed:

_____

_____

_____

SENSORY STIMULATION

_____   _____

_____   _____

_____   _____

_____   _____

How these items are stored and displayed:

_____

_____

_____

_____

MUSIC

_____   _____

_____   _____

_____   _____

_____   _____

How these items are stored and displayed:

_____

_____

_____

BLOCKS

_____   _____

_____   _____

_____   _____

_____   _____

How these items are stored and displayed:

_____

_____

_____

MANIPULATIVE TOYS

_____   _____

_____   _____

_____   _____

_____   _____

How these items are stored and displayed:

_____

_____

_____

MOTOR DEVELOPMENT

_____   _____

_____   _____

_____   _____

_____   _____

How these items are stored and displayed:

_____

_____

_____

ART

_____   _____

_____   _____

_____   _____

_____   _____

How these items are stored and displayed:

_____

_____

_____

DRAMATIC PLAY

_____   _____

_____   _____

_____   _____

_____   _____

How these items are stored and displayed:

_____

_____

_____

Improvements to the Learning Environment

Use the middle column in the chart below to identify what materials you would like to add to your environment. In the right-hand column, record your ideas for organizing and displaying the new materials in ways that will invite infants and toddlers to use and enjoy them.

CATEGORY	MATERIALS YOU WANT TO ADD	HOW YOU WILL ORGANIZE AND DISPLAY THEM
Language Development		
Sensory Stimulation		
Music		
Blocks		

CATEGORY	MATERIALS YOU WANT TO ADD	HOW YOU WILL ORGANIZE AND DISPLAY THEM
Manipulative Toys		
Motor Development		
Art		
Dramatic Play		

Discuss this activity with your trainer and the other caregivers in your room.

V. Using the Outdoors as a Learning Environment[4]

In this activity you will learn:

- to create an outdoor environment that facilitates the growth and development of infants and toddlers; and

- to provide a variety of materials, equipment, and activities in the outdoor environment.

Outdoor play is very important for infants and toddlers because it allows them to use their rapidly developing gross motor skills along with their senses to experience the natural environment. Even very young infants enjoy being outdoors. They can sleep outside in carriages or on blankets in the shade.

If possible, the play yard used by infants and toddlers should include three areas: a shaded grassy area for small babies, an area with a small climber and swings, and an area for riding toys and sand and water play. These three areas will allow for a variety of experiences that will delight infants and toddlers.

Textures and Sensory Delights

Infants use their senses to explore the world. Because the outdoor environment is already full of sensory experiences, you do not need to add much to it to encourage infants to explore. It is hard to improve on nature's natural materials and activities. Children love watching shadows created by the sun; watching and listening to the wind blowing through the trees; trying to touch and catch butterflies and other insects; and feeling the varied textures of grass, tree bark, sand, and rocks. To build on what nature has provided, you might do the following:

- **Create interesting patterns of light** by hanging colored pieces of plexiglass or a crystal from tree branches or a fence. Hang large pieces of bright fabrics to let the sun shine through and to use as temporary shade providers.

- **Add to the textures in the play yard.** Examine what textures are already included (grass, concrete, cement, chain link, wood), and add others such as rubber tires, blankets, water, indoor/outdoor carpeting, and wood chips.

---

[4]Based on Karen Miller, *The Outside Play and Learning Book* (Mt. Rainier, MD: Gryphon House, 1989), pp. 23-26, 112-113, 115, 131, and 212.

- **Hang a variety of items on a section of the fence** that is in a shady area. Place a young infant in a carriage or infant seat close to the fence where she or he can watch and reach for the items.

- **Add items that will make different sounds.** Hang a variety of wind chimes made from different materials (metal, ceramic, aluminum pie tins, sea shells), plastic streamers, and wind socks.

- **Add some pleasant smells.** You can lift up children to smell the flowers in the window box, break a leaf in half to smell the inside, or plant herbs in a protected area. If you don't have enough full sun all day to have a garden, plant one in a wheelbarrow and move the "garden" several times a day so it is always in the sun.

Gross Motor Play

Both infants and toddlers are eager to practice their gross motor skills. Moving their bodies from one place to another is an activity in and of itself. Young children are learning what their bodies can do and developing strength and coordination. To assist them, you might do the following:

- **Create safe places for young infants.** A blanket placed on the ground provides a safe place for a young infant to stretch, reach, and practice rolling over without being in the path of the older children. Some infants enjoy being right on the grass; others may not like the way the grass feels. You can place an infant on her tummy on the blanket and then take her for a "ride" by pulling the blanket around.

- **Create safe places for crawlers.** You might make a texture path for the crawlers using pieces of carpeting, tires, floor mats, and natural materials. Also, you can bring some of the indoor equipment outdoors—for example, cardboard boxes, tunnels, covered ramps, and so on.

- **Create safe places for cruisers.** Cruisers are children who have learned to pull themselves up and walk by holding on to something. You could build a cruising rail in the play yard: a low rail about 12 to 18 inches off the ground. If you have a chain link fence, children can use this for cruising. You may have to show them how at first.

- **Create safe places for climbers.** Climbing is the next milestone after learning to move on all fours. Young children seem to have a compulsion to swing one leg up and over something and then pull themselves up and onto the top. Indoors, a stool or hassock is a perfect height for this. Outdoors, you can provide "climbers" no higher than 18 inches from the ground. To ensure children's safety, they should have soft cushioning material underneath and low, wide steps. The steps should lead to a platform large enough for two or three children to use at a time. There should be handholds for children to grab when they need to steady their balance.

- **Provide plenty of wheel toys for toddlers.** It is best to select sturdy wheeled toys with wheels that turn. Many riding toys go only forward or backward. Young children soon outgrow these because they want to make turns without having to stop and pick up the riding toy to make it face another direction. Toddlers also enjoy wagons to push and pull, wheelbarrows, and doll carriages. Your play yard should have a hard dirt or paved surface for riding toys.

- **Provide open space for running.** Toddlers don't need any help running; it's a natural instinct. They might enjoy it if you blow bubbles for them to chase or jump on.

- **Hang a stuffed animal or punching ball** from a low tree branch. Children can push the stuffed animal as if it was on a swing and hit the ball with paper towel tubes.

- **Have on hand a variety of balls.** Toddlers like to kick and throw balls. These are both hard skills to master, but toddlers enjoy doing them over and over.

Fine Motor Play

There are many opportunities for infants and toddlers to use their fine motor skills as they play outdoors. Some examples follow:

- **Dumping and filling.** Toddlers and older infants will enjoy filling small wagons or baskets (or any container with a handle) with small toys or natural items, carrying them to a new place, and dumping out the contents. This activity will keep them amused for relatively long periods of time.

- **Sand play.** Older infants and toddlers enjoy pushing cars through the sand or filling containers with sand and dumping them. They also enjoy the sensory feeling of sand running through their fingers. If you sit down with them and show them how to use the sand, they will be less likely to eat it.

- **Water play.** In warm weather, water play is a favorite activity. Whether you move the water table outdoors or just put dishpans or buckets full of water on the ground, the children will be captivated. To provide variety, add some simple props such as sponges, paint brushes, and boats, or bring out the dolls and give them all baths. You also might do some laundry—children can wash the doll clothes and hang them out to dry on a clothesline. Or you might bring the dirty chairs outside and ask children to use scrub brushes and soapy water to get them clean. Help them notice what happens to the water when you wash dirty dolls, doll clothes, or chairs. In winter in a cold climate, you can bring the water table outside and fill it with snow.

In this learning activity you will conduct two five-minute observations in the outdoor learning environment. Next, you will use your observation notes to describe how the outdoor learning environment is facilitating the growth and development of the children. Finally, you will note any changes you would like to make in your outdoor environment. Begin by reviewing the example that follows.

Outdoor Learning Environment Observation

(Example)

Child(ren)   _Marisa and Terrence_   **Age(s)** _28 and 32 months_   **Date(s)** _September 10_

Setting   _Play area near pine tree_

Marisa is filling up the wheelbarrow with pine cones from under the big pine tree. She is working alone. She picks up a pine cone and smells it. Then she puts it in the wheelbarrow. She looks at the full wheelbarrow, then begins wheeling it across the pine needles and onto the path. When she gets to the grassy area, she stops. She dumps the pine cones out of the wheelbarrow. Terrence comes up to her and says, "Can I play too?" She lets him play with her. Terrence throws the pine cones in the air. Marisa picks them up and puts them back in the wheelbarrow.

How did the outdoor learning environment foster development in the following areas?

Sense of textures and sensory delights:

Marisa seemed to enjoy smelling the pine cones. It feels different to push the wheelbarrow across the bumpy pine needles under the tree than it does to push it on the hard path.

Gross motor skills:

Marisa used her gross motor skills to push the wheelbarrow. Terrence used his to throw the pine cones in the air.

Fine motor skills:

Marisa and Terrence used their fine motor skills to pick up the pine cones.

Outdoor Learning Environment Observation

Child(ren) _____ Age(s)_____ Date(s)_____

Setting _____

_____

_____

_____

_____

_____

_____

How did the outdoor learning environment foster development in the following areas?

Sense of textures and sensory delights:

_____

_____

_____

Gross motor skills:

_____

_____

_____

Fine motor skills:

_____

_____

_____

Outdoor Learning Environment Observation

Child(ren) _____ Age(s)_____ Date(s)_____

Setting _____

_____

_____

_____

_____

_____

_____

How did the outdoor learning environment foster development in the following areas?

Sense of textures and sensory delights:

_____

_____

_____

Gross motor skills:

_____

_____

_____

Fine motor skills:

_____

_____

_____

On the basis of what you have learned in completing these observations, what changes do you want to make in your outdoor environment? Write down what you want to do and why this will help create a good outdoor environment for infants and toddlers.

WHAT YOU WANT TO DO   **WHY**

_____   _____

_____   _____

_____   _____

_____   _____

_____   _____

_____   _____

_____   _____

_____   _____

Discuss your ideas with your trainer and other caregivers in the room. Decide what changes you will make.

VI. Planning Your Daily Routines and Schedule

In this activity you will learn:

- to recognize how infants and toddlers learn from daily routines; and

- to plan a schedule that meets individual needs of infants and toddlers.

Routines are the daily events that take place in your program. They include:

- arriving and leaving;
- eating;
- sleeping;
- changing diapers;
- going outdoors; and
- cleaning up.

As adults we usually don't give much thought to our own daily routines. Day after day we take showers, shop for food, fill our gas tanks, set the table, and brush our teeth. Routines are tasks that must be completed before we can get on to what we really want to do.

For infants and toddlers, however, daily routines are the major part of the day. They are wonderful opportunities for learning. By doing the same things over and over, children begin to make sense of their world.

Because routines are times when **infants** have your undivided attention, they are excellent opportunities for developing relationships. Being changed means more to Susannah (4 months) than just getting a clean, dry diaper. It is a chance to look closely at your face, hear your voice, and have a conversation of sorts. In time, she will come to learn the meaning of wet and dry. Eventually, she will be able to lift her legs as you pull out the diaper.

Repeating the same activities again and again helps **toddlers** master new skills. It takes a lot of practice to learn to pull up pants, buckle overall straps, and zip up coats. When toddlers can do these things for themselves, they feel competent.

When you wait patiently for Demian (28 months) to practice zipping up his coat, you show your respect. You are saying, "You are learning something important. I will give you the time you need."

Routines are also a major part of a caregiver's day. You may find routines more interesting if you remember that as you change diapers or ask toddlers to help you wipe up some spilled apple juice, you are teaching children very important things about themselves and the world. Review the chart that follows to see how much an infant learns from one simple act: eating a banana.

Eating a Banana: A Learning Experience

Things an Infant Might Do While Eating a Banana	Things an Infant Might Learn While Eating a Banana
Pick it up and eat it.	*I can feed myself.*
Spit it out.	*I don't like bananas.*
Finish it and ask for more.	*I love bananas.*
Squish it.	*I can change this. I am powerful.*
Drop it on the floor and watch it fall.	*When I drop something, it falls to the ground.*
Try to feed some to a caregiver.	*My caregiver really likes me. My caregiver likes bananas, too.*
Hear a caregiver call it a banana.	*This thing has a name.*
Try to say "banana."	*I can communicate.*

Here are some guidelines to help make daily routines valuable learning experiences for infants and toddlers.

- **Keep group sizes as small as possible.** Consider dividing up groups so that some children stay in while others go out. Being in a smaller group is more relaxing for both children and caregivers.

- **Treat children as partners.** Talk with infants and toddlers about what you are doing as you dress and feed them. Observe what they are doing. Let them participate as much as they are able.

- **Develop a system for each routine.** You will find it easier to focus on each child if you aren't jumping up to find a spoon or a lost mitten.

- **Don't rush**. Take time to talk, snuggle, tickle a tummy, or sing a song as you change a diaper or feed an infant. Give toddlers plenty of time to practice new skills.

Doing these things will make daily routines more enjoyable for you as well as for the children in your care.

The Daily Schedule

The schedule defines the events of the day. It shows how you expect the day's activities to flow, in what order, and for how long.

When you care for infants, you're likely to have as many schedules as you have infants. Each one has a personal schedule. You can't decide when an infant will get tired or hungry or need a diaper changed. For toddlers, you can plan how the day will go—but even so, you need to be flexible. You can't predict when one of the toddlers will decide to put her socks in the toilet, causing it to overflow. Your schedule will have to accommodate the arrival of the maintenance crew to clean up the spill. The toddlers won't mind because they will find this event very interesting. You, however, may have to reschedule finger painting with shaving cream for another day.

So why bother having a schedule? Here are some reasons why a daily schedule is important.

- A schedule helps children learn that their world is predictable. Knowing what comes next gives children a sense of predictability and helps them develop a sense of trust in the world.

- Having a schedule gives you a sense of order, which is important when you take care of very young children.

- A schedule gives each parent a picture of what their child's days are like. You can give each parent a copy of the daily schedule or post it in the room where they can read it.

What is a good schedule for infants and toddlers? No one schedule will work for all groups and all caregivers, but there are some guidelines to follow in planning your schedule. A good schedule should provide the following:

- an overall daily plan that can be changed to meet the individual needs of children and caregivers;

- sufficient time for daily routines;

- outdoor and indoor play times;

- opportunities to be in small groups or alone with special caregivers;

- a balance between free-choice activities, caregiver-directed activities, and small group activities; and

- time for cleaning up and other household chores.

When you develop a schedule, it's important to be consistent from day to day and week to week. As noted above, children feel more secure when they can predict events during the day: "After lunch we wash our hands, and then we get ready to take our naps." By knowing what comes next, they learn to rely on both their environment and their caregivers.

Consistency, however, does not mean that the schedule should not be flexible. If it turns out to be too windy for a walk outside or a movement activity has lasted longer than originally planned for, you can adapt the schedule accordingly. Also, it is appropriate to completely abandon your original plans in order to take advantage of "teachable moments," such as the appearance of a rainbow during a walk or the arrival of a new piece of equipment at the center. Thus, a daily schedule is a tool to help you; you should use it and bend it to meet your needs and those of the children.

In this activity you will first consider how well your schedule meets the needs of the children in your care. Write down your schedule on the chart that follows. Then use the checklist that follows to assess your schedule. Finally, rewrite your schedule, making any necessary changes.

Daily Schedule

TIME	ACTIVITY
_____	_____
_____	_____
_____	_____
_____	_____
_____	_____
_____	_____
_____	_____
_____	_____

Daily Schedule Checklist

1. The schedule has sufficient time for routines. _____

2. There is a balance between active and quiet times. _____

3. There are times for children to play alone. _____

4. There are times for children to play together. _____

5. There are times for children to play with caregivers. _____

6. There are caregiver-directed activities. _____

7. There are times for free play. _____

8. Outdoor activities are scheduled twice a day. _____

9. The major events of the day occur in the same order each day. _____

10. Sufficient time is allowed for transitions from one activity to the next. _____

Revised Daily Schedule

TIME		ACTIVITY	
_____		_____	
_____		_____	
_____		_____	
_____		_____	
_____		_____	
_____		_____	
_____		_____	
_____		_____	

Discuss your ideas with the other caregivers in your room and decide together if you will change the daily schedule.

Summarizing Your Progress

You have now completed all of the learning activities for this module. Whether you are an experienced caregiver or a new one, this module has probably helped you develop new skills in creating a learning environment for infants and toddlers. Before you go on, take a few minutes to summarize what you've learned.

- Turn back to Learning Activity I, Using Your Knowledge of Infant and Toddler Development to Create a Learning Environment, and add to the chart specific examples of how you created a good learning environment during the time you were working on this module.

- Next, review your responses to the pre-training assessment for this module. Write a summary of what you learned, and list the skills you developed or improved.

_____

_____

_____

_____

_____

_____

Your final step in this module is to complete the knowledge and competency assessments. Let your trainer know when you are ready to schedule the assessments. After you have successfully completed these assessments, you will be ready to start a new module. Congratulations on your progress so far, and good luck with your next module.

196

Answer Sheet: Creating and Using an Environment for Learning

Organizing Indoor and Outdoor Areas That Encourage Play and Exploration

1. **What did Mr. Jones know about the toddlers in his group?**

    a. The children were frustrated when they could not get the equipment they wanted to use.

    b. Some children's play and work were being interrupted by other children riding bikes or playing ball.

2. **What are examples of quiet and active things that children might have wanted to play with or explore in this play yard?**

    a. Quiet things would include playing with sand and taking care of the plants.

    b. Active things would include riding bikes and playing ball.

3. **How did Mr. Jones use this information about toddlers and different activities to organize an outdoor area that would encourage play and exploration?**

    a. He organized toys and equipment so things were easy to see and within children's reach.

    b. He designated certain areas for certain activities to protect quiet play and to give children space for active play.

Selecting and Arranging Appropriate Materials and Equipment That Foster Growth and Learning

1. **What did Ms. Gonzalez observe to make her think that the stacking toy needed to be replaced?**

    a. Mike couldn't push the blue ring all the way down.

    b. Mike looked frustrated and tossed the toy aside.

2. **Why would a stacking toy with a straight post be better?**

    a. The rings could go on in any order.

    b. Children would feel successful rather than frustrated.

Planning and Implementing Schedules and Routines That Respond to the Needs of Children Under Three

1. How did Ms. Bates and Ms. Moore know that Randy and Pam were tired?

    a. They saw Randy rub his eyes and cry and Pam whine and rub her ear.

    b. The children's mothers had told the caregivers that their children didn't sleep well.

2. How did the caregivers change their daily routine to meet the needs of the young children in their care?

    a. They decided to divide the group of children.

    b. Instead of having them all go outside at the same time, some children would go out then and some later.

Using Your Knowledge of Infant and Toddler Development to Create a Learning Environment

WHAT YOUNG INFANTS DO (0-8 MONTHS)	HOW CAREGIVERS CAN USE THIS INFORMATION TO CREATE A LEARNING ENVIRONMENT
They feel most secure at home with their parents.	Make the environment welcoming and homelike for infants and their parents so they feel secure.
They begin to reach for objects.	Place a variety of washable toys within reach of infants to encourage them to look at and stretch for objects.
They like being held and looking at faces.	Sit in a comfortable place while holding and feeding infants and look directly into their faces.
They listen to noises around them and are interested in sounds. They look to see where sounds come from.	Talk to infants. Occasionally play music. Provide toys that rattle and squeak so they can listen to different sounds.
They begin creeping and crawling.	Provide open spaces with a variety of textures to move on—hard floors, rugs, grass—so infants can move about safely.
WHAT MOBILE INFANTS DO (9-17 MONTHS)	HOW CAREGIVERS CAN USE THIS INFORMATION TO CREATE A LEARNING ENVIRONMENT
They grow and change in their abilities and interests quickly from one week to the next.	Make changes in the environment often to keep up with each infant's growth.

They sometimes need to get away from the group and be alone or with a special caregiver.	Set up safe areas within your sight where infants can have privacy—a cardboard box or secluded corner of the room—so they can be alone when they want to.
They being pulling themselves up to stand and then begin walking.	Provide handholds or low furniture to grab onto. Low platform ramps can be added to provide interesting new places to explore.
WHAT TODDLERS DO (18-36 MONTHS)	**HOW CAREGIVERS CAN USE THIS INFORMATION TO CREATE A LEARNING ENVIRONMENT**
They copy the behavior of adults.	Provide simple materials for dramatic play (bags, hats, dishes, dolls) so toddlers can explore the adult world.
They talk, run, and climb—they are very active.	Provide open spaces where toddlers can move freely. Have lots of things to climb on and places to hide.
They like to do things themselves.	Give toddlers chances to practice self-help skills. Keep coats where toddlers can reach them.
They may have trouble sharing. They can be very possessive.	Provide more than one of favorite toys to lessen conflicts. Give toddlers space to store their special things from home.
They can make simple decisions.	Arrange the room so toddlers can see into every area and decide where to go next. Arrange toys and materials clearly so toddlers can choose what they want.
They are becoming toilet-trained.	Have a bathroom area with toilet and sinks that toddlers can use by themselves.
They like to play with toys.	Provide simple puzzles with three to five whole pieces, cardboard boxes to build with, push-and-pull toys, and sturdy books.

Glossary

Daily schedule	How you anticipate and plan for the day's activities. The schedule includes the times of day and the order in which activities will occur.
Learning environment	The complete makeup of each room in a child development center. The learning environment includes the space and how it is arranged and furnished, routines, materials and equipment, planned and unplanned activities, and the people in the room.
Routines	Scheduled activities that occur every day, including meals, naps, toileting, washing hands, and going outdoors, which can all offer opportunities for children to learn.

Module 4
Physical

What Is Physical Development and Why Is It Important?

Physical development refers to the gradual gaining of control over large and small muscles. It includes acquiring gross motor skills such as sitting, crawling, walking, running, and throwing, and fine motor skills such as holding, pinching, and flexing fingers and toes. Coordinating movement is also an important part of physical development. We use our senses—especially sight, sound, and touch—to coordinate the movement of our large and small muscles.

Adults use a wide range of physical skills every day. We walk and run, often several miles a day, in our homes and at our work sites. We lift and manipulate large and small objects. We grasp pencils, pens, cups, and other small items. Because we regularly use our large and small muscles, we often don't think about the skills involved. But in fact, we developed these skills through many years of practice.

A tremendous amount of physical development takes place during a child's first three years of life. During this time children learn to control their body muscles and practice the physical skills they will use for the rest of their lives. These skills may be refined during adolescence and adulthood. Therefore, it is crucial for young children to have many opportunities to learn and practice basic physical skills.

When we look through a child's eyes, we see how much there is to learn. Things we adults do automatically, such as picking up and eating a cracker, are actually complex skills that have many steps. To eat a cracker at snacktime, Rebecca (8 months) must be able to see the cracker, reach for it, grasp it, bring it to her mouth, open her mouth, and put the cracker in even before she moves her tongue and lips to taste it.

Young children do not have to be reminded to practice physical skills. Most infants will gleefully kick their legs and reach for objects. Toddlers love to push, pull, shake, dump, and pour. They delight in running and climbing as well as in building and knocking down.

Physical development is important for developing self-esteem. Young children use their large and small muscles, along with all their senses, to discover their world and the effects they can have on it. Creating a sound by kicking a mobile made of juice lids, reaching for a toy to play with, pouring a cup of juice, and carrying a roll of paper towels into the kitchen are all examples of activities that help children feel that they have an effect on their world and that they are competent human beings. Feeling good about themselves means they will be more likely to try using their physical skills in new ways.

Adults play an important role in promoting children's physical development. They provide safe spaces indoors and outdoors for children to move their bodies. As a caregiver you provide children with opportunities to use and practice skills they are working on throughout the day. You can reinforce fine and gross motor skills by sharing your interest, excitement, and pleasure in children's accomplishments.

You also set the stage for children to experience success as they refine their large and small muscles. As in other areas of development, children attain and refine their physical skills gradually. By selecting materials and equipment matched with each child's developmental level, you help children learn to use their muscles safely. In this way children can practice skills such as sitting, running, and climbing.

Promoting infants and toddlers physical development involves:

- reinforcing and encouraging physical development;

- providing equipment and opportunities for gross motor development; and

- providing equipment and opportunities for fine motor development.

Listed below are examples of how caregivers demonstrate their competence in promoting the physical development of infants and toddlers.

Reinforcing and Encouraging Physical Development

Here are some examples of what caregivers can do.

- Schedule time for active play every day. "It's raining hard today, Shawn, so help me move this table and we'll set up the climber over here where we won't get wet."

- Help and encourage children when they are learning new skills. "Do you want to hold your bottle, Annie? You can hold the bottle while I hold you."

- Encourage children to use their large and small muscles in coordinated ways. "I see you watching Sarah flattening the playdough with the wooden mallet, Jared. Would you like to use one of the other mallets?"

- Help children develop an awareness of rhythm so they can coordinate their body parts. "I see you dancing to the music, Tommy!"

- Encourage children to use all their senses to explore size, shape, volume, and other characteristics of objects. "Chaundra, here's a pine cone for you. How does it feel? What does it smell like?"

- Step back to give children the time and opportunity they need to practice new skills. "I see Danny reaching for the rattle at the edge of his blanket. Instead of jumping in, I'll give him the chance to get it himself."

Providing Equipment and Opportunities for Gross Motor Development

Here are some examples of what caregivers can do.

- Set up the room so that infants have freedom and opportunities to explore in a variety of safe places. "Now that several infants have learned to crawl, Ms. Bates, let's divide the open space so that the infants who don't crawl yet won't get hurt by children who can move on their own."

- Use a variety of materials and equipment that require children to use their large muscles. "Felipe and Tamila certainly enjoy pushing the chairs around the room. What else could they safely move around?"

- Play indoor and outdoor noncompetitive games with children. "In this game we'll all take turns going from here to the tree in a different way. Crystal, how are you going to move to the tree?"

- Encourage the development of self-help skills using large muscles. "How can you make yourself taller, Joseph, so that you can reach the sink? That's right, you can get the hollow block and stand on it."

- Plan and implement increasingly difficult activities in which large muscles are used. "Let's arrange the large cushion wedges in a new way for infants to crawl and tumble on."

Providing Equipment and Opportunities for Fine Motor Development

Here are some examples of what caregivers can do.

- Use a variety of materials that require children to use their small muscles. "Lloyd and Maddie, would you like to use the fingerpaints today?"

- Provide infants with opportunities to develop small muscles by grasping, dropping, pulling, and fingering. "I've collected lids from margarine tubs. Let's decorate them and suspend them from the ceiling for the infants to reach for."

- Encourage the development of self-help skills using small muscles. "Theresa, you pulled off your sock. Good for you!"

- Plan and implement increasingly difficult activities in which small muscles are used. "This fingerplay is about catching a bee. I'll teach you hand movements and then sing you the words."

Promoting Physical Development

In the following situations, caregivers are promoting the physical development of infants and toddlers. As you read each one, think about what the caregivers are doing and why. Then answer the questions that follow.

Reinforcing and Encouraging Physical Development

Lionell (5 months) is fussing. He has been sitting in Ms. Bates' lap drinking his bottle. "I think you want to get down," Ms. Bates says. "Let's put you on a blanket near the low mirror on the floor. You'll have plenty to do and see." She places Lionell on his tummy. "Look, there you are." She kneels down and points to his reflection. He pushes up on his forearms, lifting his head and babbling, and reaches to touch the mirror. He lowers himself down and starts to roll over. Ms. Bates watches to see if he needs help. He has just begun rolling over and sometimes gets stuck. "You did it!" Ms. Bates says. "Hurray!" Lionell waves his arms and kicks his feet in the air. "Ahhhh," he says. Then he grabs one of his feet and begins sucking on it.

1. **What are some of Lionell's physical skills?**

   _____

   _____

   _____

   _____

2. **How did Ms. Bates encourage his physical development?**

   _____

   _____

   _____

   _____

Providing Equipment and Opportunities for Gross Motor Development

"It must be something about the rain!" Ms. Lewis says to Ms. Gonzalez. "The children seem restless. Perhaps they need some exercise. This is the second day we've had to stay indoors. I think we need to try some new ways to move around inside." "I agree," says Ms. Gonzalez. "Let's clean up, then we can find some new ways for these crawlers and walkers to move their bodies." When the last toys are put away, Ms. Lewis and Ms. Gonzalez push the shelves against the wall to make more room. "We need this space for dancing," they tell the children. Ms. Lewis puts on a record and several children begin swaying to the music. She picks up Michael and dances with him. As they move about, Ms. Lewis says, "Dora is jumping! And Sam is waving his arms! Joe is bending his knees!" Meanwhile, Ms. Gonzalez sits down with the crawlers and moves to the music. They all laugh and squeal. "What terrific dancers!" she exclaims. After five minutes of energetic movement, the children tire of the activity. Ms. Lewis says, "It's not raining any more. If you take the older ones outside for a few minutes, I'll get the others ready for lunch." Ms. Gonzalez takes four walkers outside for a march around the playground.

1. **How did Ms. Lewis and Ms. Gonzalez know the children were ready for gross motor activities?**

_____

_____

_____

_____

2. **What gross motor activities did Ms. Lewis and Ms. Gonzalez provide?**

_____

_____

_____

_____

Providing Equipment and Opportunities for Fine Motor Development

Mr. Jones and Ms. Moore are expanding the variety of fine motor activities in the toddler room. Ms. Moore crouches next to Becky (30 months) and says, "Becky, I see what you've done with the shaving cream! You've smeared it on the table, on your arms, and on your cheeks. Now you're running your finger through a mountain of cream on the table. How does that feel?" "Cold," answers Becky. As Ms. Moore watches, Becky continues to move her finger through the shaving cream mound. She slowly brings her left hand up to the table top, sticks out her index finger, and traces straight and curved lines through the shaving cream. Then she uses her two fingers to make white trails on the table. "Look what you did, Becky," Ms. Moore tells her. "You used your fingers to make two lines that are the same."

Nearby, Mr. Jones sits in the block area with several toddlers. "Vroom," Andy (28 months) says, as he pushes a car between two walls of blocks. Some of the blocks begin to tumble, and Sarah (31 months) and Jerome (32 months) move their wooden people out of the way. "Fall, they fall!" Sarah says. She, Jerome, and Andy push their cars and people on the floor to move them around the fallen blocks. "Your cars are riding and your people are walking around a lot of obstacles. Good work, kids," Mr. Jones says.

1. **What activities did Ms. Moore and Mr. Jones provide for fine motor development?**

    _____

    _____

    _____

    _____

2. **How did they reinforce the children's small muscle play?**

    _____

    _____

    _____

    _____

Compare your answers with those on the answer sheet at the end of this module. If your answers are different, discuss them with your trainer. There can be more than one good answer.

Taking Care of Your Own Body[1]

As a caregiver, you are concerned about children's physical development. Yet to work well, it's essential that you take care of yourself, too. How many times a day do you:

- pick up a child?

- lean over a stepstool in front of a sink to wash your hands?

- sit on the floor and bend forward to play with a child?

- sit on a child-sized chair?

These are normal activities for caregivers of young children. They are also activities that can produce sore backs and limbs. There are many ways to maintain good posture and flexibility and to avoid physical pain as you provide care for children. Here are some suggested practices:

- Keep your lower back as straight as possible and avoid slouching when sitting or standing.

- Put one foot up on a stool or step when standing for a long time.

- Bend your knees, not your back, when you are leaning forward.

- Wear low-heeled, soft-soled, comfortable shoes to maintain proper posture.

- Bend your knees, tuck in your buttocks, and pull in your abdominal muscles when lifting a child or a heavy object.

- Avoid twisting when lifting or lowering a child or a heavy object. Hold the child or object close to you.

- Avoid standing for long periods with a child on your hip.

- For yourself in the children's room, use a low chair with an adult-sized seat and backrest.

- Use adult-sized tables and chairs, if possible, when meeting with other adults, when participating in training, or during planning and paperwork time away from the children.

- Talk with your supervisor and colleagues about staff coverage for short morning and afternoon breaks. Relax during these breaks! (Doing some stretching exercises is also a good way to spend breaks.)

[1]Based on Susan S. Aronson, M.D., "Coping with the Physical Requirements of Caregiving," *Child Care Information Exchange* (Redmond, WA: Exchange Press, May 1987), pp. 39-40.

Caregiving is a physically demanding job. For you to help children grow and develop in appropriate ways, you need to be in good physical shape. Think about your daily movements and your environment, and answer the questions below.

1. **How can you improve your posture and movements throughout the day?**

_____

_____

_____

_____

2. **What changes to the environment or the schedule can you suggest so that you and your colleagues can avoid sore backs and limbs?**

_____

_____

_____

_____

The suggestions you have just read and the ones you noted, along with regular exercise and good health and nutrition practices, can help you promote your own physical development as you promote the physical development of young children.

When you have finished this overview section, you should complete the pre-training assessment. Refer to the glossary at the end of this module if you need definitions of the terms that are used.

Pre-Training Assessment

Listed below are the skills that caregivers use to promote the physical development of infants and toddlers. Think about whether you do these things regularly, sometimes, or not enough. Place a check in one of the columns on the right for each skill listed. Then discuss your answers with your trainer.

SKILL	I DO THIS REGULARLY	I DO THIS SOMETIMES	I DON'T DO THIS ENOUGH
REINFORCING AND ENCOURAGING PHYSICAL DEVELOPMENT 1. Scheduling time for outdoor play every day.			
2. Helping and encouraging young children when they are learning new skills.			
3. Providing safe places for infants and toddlers to move about.			
4. Providing safe and interesting objects for infants and toddlers to explore with their senses.			
5. Observing and recording information about each child's physical strengths, interests, and needs.			
6. Helping young children develop an awareness of rhythm through music and movement activities.			
7. Arranging the room with a variety of textures and heights for young and mobile infants to lie and crawl on.			

SKILL	I DO THIS REGULARLY	I DO THIS SOMETIMES	I DON'T DO THIS ENOUGH
PROVIDING EQUIPMENT AND OPPORTUNITIES FOR GROSS MOTOR DEVELOPMENT			
8. Using a variety of materials and equipment to promote gross motor development.			
9. Playing indoor and outdoor noncompetitive games with children.			
10. Encouraging the development of self-help skills that use large muscles.			
11. Planning and implementing increasingly difficult activities in which large muscles are used.			
12. Using a variety of materials that require infants and toddlers to use their small muscles.			
PROVIDING EQUIPMENT AND OPPORTUNITIES FOR FINE MOTOR DEVELOPMENT			
13. Providing children with opportunities to develop small muscles by grasping, pulling, fingering, pinching, rolling, squeezing, zipping, turning pages, and so on.			
14. Encouraging the development of self-help skills that use small muscles.			

SKILL	I DO THIS REGULARLY	I DO THIS SOMETIMES	I DON'T DO THIS ENOUGH
15. Planning and implementing increasingly difficult activities in which small muscles are used.			
16. Encouraging children to participate in daily routines (such as wiping up a spill, brushing their teeth, or cleaning up the toys) as much as their developing small muscle skills allow.			

Review your responses, then list three to five skills you would like to improve or topics you would like to learn more about. When you finish this module, you will list examples of your new or improved knowledge and skills.

_____

_____

_____

_____

Now begin the learning activities for Module 4, Physical.

I. Using Your Knowledge of Infant and Toddler Development to Promote Physical Development

In this activity you will learn:

- to recognize some typical behaviors of infants and toddlers; and

- to use what you know about infants and toddlers to promote their physical development.

Very young **infants** do not have control over how they move. Some of their kicking, squirming, and wiggling is random, without purpose. Most of a newborn's first movements are reflexive, which means they happen automatically, without the infant's thinking about them. For example, if you touch the area around an infant's lips or cheeks, the infant will turn toward you and begin moving his or her mouth as if sucking.

As infants develop, they begin to gain control over how they move. Although infants develop at different rates and have different abilities, physical growth follows a general pattern. For instance, control develops from head to toe. At first infants need you to support their heads, but soon they learn to do this themselves. As infants learn to lift their heads, sit, crawl, and walk, we see them gaining control of their bodies from head to toe.

As they gain large muscle control, infants also are working on small muscle development and eye-hand coordination. In the first 18 months of life, an infant will develop from a tightly fisted newborn to a mobile infant who can point, climb stairs, and scribble. Although they sound simple, these skills are built upon many others. For example, infants must learn to bring their hands to their mouth, to reach for things, to let go of things, to move a toy from one hand to another, and to grasp things between their fingers and thumbs.

As infants develop new physical skills, the world opens up to them. Being able to reach out and grab something allows young infants to have physical contact with a piece of their world: a rattle, a bell, or a book. Crawlers can feel the soft rug, cool hard floor, and spongey pillows they crawl over. New walkers can travel to different sections of the room and discover books and toys that they never noticed before. By promoting their physical development, you can help infants learn about themselves and the world.

Toddlers have acquired a wide range of large and small muscle skills. Most toddlers walk very steadily, and they can run, climb, squat, and jump. They can fit pieces into a simple puzzle, build with blocks, and pour juice from a small pitcher. Now that they can move about without using their hands to support themselves, their hands are free to touch, lift, grasp, push, and so on. By the time they are 3 years old, toddlers develop a preference for using their right or left hands most of the time.

As toddlers develop new physical skills, these skills are used to achieve other goals. Learning to climb on a stepstool is followed by carrying the stepstool to the window and climbing up to look outside. Toddlers learn to coordinate their fine motor skills so they can reach for and pick up objects. They learn to eat using utensils, to turn the pages of books, and to begin to draw, pretend write, and paint.

Because infants and toddlers learn by doing, their physical development is closely connected with every other aspect of their development. Infants feel good about themselves when they gain new skills, such as rolling over or crawling. Toddlers learn to relate to other people when they do physical things together—jumping on a bouncy pillow with a friend or waiting for a turn on a riding toy. As they try to balance on one foot or build ramps for their cars to roll down, they are gaining an understanding of how things work. By promoting the physical development of infants and toddlers, you are helping them learn about themselves, about other people, and about their world.

The chart on the next page lists some typical behaviors of infants and toddlers. Included are behaviors relevant to physical development. The right-hand column asks you to identify ways that caregivers can use this information about child development to promote young children's physical development. Try to think of as many examples as you can. As you work through the module, you will learn new strategies for promoting physical development, and you can add them to the child development chart. You are not expected to think of all the examples at one time. If you need help getting started, turn to the completed chart at the end of the module. By the time you complete all the learning activities, you will find that you have learned many ways to promote children's physical development.

Using Your Knowledge of Infants and Toddlers Development to Promote Physical Development

WHAT YOUNG INFANTS DO (0-8 MONTHS)	HOW CAREGIVERS CAN USE THIS INFORMATION TO PROMOTE PHYSICAL DEVELOPMENT
They have reflexive arm and leg movements that are not under their conscious control.	
They gain control of their heads.	
They begin to coordinate their eyes and to stare at objects, especially faces.	
The gain voluntary control of their arms and legs.	
They reach out with one hand to pick up a toy.	
They begin turning from back to belly and belly to back.	

WHAT MOBILE INFANTS DO (9-17 MONTHS)	HOW CAREGIVERS CAN USE THIS INFORMATION TO PROMOTE PHYSICAL DEVELOPMENT
They can sit in chairs.	
They hold objects and manipulate them.	
They creep or crawl.	
They hold onto furniture to pull themselves up to standing.	
They pick up small objects using a thumb and forefinger.	
They walk but may still prefer crawling.	
They may begin dressing and undressing themselves.	

WHAT TODDLERS DO (18-36 MONTHS)	HOW CAREGIVERS CAN USE THIS INFORMATION TO PROMOTE PHYSICAL DEVELOPMENT
They walk well.	
They enjoy sensory experiences.	
They develop new skills, such as throwing, catching, and hopping.	
They gain control of bladder and bowel muscles.	
They grip with thumb and forefinger (pincer grasp) effectively.	
They manipulate objects with hands and fingers.	

When you have completed as much as you can do on the chart, discuss your answers with your trainer. As you proceed with the rest of the learning activities, you can refer back to the chart and add more examples of how caregivers promote infants' and toddlers' physical development.

II. Observing Children's Physical Development

In this activity you will learn:

- to identify children's large and small muscle skills; and

- to observe individual differences in children's physical development.

Observing Gross Motor Development

In any group of infants and toddlers, the children will have a wide range of fine and gross motor skills. In order to decide how best to respond to children's needs, you must first observe to see what skills a child has and what skills he or she is currently working on.

Learning to move occupies an important part of the day for every **infant**. Young infants develop new muscles and skills as they reach for the mobile hanging over the changing table or roll over to get the rattle that tumbled to the edge of their blanket. Mobile infants pull themselves up on chairs, sofas, and caregiver's legs, and—to the excitement of their families and caregivers—soon take their first steps.

During the first 18 months of their lives, infants develop from having little control over how they move to being able to walk with increasing ease and speed. The infants in your room will probably have a wide variety of large muscle skills. Sammy (4 months) may be beginning to lift his head, while Peter (14 months) may be walking and climbing in and out of his car made from a box.

As **toddlers** walk, run, climb, push, and pull, they are learning about themselves and their world. Sally (20 months) is learning how big she is as she climbs in and out of boxes and through a cloth tunnel. Jessica (34 months) feels proud of herself as she tries to do a forward roll—something she has watched her older sister do many times. Ricky (28 months) and his new friend, Adam (30 months), like to climb to the top of the outdoor climber. Toddlers need many opportunities to practice their gross motor skills so they can gain more control over their movement. Observe the toddlers in your group to determine who needs encouragement to try new things and who needs to be reminded to slow down.

On the next page is a chart listing the major large muscle skills that infants and toddlers acquire and the average age at which these skills appear. Use this chart as a guide, but remember that there are large differences in the rates at which individual children develop.

Gross Motor Skills[2]

BEHAVIOR	AVERAGE AGE
Gains control of head	3-6 months
Turns from back to belly and belly to back	5-6 months
Sits alone	8-10 months
Crawls	9-12 months
May pull self to standing by holding onto furniture	9-12 months
Stands without holding	9-12 months
May walk	10-15 months
Walks fast and well	12-18 months
Walks up stairs holding a hand	12-18 months
Has jumping and climbing skills (for example, gets in and out of a low chair)	15-18 months
Demonstrates coordination skills (for example, walks with a pull toy or kicks a ball)	15-18 months

[2]Based on Janet Gonzalez-Mena and Dianne Widmeyer Eyer, *Infancy and Caregiving* (Palo Alto, CA: Mayfield, 1980), pp. 143-153, and Christine Z. Cataldo, *Infant and Toddler Programs* (Reading, MA: Addison-Wesley, 1983), pp. 215-216.

BEHAVIOR	AVERAGE AGE
Walks fast and well, in an increasingly well-organized and smooth way, with feet close together	18-20 months
Runs for short distances, with frequent starts and stops	20-22 months
Walks up and down stairs, negotiating one step at a time	23-25 months
Kicks and throws objects, either in play or in anger, with increasingly accurate aim	18-30 months
Has some balance in walking, jumping, and hopping (for example, jumps with both feet, hops briefly on one foot, walks a low balance beam)	18-30 months
Coordinates a series of physical skills in play (for example, lifts, carries, pushes, and arranges heavy objects, such as hollow blocks)	18-36 months
Vigorously pursues, with some success, physical activities such as tumbling, rolling, rolling sideways and doing forward rolls, throwing, stretching, and roughhousing	18-36 months

Observing Fine Motor Development

Young children need to develop their small muscles for many tasks. Coordinating hands, fingers, and wrists is necessary for writing and drawing. Strength in the small muscles is needed for cutting with scissors and using tools. Control and agility are required for buttoning, zipping, holding utensils, and other tasks. These fine motor skills are an important part of the early years, and they are refined, adapted, and used later in life for tasks such as typing, driving, and cooking.

During the first 18 months of life, **infants** develop from having their fists clenched to being able to hold a large crayon and make large marks. The infants in your room probably have a wide range of fine motor skills. Jon (4 months) may be able to reach for a dangling toy, while Shelley (10 months) may be able to pick up small pieces of carrot from her plate using her thumb and forefinger.

Infants use their fine motor skills to get information about their world. They also use their senses to learn about themselves and the people and objects around them. Hands and mouths are used together to explore a food. Eyes and ears are used together to identify the location of a sound. As Becky (6 months) learns to use her fingers, hands, and wrists, she can reach out and touch a soft stuffed animal or shake a rattle and listen to the sound it makes. She brings things to her mouth to see how they feel and taste. Tearing crunchy lettuce leaves helps Roger (17 months) learn to coordinate small muscle movements.

Between the ages of 18 months and 3 years, **toddlers** perfect the fine motor skills they already have and learn new ones. The toddlers in your room probably have a wide range of fine motor skills. Karen (18 months), who first scribbled when she was 14 months old, can now coordinate her eyes, arm, and hand well enough to make a single mark. Leslie (26 months) can coordinate her hand, arm, and wrist well enough to fill a page with scribbles, while Mary (35 months) can make circles.

The chart that follows can help you keep track of individual children's developing skills. Keep in mind, however, that this chart—and any developmental chart—can provide only guidelines. Every child develops at his or her own pace!

Fine Motor Skills[3]

BEHAVIOR	AVERAGE AGE
Holds hand clenched in fist or partially open	1-2 months
Grasps voluntarily when toy is placed in hand	2-3 months
Clasps hands together in play	4 months
Grasps object held near hand	5 months
Reaches block or toy (mittenlike grasp)	6 months
Transfers toy from one hand to the other	6-7 months

[3] Based on Sally Provence, *Guide for the Care of Infants in Groups* (New York, NY: Child Welfare League of America, 1975), p. 73-75.

BEHAVIOR	AVERAGE AGE
Holds two toys at once	7-8 months
Bangs two toys together	9-10 months
Grasps small object with index finger and thumb (pincer grasp)	10-11 months
Takes covers off containers	13-14 months
Scribbles with crayon	13-14 months
Turns pages in a book, two or three at a time	15 months
Piles three or four blocks	18 months
Makes strokes with crayons on paper	18 months
Piles five or six blocks	21 months
Turns pages of a book, one at a time	22-23 months
Makes large circular strokes with a crayon	24 months
Can roll, pound, squeeze, and pull playdough	24-29 months
Fills and dumps containers with sand, water, toys, etc.	24-29 months
Enjoys finger painting	30-35 months

BEHAVIOR	AVERAGE AGE
Makes mud and sand pies	30-35 months
Paints strokes, dots, and circular shapes on easel	30-35 months
Cuts with scissors	35 months

In this learning activity you will observe and take notes on two children of the same age over a three-day period to see individual differences in the development of large and small muscle skills. Begin by reading the example that follows this page.

Gross Motor Skills
(Example)

Child(ren) *Frank, Jesse*   **Age(s)** *12 months*   **Date(s)** *March 15-17*

Setting *Infant room carpeted area*

Write two brief observations of how each child used physical skills over the past three days.

Child 1: *Frank*

Frank takes eight steps, then plops down on the floor near a coffee can filled with small plastic blocks. He dumps out the blocks. He picks up one and drops it back in the can. Then he gets up and takes off, walking quickly across the room.

Frank laughs as he pushes a chair across the room.

Child 2: *Jesse*

Jesse sits on the floor with the coffee can of blocks. He takes the cover off, dumps out the blocks, then one by one puts each block back in the can.

Jesse pulls himself up and, holding onto furniture, cruises over to the table. He picks up a crayon and scribbles all over a sheet of paper that a caregiver holds for him.

What large and small muscle skills are each child working on?

Child 1: *Frank*

Frank is walking quickly and pushing things. I also saw him grasping a block.

Child 2: *Jesse*

Jesse pulls himself up and moves holding onto furniture. He can take a cover off a can, grasp small blocks, and scribble with a crayon.

Describe the differences you see in the two children's physical development.

Frank is a good walker. He spends most of his time on the move.

Jesse still holds onto furniture when he walks. He is very skilled with his fingers. During most of the time I observed him, he was working on fine motor skills.

Discuss your observations with your trainer.

Gross Motor Skills

Child(ren) _____ Age(s)_____ Date(s) _____

Setting _____

Write two brief observations of how each child used physical skills over the past three days.

Child 1: _____

_____

_____

_____

Child 2: _____

_____

_____

_____

What large and small muscle skills is each child working on?

Child 1: _____

_____

_____

_____

Child 2: _____

_____

_____

_____

Describe the differences you see in the two children's physical development.

_____

_____

_____

Discuss your observations with your trainer.

III. Promoting Physical Development

In this activity you will learn:

- to help infants and toddlers develop and refine their physical skills; and

- to encourage children's physical development during daily routines.

As you think about ways to promote physical development, remember that nothing is more important than your relationships with children. Infants and toddlers need to feel safe and secure to do the exploring and experimenting that are necessary to learn new physical skills. By building trusting, caring relationships, you help them feel at home in child care. Your interest in and encouragement of what they are doing—be it learning to grasp an object or pull down their pants to use the toilet—promotes their physical development more than any activity or toy possibly could.

The first task, therefore, is to be involved with each child in your care. Here are some suggestions of ways to promote physical development as you interact with children:

- **Pay attention to what children are doing and encourage them.** To 5-month-old Jerry you might say, "Look at you reaching, Jerry! Just a little further and you'll have that rattle." To 20-month-old Jenny you might say, "You sure are balancing, Jenny! Why don't you try walking to the other end of the board again?"

- **Use your knowledge about child development and about the individual children in your room to decide when to intervene directly and when to let a child work out a problem.** You may decide to let Kenny (16 months) figure out how to climb into a box but might step in when you see him trying to climb into his crib. Give Jessica (34 months) the chance to figure out how to climb down from the climber before offering help. If you think she is in danger, be available to help her.

- **Set clear limits to help children begin learning how to use their large muscles safely.** Tell two toddlers, "When you rock in the rocking boat, hold on with two hands so you don't fall." Tell an infant, "You can crawl over here on the carpet, away from the walking children."

- **Move yourself. Show children that moving is an enjoyable part of life.** Ms. Gonzalez does a few of her daily exercises with the infants in her room. Kevin (15 months) laughs as he sits on her stomach while she does her sit-ups. Mr. Jones enjoys playing actively with the toddlers in his room. Everyone enjoys crawling, jumping, and walking on tiptoe while playing "Follow the Leader," chasing bubbles, rolling hoops, and jumping on pillows.

Taking Advantage of Daily Routines

Each day you and the infants and toddlers in your group spend much of your time together involved in daily routines of dressing, toileting, and eating. It is tempting to hurry through these chores, but they deserve the same care and attention as any other activity you do with children. Each provides rich opportunities for developing large and small motor skills. And as children grow, these daily routines offer new physical challenges.

Dressing

Dressing offers children of different ages different opportunities to practice physical skills. Jeremy (3 months) becomes more aware of his body and works on controlling his head as he holds it up for a second while his caregiver pulls on his shirt. Mike (15 months), to the dismay of his caregiver, uses getting dressed as a time to practice walking. At 24 months, Jerry is coordinated enough to put his foot into his boots, while Laura (32 months) can zip up her own jacket after her caregiver gets it started.

Toileting

Shelley (5 months) discovers her feet and sucks on her toes as her caregiver tries to fasten her dry diaper. Andrew (8 months) opens and closes his fingers, tightly grasping his caregiver's necklace, as she leans over him. Alison (18 months) climbs up the footstool to the sink and turns on the faucet after getting a new diaper, and she and her caregiver wash their hands.

Using the potty—an event caregivers and parents look forward to—requires that children be aware of and able to control their bladder and bowel muscles. Every child develops at his or her own pace, but typically between 24 and 30 months, children are physically mature enough to begin using the toilet. Greta (29 months) tells her caregiver when she has to "pee pee" during the day. She, like many of her peers, enjoys practicing her small motor skills by flushing the toilet. Arnie (33 months) walks into the bathroom himself. He is able to pull his pants down and up again on his own. He can follow directions displayed in simple pictures on the bathroom wall that remind him to flush the toilet and wash his hands.

Eating

Breakfast, lunch, and snack times are wonderful opportunities for physical development. Carla (4 months) brings her hands to midline as she explores the bottle her caregiver holds for her. Josie (9 months) sits up straight in her highchair and uses her pincer grasp to pick up a piece of toast. Whether she eats it or throws it on the floor depends on her mood. Harry (14 months) insists on having his own spoon. He can sometimes get a little applesauce in his mouth, though most of it ends up on his shirt. John (22 months) loves stirring and pouring when he helps make French toast for a snack. At 30 months, Karen proudly sweeps with a broom and holds the dustpan as she helps her special caregiver clean up after lunch.

In addition to taking advantage of daily routines, you can also plan activities such as playing with dough and going outdoors.

Playing with Dough

Playdough is an ideal material for toddlers. It is much better than other modeling materials. Modeling clay, or plasticene, is too hard for toddlers to manipulate when it gets cold. Earth clay, or potters' clay, can be very messy and is sometimes hard to get. Silly Putty does not keep its shape, is not a great thing for toddlers to taste, and can be hard to get out of clothing and hair.

Toddlers love to touch, squeeze, roll, pound, and poke holes in dough. They are not interested in making things; they are interested in the changes they can make in the dough.

To vary and extend children's experiences, you can offer any of the following:

- Things to poke, such as popsicle sticks, tongue depressors, large pegs, candles, and plastic animals. Toddlers love making things stand up in the dough like a "birthday cake."

- Things for pounding or rolling. Toddlers sometimes enjoy pounding the dough with small wooden mallets or rolling it out with a wooden roller. Dowels, particularly spiral dowels, make great marks in the dough.

- Things to make impressions. All kinds of junk materials are fun for older toddlers to stick in the dough and pull out again to see what kind of mark they make: large bottlecaps, jar lids, forks, a potato masher, or a garlic press.

Here are a few simple recipes for making playdough.

Uncooked Playdough

Mix together 2 parts flour, 1 part water, and 1 part salt. Add a little more flour if it is sticky. Store in a plastic bag or covered container. Add food coloring to the water for color if you like.

Cooked Playdough

> 4 cups flour
> 2 cups salt
> 4 tablespoons cream of tartar
> 4 cups water (plus food coloring if desired)
> 2 tablespoons oil

Cooked playdough lasts longer than uncooked, especially if stored in a closed plastic container or plastic bag. Cook over medium heat, stirring constantly until stiff. Let cool and knead.

Baking Soda and Cornstarch Playdough

>2 cups baking soda
>1 cup cornstarch
>1-1/3 cups warm water (plus food coloring if desired)

Mix baking soda and cornstarch in a pan. Add water. Bring it to a boil over medium heat and stir constantly until it thickens. Remove from heat and pour onto a board to cool. Knead it when it is cool enough, and store it in a plastic bag or container.

Providing Opportunities for Outdoor Play

Probably the best opportunities for gross motor development occur in the outdoor play area. Going outdoors is important for children and caregivers alike. Spending all day inside in a large group is stressful for everyone. It is refreshing to go outside, if only briefly, every day. Outside the young infants can enjoy new sights and sounds, and the mobile infants and toddlers can truly be free to move and use their bodies in space. The outdoor environment is a world to explore and learn about as well as a place to release pent-up energy. Using the outdoors as a learning environment is also discussed in Module 3.

The selection and placement of large fixed equipment is not usually a responsibility of caregivers. Most often the outdoor area is equipped with wheel toys and stationary swings, slides, climbers, and a sand box. In addition, the children will enjoy playing with a variety of materials such as playground rubber balls, tunnels, riding toys, wagons, and cardboard boxes to climb into and out of.

Young infants can be placed on a blanket in a safe area outdoors. Even if they don't move much, the trip outdoors lets them know that there is a whole world to explore, and they enjoy the warmth of the sun and the way the wind feels on their bodies. This is an important message for children who will soon be literally moving into the world. Mobile infants enjoy crawling and walking on sand and grass. Toddlers like to ride and climb on toys that they may not be able to use inside.

As you play with the children and encourage their play with others outdoors, keep the following suggestions in mind:

- **Pay attention to what the children are doing and participate with them.** Avoid thinking that being outdoors is a time to stand and talk with other caregivers.

- **Accept children's fears as real.** Offer a hand as encouragement for a child who is hesitant to go down the slide alone.

- **Participate at the children's level as much as possible.** Kneel or crouch and roll balls or toss bean bags to the children. Sit down on a blanket with an infant and talk to her about the things she is seeing and hearing.

- **Arrange with other caregivers to take your place occasionally so you have time to move, stretch, or take a short run around the yard.** You will probably have lots of company. Getting a little exercise during the day will help you feel refreshed. At the same time you will be showing the children that using large muscles is a part of your life, too.

In this learning activity, you will look at ways you can support the physical development of infants and toddlers through daily routines. Begin by identifying fine and gross motor skills being worked on by two children in your group. Arrange a time to observe another caregiver interacting with each child during a daily routine. After completing each observation, identify ways that the caregiver promotes an infant's or toddler's physical development during that routine, and other ideas you might try.

Promoting Physical Development During Daily Routines
(Infant Example)

Child _Dennis_   **Age** _4 months_   **Date** _August 16_

Setting _Indoor play area_   **Caregiver** _Ms. Edwards_

Write a brief observation of this child during a daily routine. Underline the routine you are observing: dressing, eating, <u>diapering</u>.

> *Dennis is lying on a blanket on the floor. Ms. Edwards kneels down next to him and says, "I'm going to change you now, Dennis." She waits a moment as Dennis turns his head to look at her and then picks him up, supporting his head with her hand. She carries him to the changing table. As she changes Dennis, he touches his hands together over his stomach. Ms. Edwards begins playing pat-a-cake, touching her hands together. Dennis coos.*

What gross motor or fine motor skills is this child working on?

> *Dennis is learning to control his head. He lifts his head up when I am sitting with him in the rocking chair.*

> *His fingers aren't always in a fist any more. He is bringing his hands together over the middle of his body.*

What did the caregiver do to support this child's physical development?

> *She encouraged him to practice controlling his head by kneeling down, talking to him, and waiting for him to look at her. She played pat-a-cake to encourage him to bring his hands together.*

What else might a caregiver do to promote the physical development of a child this age during this daily routine?

> *She might offer him something to hold so he can practice holding something in his fingers.*

Promoting Physical Development During Daily Routines
(Toddler Example)

Child _Kenny_ **Age** _32 months_ **Date** _August 18_

Setting _Indoor entrance area_ **Caregiver** _Ms. Jacobs_

Write a brief observation of this child during a daily routine. Underline the routine you are observing: <u>dressing</u>, eating, diapering.

> _Kenny and two other toddlers are going for a neighborhood walk with Ms. Jacobs. Kenny concentrates as he works on pulling up the zipper of his jacket. After helping the other children get ready, Ms. Jacobs asks if she can start it for him. He nods. "I did it," he says proudly as he pulls the zipper up to his chin._

What gross motor or fine motor skills is this child working on?

> _Kenny is working on the fine motor skill of zipping his jacket._

What did the caregiver do to support this child's physical development?

> _She gave him time to work on his new skill. She helped him do the part he couldn't do (begin the zipper) and let him do the rest._

What else might a caregiver do to promote the physical development of a child this age during this daily routine?

> _She could continue to observe other times when he is getting dressed as he uses buttons, snaps, and buckles so she can offer help when he needs it and let him do as much as he can on his own._

Promoting Physical Development During Daily Routines

Child _____ Age _____ Date _____

Setting _____ Caregiver _____

Write a brief observation of this child during a daily routine. Underline the routine you are observing: dressing, eating, diapering.

_____

_____

_____

_____

What gross or fine motor skills is this child working on?

_____

_____

_____

_____

What did the caregiver do to support this child's physical development?

_____

_____

_____

_____

What else might a caregiver do to promote the physical development of a child this age during this daily routine?

_____

_____

_____

_____

Promoting Physical Development During Daily Routines

Child _____ Age _____ Date _____

Setting _____ Caregiver _____

Write a brief observation of this child during a daily routine. Underline the routine you are observing: dressing, eating, diapering.

_____

_____

_____

_____

What gross or fine motor skills is this child working on?

_____

_____

_____

What did the caregiver do to support this child's physical development?

_____

_____

_____

_____

What else might a caregiver do to promote the physical development of a child this age during this daily routine?

_____

_____

_____

_____

Review your responses with your trainer.

IV. Helping Infants and Toddlers Develop Strong Self-Concepts Through Physical Development

In this activity you will learn:

- to recognize how physical development helps young children develop socially and emotionally; and

- to interact with infants and toddlers in ways that encourage them to develop positive self-concepts.

Early childhood educators have long recognized the important role that physical development plays in helping children feel good about themselves. When a child learns to hold a bottle, pull himself or herself up in the crib, or jump down from a step, the sense of accomplishment is enormous. The pride that comes from successfully mastering physical skills makes children feel good about themselves. This sense of confidence and competence leads to emotional security and a willingness to risk learning difficult cognitive tasks. Thus, by encouraging the physical development of infants and toddlers, you are promoting their growth in all areas and contexts.

Encouraging Strong Self-Concepts Through Interactions with Children

Because you are so important to the children you care for, how you respond to them as they are learning new physical skills will influence how they feel about themselves. Here are some ways you can help children feel good about who they are as you encourage their new skills.

- **Respect children's individual differences** in terms of their physical development. Praise a child's progress without making comparisons to other children: "You balanced on one foot today, Luis (30 months), and you didn't fall down."

- **Help children sometimes by teaching directly.** You may, for example, want to review with a toddler how to catch a ball before you throw it: "I'm ready to throw the ball to you. Keep your arms stretched out. Here it comes."

- **Verbally reassure a child who is reluctant or frightened:** "Let me hold your hand while you jump off the wooden box."

- **Know when to stand back.** Sometimes the most supportive thing you can do is to give children an uninterrupted opportunity to work on a new skill as you watch to be sure they are safe: "I'll wait a few minutes to see what happens. If I rush in to help, I may take away from Carl the satisfaction of getting the last piece of the puzzle in place."

- **Encourage children to try new activities:** "Would you like to help scrub these carrots?"

- **Follow children's leads** about what they feel comfortable to try. Be there to offer assistance and encouragement, but do not force children when they are reluctant: "If you don't want to go up the steps to the slide, maybe you would like to come play in the sandbox."

- **Suggest how a child can overcome an obstacle.** No one can learn if he or she is too frustrated: "Hold your cup with both hands so your milk doesn't spill again."

Encouraging Strong Self-Concepts Through Materials and Activities

Like us, infants and toddlers feel proud and excited about making new discoveries and developing new skills. You can help children feel good about themselves and encourage them to reach out into their world by offering materials and activities that reflect and respond to who they are. This means knowing children as individuals as well as about their developmental stages. It means observing to see when children need a new challenge and being able to help them extend and work on new skills without becoming too frustrated.

In the following example, Ms. Oanh, a caregiver, encourages Tensi to work on her fine motor skills and to feel good about herself by observing and making choices that respond to Tensi's needs:

> As Ms. Oanh watches Tensi (29 months) at the easel, she notices that Tensi seems very hesitant. When she gets paint on her fingers, she puts down her brush and goes to wash it off. She doesn't come back to paint. Ms. Oanh wonders what is going on. This child is very different from the Tensi of a few months ago, who would laugh and talk as she filled her paper with colorful swirls and splotches.

> After talking with colleagues, Ms. Oanh wonders if Tensi's concern with getting "dirty" has something to do with the fact that she is now really working hard on toilet training. Keeping clean and dry is very important to her. She continues to observe and finds that Tensi stays away from the easel.

> Ms. Oanh decides she will keep her eye on Tensi and the easel over the next few weeks to see what happens. In the meantime she decides to offer Tensi beads to string and simple puzzles—materials with which she can still work on fine motor skills and not worry about keeping neat.

In this activity, you will read several descriptions of children and decide what activities you could offer and what you would say to help each child feel successful and competent.

Promoting Self-Concepts Through Physical Development

WHAT THE CHILD IS DOING	WHAT ACTIVITIES/ MATERIALS YOU WOULD OFFER THIS CHILD	WHAT YOU COULD SAY TO ENCOURAGE THE CHILD
Janet (32 months) likes to try to use scissors but ends up getting frustrated and tearing up her paper.		
Leroy (5 months) likes to hold his rattle, shaking and sucking it. If he drops it, he cries until his caregiver gives it back to him.		
Maria (24 months) likes to throw beanbags in a box on the floor. Every time she tries to throw a beanbag in the box, she misses. When she misses, she picks up the beanbag and throws it again.		
Lucy (22 months) enjoys sitting on the floor and stacking the small colored blocks. She can make a pile of four or five blocks. One time she tried to make a larger stack. When it fell down, she got frustrated and knocked the blocks all over the floor.		
Isolina (10 months) likes to hold her own spoon when her caregiver feeds her. However, every time she takes a turn at helping feed herself, a large amount of food ends up on her highchair tray. Still, she loves to feed herself.		

Review your responses with your trainer.

Summarizing Your Progress

You have now completed all of the learning activities for this module. Whether you are an experienced caregiver or a new one, this module has probably helped you develop new skills for promoting the physical development of infants and toddlers. Before you go on, take a few minutes to summarize what you've learned.

- Turn back to Learning Activity I, Using Your Knowledge of Infant and Toddler Development to Promote Physical Development, and add to the chart specific examples of how you promoted physical development during the time you were working on this module.

- Next, review your responses to the pre-training assessment for this module. Write a summary of what you learned, and list the skills you developed or improved.

_____

_____

_____

_____

_____

_____

Your final step in this module is to complete the knowledge and competency assessments. Let your trainer know when you are ready to schedule the assessments. After you have successfully completed these assessments, you will be ready to start a new module. Congratulations on your progress so far, and good luck with your next module.

Answer Sheet: Promoting Physical Development

Reinforcing and Encouraging Physical Development

1. **What are some of Lionell's physical skills?**

   a. He can lift his head.

   b. He can roll over.

   c. He can kick his feet and wave his arms in the air.

   d. He can reach out and touch the mirror.

2. **How did Ms. Bates encourage his physical development?**

   a. She put him down on a blanket where he could move freely.

   b. She put him in front of a low mirror so he could see himself move.

   c. She waited to see if he could roll over by himself.

   d. She got excited when he rolled over.

Providing Equipment and Opportunities for Gross Motor Development

1. **How did Ms. Lewis and Ms. Gonzalez know the children were ready for gross motor activities?**

   a. They were restless.

   b. They had been indoors for two days.

2. **What gross motor activities did Ms. Lewis and Ms. Gonzalez provide?**

   a. They put on some music to dance to.

   b. They let the older children run around the playground briefly in their rain gear.

Providing Equipment and Opportunities for Fine Motor Development

1. **What activities did Ms. Moore and Mr. Jones provide for fine motor development?**

   a. Fingerpainting with shaving cream.

   b. Playing with cars, wooden people, and blocks.

2. **How did they reinforce the children's small muscle play?**

   a. They described children's actions and asked questions to let the children know they were aware of what the toddlers were doing.

   b. They praised the children's work.

PHYSICAL

Using Your Knowledge of Infants and Toddlers Development to Promote Physical Development

WHAT YOUNG INFANTS DO (0-8 MONTHS)	HOW CAREGIVERS CAN USE THIS INFORMATION TO PROMOTE PHYSICAL DEVELOPMENT
They have reflexive arm and leg movements that are not under their conscious control.	Observe infants to see what they need. Help infants feel secure by putting them in safe, peaceful spots. For example, place a blanket on the floor or make a nest made of pillows so that infants won't be overstimulated.
They gain control of their heads.	Prevent neck injuries by supporting the head as you move, lift, and carry an infant. Hang interesting pictures or mobiles in and near cribs and changing tables to encourage infants to lift their heads to look.
They begin to coordinate their eyes and to stare at objects, especially faces.	Give individual attention to infants to encourage them to look at your face as you talk, hold, and care for them.
The gain voluntary control of their arms and legs.	Lay infants on rugs or mats so they have freedom to explore by looking, sucking, stretching, and reaching.
They reach out with one hand to pick up a toy.	Place a variety of washable objects within reach so infants can look at them and practice reaching for them.
They begin turning from back to belly and belly to back.	Provide a safe space so infants have freedom to practice moving. Be aware of what infants are doing in case they get stuck while rolling over and need help.

245

WHAT MOBILE INFANTS DO (9-17 MONTHS)	HOW CAREGIVERS CAN USE THIS INFORMATION TO PROMOTE PHYSICAL DEVELOPMENT
They sit in chairs.	Provide low, sturdy seats for infants to sit in and practice getting in and out of.
They hold objects and manipulate them.	Place interesting objects a little out of reach to encourage infants to move and get them. Be sure not to put them so far away that the infants become frustrated.
They creep or crawl.	Provide a safe environment so infants can move and explore with little adult interference. Add a variety of levels using pillows and small platforms to encourage infant's interest in crawling and moving. Provide balls for infants to chase.
They hold onto furniture to pull themselves up to standing.	Keep mobile infants safe by making sure that the furniture in your room is steady. Watch infants in case they get up but can't sit back down. Encourage infants to problem-solve and gain confidence by helping them figure out what to do and letting them do it.
They pick up small objects using a thumb and forefinger.	Help infants develop small muscle skills with activities such as helping them take off their socks, playing with nesting toys, and turning the pages of books. Offer "finger foods" at snacks and meals.
They walk but may still prefer crawling.	Give mobile infants lots of indoor and outdoor space to enjoy crawling and to practice walking. Allow children to decide when they are finished with crawling.

WHAT TODDLERS DO (18-36 MONTHS)	HOW CAREGIVERS CAN USE THIS INFORMATION TO PROMOTE PHYSICAL DEVELOPMENT
They walk well.	Take toddlers on short walks in and around the center so they can be free to move and explore with a minimum of restriction.
They enjoy sensory experiences.	Encourage small muscle development by offering a variety of sensory experiences such as water play, scribbling, and playing with playdough. Talk with toddlers about what they are doing, and sit with them to show you are interested in and value their work and play.
They develop new skills, such as throwing, catching, and hopping.	Plan daily large muscle activities indoors and outdoors, such as jumping, playing ball, and climbing. Participate for your own fun and exercise and to show toddlers that you value physical activity.
They gain control of bladder and bowel muscles.	Encourage toddlers to use the toilet when they are ready. Work with parents to develop a consistent approach to toilet training so that it is a positive experience that helps toddlers feel good about themselves.
They grip with thumb and forefinger (pincer grasp) effectively.	Offer materials and activities that encourage toddlers to practice their pincer grasp, such as turning the pages of books and zipping jackets (after you connect the bottom of the zipper).
They can manipulate objects with hands and fingers.	Provide simple puzzles, table toys, house corner props, and art materials for children to practice picking up and placing small objects to help them develop eye-hand coordination. Offer self-serve opportunities at snacks and meals.

Glossary

Eye-hand coordination	The ability to direct finger, hand, and wrist movements to accomplish a fine motor task—for example, fitting a peg in a hole, piling blocks, or picking up a piece of dry cereal.
Fine motor skills	Movements that involve the use of small muscles of the body, hands, and wrists—for example, picking up puzzle pieces or cutting with a pair of scissors, or using a spoon to feed yourself.
Gross motor skills	Movements that involve the use of large muscles of the entire body or large parts of the body—for example, running, hopping, or climbing.
Physical development	The gradual gaining of control over large and small muscles.
Sensory awareness	The gaining of information through sight, sound, touch, hearing, and smell—for example, smelling spices or turning in the direction of a voice.
Spatial awareness	The knowledge that the body takes up space and can move in space—for example, crawling inside a box.

Module 5
Cognitive

What Is Cognitive Development and Why Is It Important?

Cognitive development is the process of learning to think and to reason. We have learned a great deal about cognitive development from the work of Jean Piaget, who carefully observed young children to find out how they think at different ages and how they learn. He defined a series of stages that all children progress through from birth to maturity. Through his research, he noticed that children think differently from adults. For example, young children believe that water in a short, wide glass increases in amount if it is poured into a tall, thin glass. This is because children think it looks like there is more water in the tall glass; they can't remember that the same amount of water has been poured into a different glass. Eventually, they understand that the amount of water remains the same. This understanding comes when children are old enough to be able to think more abstractly and after they have had many experiences playing with water. It is through their play with real objects and materials that children come to understand the world around them.

Children develop their cognitive skills in everything they do. They are continually exploring and investigating everything around them. You have undoubtedly experienced how many things young children notice. They see the smallest caterpillar that you overlook. And for them it's not enough to see the caterpillar; they have to touch it, pick it up, examine it closely, even smell it. By using all their senses, young children develop a real understanding of caterpillars. When they hear the word caterpillar, they learn a label for this object they have explored. And on another day, when they see a worm, the same children may say, "Look at the caterpillar!" This is because they have noticed that a worm and a caterpillar have some characteristics in common. Although they are not actually correct, they are using their cognitive skills.

A child's cognitive development is not measured only by what information the child knows. A very important factor is whether a child has the self-confidence and skills to explore, to try out ideas, to solve problems, and to take on new challenges. Helping children develop and use their cognitive skills is a crucial part of being a caregiver. If you can help children begin to see themselves as successful learners, you will prepare them for school and for life.

In caring for infants and toddlers, you have many opportunities to promote their cognitive development. Most young children are eager to explore the world around them, to find out how things work. They want to learn what they can do with things they see in the world. You can build on this natural curiosity to promote cognitive development. You can provide opportunities for children to use all their senses to explore their environment. You can help children feel good about expressing their ideas and solving problems on their own. And finally, you can help children develop new concepts and acquire thinking and reasoning skills appropriate for their age and stage of development.

Promoting young children's cognitive development involves:

- providing opportunities for infants and toddlers to use all their senses to safely explore their environment;

- interacting with infants and toddlers in ways that promote their confidence and curiosity; and

- providing opportunities for infants and toddlers to develop new concepts and skills.

Listed below are examples of how caregivers demonstrate their competence in promoting cognitive development.

Providing Opportunities for Infants and Toddlers to Use All Their Senses to Explore Their Environment

Here are some examples of what caregivers can do.

- Include children in simple food-preparation activities, letting them see, touch, taste, and smell a variety of foods.

- Call attention to sensory experiences in the course of daily routines with children. "Doesn't the finger paint feel smooth?" "The snap on your jacket goes 'pop' when it opens." "Your orange smells delicious."

- Take a "listening walk" with a small group of children to discover different sounds.

- Provide musical instruments so children can make various sounds and explore the meaning of loud and quiet.

- Make matching games. "You put two circles in the box! Can you find any more circles?"

- Hang interesting things to touch over infants' cribs such as a vegetable brush and a piece of velvet. "Tom, you can reach up and touch the vegetable brush. Does it feel prickly?"

- Provide pillows covered in different textured fabrics for infants to crawl on. "The velour pillow feels soft on your knees when you crawl on it."

- Give infants finger foods so they can squish bananas, smell a slice of peach, and taste cooked green beans. "Nadia, you have smooshed peach all over your nose. You must have been enjoying the smell."

Interacting with Infants and Toddlers in Ways That Promote Their Confidence and Curiosity

Here are some examples of what caregivers can do.

- Show respect for and interest in a child's ideas. "You made a train out of those blocks. What a good idea!"

- Share children's curiosity about the world. "Do you want to come and help me watch to see how our hermit crab eats? I've always wanted to know about hermit crabs."

- Stretch children's thinking by asking questions. "Remember what we saw last time we came to this park?"

- Extend dramatic play. "I see your baby is sick today. What do you think we should do to help him feel better?"

- Comment on an infant's successes, such as holding on to a toy, rolling over, or sitting up. "Jonathan, you worked hard to pick up that rattle. You're really holding on to it now."

- Wear beads, scarves, and colorful clothes of different textures that infants can explore while you hold them. "Laura, I see you looking at my beads. I'm going to gently put your hand on them. They feel cold and smooth."

- Include children in solving problems. "What can we do to make this playdough less sticky?"

- Encourage children to ask questions by answering the many questions they ask.

Providing Opportunities for Infants and Toddlers to Develop New Concepts and Skills

Here are some examples of what caregivers can do.

- Offer children simple, clear choices when the decision can be theirs. "Do you want to paint at the easel or use the finger paints?"

- Provide everyday materials to extend children's dramatic play. "Here are some pots, pans, and spoons for you to play with."

- To introduce the idea of cause and effect, talk with children about what they are doing and why. "Let's pick up the blocks so no one trips and falls."

- Provide basins of water and objects so children can discover what sinks and what floats.

- As you hold a baby securely, lift her up into the air and bring her down as you say "up" and "down."

- As you change and dress infants, name parts of their bodies. Comments such as "I'm putting your arm in the sleeve" or "I'm going to tickle your tummy" will help children become more aware of their bodies.

- Join games of "peek-a-boo" to help children begin learning that things exist even when they are out of sight. "Where is Roger's teddy bear? Where did he go? Here he is. Uh-oh, now he's gone again!"

Promoting Cognitive Development

In the following situations, caregivers are promoting infants' and toddlers' cognitive development. As you read each one, think about what the caregivers are doing and why. Then answer the questions that follow.

Providing Opportunities for Infants and Toddlers to Use All Their Senses to Explore the World

"Would you like a cracker?" Ms. Bates asks George (8 months). She puts a cracker on his highchair tray. George looks at Ms. Bates and then down at the cracker. He tries to pick up the cracker, and it crumbles in his fingers. Ms. Bates reaches for a sponge but then decides to forget it. A little crumbled cracker isn't a big problem, she thinks. And besides, George seems to be interested in it. She watches as he first pushes the pieces of cracker across his tray and then chews on a piece of cracker. He catches her eye and smiles. "Does that cracker taste good?" Ms. Bates asks him. George offers her a piece of the soggy cracker to taste. "No, thank you, George," Ms. Bates says. "That cracker is for you. That's your cracker."

1. **Why did Ms. Bates decide not to stop George and wipe up the cracker crumbs?**

_____

_____

_____

2. **What did George learn about a cracker through his senses?**

_____

_____

_____

Interacting with Infants and Toddlers in Ways That Promote Their Confidence and Curiosity

When Ms. Lewis sets up the play tunnel for the first time this year, several children come right over to check it out. Will (11 months) just stares at the tunnel from across the room. Ms. Gonzalez nods in his direction and smiles at Ms. Lewis. They know it takes Will time to get used to something new. He always watches for a while before he joins in a new activity. Ms. Lewis, who is rolling balls through the tunnel with Tammy (14 months), asks, "Would you like a ball, Will?" Seeing his sudden smile, she rolls a red one to him. When Tammy chases a stray ball, Ms. Lewis looks through the tunnel. "Peek-a-boo, Will," she calls. Will peeks through and squeals with delight. A few minutes later, he crawls closer and peeks at Ms. Lewis again. "I see you, Will," she says. "Peek-a-boo!"

1. **What is Will's way of dealing with something new?**

_____

_____

_____

2. **How did Ms. Lewis encourage Will's curiosity and confidence?**

_____

_____

_____

Providing Opportunities for Infants and Toddlers to Develop New Concepts and Skills

Jerome (22 months) is sobbing. His daddy has just said good-bye and has gone to work. Mr. Jones kneels down next to Jerome. "Your daddy went to work. I know it makes you sad to say goodbye. Would you like to come over and look at a picture of your daddy?" he asks. Jerome nods through his tears. They walk over to where pictures of children and their families are hanging on the wall at a child's level. "Daddy," says Jerome pointing to his father's picture. Jerome picks up the toy telephone and hands the receiver to Mr. Jones, who says into the phone, "Jerome was sorry to see you leave this morning. We've been looking at your picture." He then hands Jerome the phone. Jerome holds it to his ear and smiles. Later in the day, Mr. Jones notices Jerome playing "peek-a-boo" with Sarah (24 months). Although it is snack time, he doesn't interrupt their game. He knows playing "peek-a-boo" gives Jerome a chance to feel in control of someone's leaving and coming back.

1. **How was Jerome's sadness about separating from his daddy related to his cognitive development?**

_____

_____

_____

2. **What things in the environment helped Jerome deal with separation?**

_____

_____

_____

3. Why didn't Mr. Jones interrupt Jerome when he was playing "peek-a-boo?"

_____

_____

_____

Compare your answers with those on the answer sheet at the end of this module. If your answers are different, discuss them with your trainer. There can be more than one good answer.

Your Own Experiences with Learning

Cognitive development continues throughout life. People don't stop learning when they leave school. They continue to develop their ability to think and to reason. You probably know people you feel are good learners and thinkers. You probably consider yourself a good learner. People who have confidence in their ability to learn generally have some of the following characteristics:

- They are not afraid to accept a challenge. "I don't know the answer, but I'll find out."

- When they confront a problem, they don't give up if they can't resolve it right away. They try to figure out what to do. If a child's behavior is continually annoying them, they try to find out what is causing the behavior and what they can do to improve the situation.

- They are curious and interested in learning new things. "I hear that book is really interesting. I'd like to read it when you are finished."

- They are creative thinkers—they can look at something and see lots of possibilities. "I think the children would use the house corner more if we reorganized it and moved it closer to the block area."

- They speak up and say what they think. "I'm not sure I agree with you. Here's what I see happening."

It's not how much information people have but how they use their thinking abilities that is important. We don't all know the same things, nor do we need to. A car mechanic knows a lot about the parts of a car, what makes it go, and how to fix it. When there's a problem, the mechanic tries to figure out the cause. If you know very little about how a car operates, this doesn't make you less smart. You know other things that the car mechanic doesn't know. What's important is whether you each have the confidence and skills to learn what you need in your own life.

Many factors affect our ability to learn something new. Most important is whether the new information is useful to us. If we can see a way to use what we are learning, we are likely to be more interested in putting forth the effort. It helps if the new information is related to something we already know about, or know how to do—or to something we've wanted to know for some time.

Each of us has a different style or way of learning that works best for us. Some of us need to read over directions and think about them for a while. Some of us need to watch someone else demonstrate a task. Some of us need to hear directions explained a couple of times.

As an adult you are aware of what helps you learn a new skill or new idea. Think of a time recently when you were in a learning situation—for instance, learning to swim, taking an adult education course, or going through these modules. List five factors that made it easier for you to learn in that situation.

Learning Situation _____

Factors:

1. _____
   _____

2. _____
   _____

3. _____
   _____

4. _____
   _____

5. _____
   _____

Some factors that affect our ability to learn relate to our trainers or to the material itself: how the information is presented, how it is organized, and whether it is on our level. Our readiness to learn is also affected by how we feel at the time. If we are tired, distracted, uncomfortable, or unsure of what is expected of us, we are less likely to learn.

This training program is designed to help you learn new concepts and skills and feel good about yourself as a learner. The training program design includes a number of strategies to make it a positive learning experience.

- The information is organized into individual modules so you won't be overwhelmed with too much information at once.

- All the modules relate to your work and should be immediately useful.

- You may use the modules in whatever order you prefer.

- There are lots of examples within each module to help you understand the content.

- Answer sheets are provided so you can get immediate feedback on your responses.

- You receive your own set of materials to keep as an ongoing reference for your job.

- You complete many of the learning activities with the infants and toddlers you care for.

As you enhance your skills and knowledge in ways that make you feel confident, you will be able to do the same thing for children. Like you, young children learn best when they are interested in and ready to receive new information. They like to try out new ideas and discover what works and what doesn't on their own. As you go through these modules, you will try out many ideas and discover for yourself what approaches work best for you and for the infants and toddlers in your care.

When you have finished this overview section, you should complete the pre-training assessment. Refer to the glossary at the end of this module if you need definitions of the terms that are used.

Pre-Training Assessment

Listed below are the skills that caregivers use to promote infants' and toddlers' cognitive development. Think about whether you do these things regularly, sometimes, or not enough. Place a check in one of the columns on the right for each skill listed. Then discuss your answers with your trainer.

SKILL	I DO THIS REGULARLY	I DO THIS SOMETIMES	I DON'T DO THIS ENOUGH
PROVIDING OPPORTUNITIES FOR INFANTS AND TODDLERS TO USE ALL THEIR SENSES TO EXPLORE THE WORLD 1. Planning experiences and activities that allow young children to touch, taste, hear, feel, and smell safely.			
2. Talking to children about what they are learning through their senses.			
3. Providing materials that encourage infants and toddlers to explore using all their senses.			
INTERACTING WITH INFANTS AND TODDLERS IN WAYS THAT PROMOTE THEIR CONFIDENCE AND CURIOSITY 4. Observing children carefully to understand how best to help each child learn.			
5. Respecting children's different styles of responding to something new.			

SKILL	I DO THIS REGULARLY	I DO THIS SOMETIMES	I DON'T DO THIS ENOUGH
6. Recognizing when to intervene and when to hold back and let infants and toddlers solve their own problems.			
7. Asking open-ended questions to stretch young children's thinking.			
8. Providing experiences that challenge children and also allow them to experience success.			
PROVIDING OPPORTUNITIES FOR INFANTS AND TODDLERS TO DEVELOP NEW CONCEPTS AND SKILLS 9. Using daily routines to help infants and toddlers learn about themselves and the world around them.			
10. Setting up an environment to help infants and toddlers accept limits and to give them choices.			
11. Selecting materials that encourage dramatic play.			
12. Encouraging the use of language.			

Review your responses, then list three to five skills you would like to improve or topics you would like to learn more about. When you finish this module, you will list examples of your new or improved knowledge and skills.

_____

_____

_____

_____

Now begin the learning activities for Module 5, Cognitive.

I. Using Your Knowledge of Infant and Toddler Development to Promote Cognitive Development

In this activity you will learn:

- to recognize some typical behaviors of infants and toddlers; and

- to use what you know about infants and toddlers to promote their cognitive development.

Infants and toddlers learn about themselves and the people and things in their world as they live every day with the adults who are important to them. As they eat, get dressed, look around, have their diapers changed, sit on a potty, or move a chair across the room, they are collecting information and learning to think.

They also learn as they play. As Gary (4 months) plays with his hands, Ellen (9 months) bangs two blocks together, and Rachel (20 months) hangs three pocketbooks over her shoulder and tells you she is going to the "oppice," they are each increasing their understanding of the world.

At first children learn about the world through their senses. They need to see, touch, taste, hear, and smell things to learn about them. Later, they also begin to gather information through language. Bit by bit they organize and reorganize what they learn, developing their first ideas about themselves and the world around them.

Children learn by doing. Through active involvement with their environment, they make sense of the world around them. They learn by observing what happens when they interact with objects and other people. When they spontaneously involve themselves in activities such as crawling, painting, or imitations, they add pieces of information to what they already know and generate new information. Children learn simple concepts and then use these concepts to understand more complex ideas.

At the same time that children are working through the early stages of cognitive development, they are also growing socially and emotionally. As they play with other children, infants and toddlers begin to learn about sharing and cooperation. They test bounds and learn which behaviors are acceptable and which are not. They take pride in their accomplishments and develop a sense of competence.

Young children learn best when they feel safe and secure. Having a safe physical environment to explore is not enough. Children need a relationship with a special adult they can trust and depend on. Developing trusting and caring relationships with infants and toddlers is one of the most important ways in which you can help them learn.

The chart on the next page lists some typical behaviors of infants and toddlers. Included are characteristics related to cognitive development. The right-hand column asks you to identify ways that caregivers can use this information about child development to promote children's cognitive development. Try to think of as many examples as you can. As you work through the module, you will learn new strategies for promoting children's cognitive development, and you can add them to the child development chart. You are not expected to think of all the examples at one time. By the time you complete all the learning activities, you will find that you have learned many ways to promote infants' and toddlers' cognitive development.

Using Your Knowledge of Infant and Toddler Development to Promote Cognitive Development

WHAT YOUNG INFANTS DO (0-8 MONTHS)	HOW CAREGIVERS CAN USE THIS INFORMATION TO PROMOTE COGNITIVE DEVELOPMENT
They visually follow and respond to objects or faces as they move.	
They hold and manipulate objects; they suck on everything.	
They vocalize to themselves, people, and toys.	
They begin understanding that objects or people exist even when they are out of sight.	

WHAT MOBILE INFANTS DO (9-17 MONTHS)	HOW CAREGIVERS CAN USE THIS INFORMATION TO PROMOTE COGNITIVE DEVELOPMENT
They learn to crawl, stand up, and walk.	
They begin to remember more from one day to the next.	
They are able to make choices between clear alternatives.	
They begin to solve problems on their own.	
They begin to develop language.	

WHAT TODDLERS DO (18-36 MONTHS)	HOW CAREGIVERS CAN USE THIS INFORMATION TO PROMOTE COGNITIVE DEVELOPMENT
They learn by helping.	
They learn to talk more.	
They learn about concepts such as size, shape, and weight by using their bodies as they move and play with toys and things in the environment.	
They can concentrate for longer periods of time.	
They sometimes think about actions before doing them.	
They enjoy and learn through role playing and dramatic play.	

When you have completed as much as you can do on the chart, discuss your answers with your trainer. As you proceed with the rest of the learning activities, you can refer back to the chart and add more examples of how caregivers can promote infants' and toddlers' cognitive development.

II. Helping Infants and Toddlers Make Sense of the World

In this activity you will learn:

- to observe how infants and toddlers make sense of the world around them; and

- to recognize how infants and toddlers learn to think.

Infants are constantly learning about the world around them. They learn through everyday experiences. As infants develop, the same experiences take on new meanings for them. While Lisa (3 months) may be learning about the feel of her stretch suit when she is dressed, Sam (16 months) may be learning about snaps and zippers.

Infants are not too young to think. You can see them thinking during daily routines and as they play.

- Infants think of many ways to explore: mouthing, dropping, banging, and squeezing. Shaunte (8 months) has a new toy. She looks at it, then begins shaking it. When she drops it, she learns that it rolls and makes a clicking noise.

- Infants are learning "object permanence." They are learning that something or someone continues to exist even when out of sight. Jake (10 months) plays "peek-a-boo" whenever he can. He holds his bib up in front of his eyes and peeks out at Sandy, his favorite caregiver. He peeks at her from around the book case.

- Infants are beginning to understand that actions have results: something they do causes something else to happen. Sarah (6 months) has learned that every time she hits her mobile, it moves.

- Infants learn how to use one object to get another. This is called "means-end." A tool or action is a means to reach a certain end or goal. Ralph (14 months) wants the toy across the table. He pulls on its string to bring it over to him.

Toddlers are learning all the time. At the center or at home, toddlers learn from special planned activities as well as from daily-life experiences. As toddlers develop, the same experiences take on new meanings for them. While Jerry (18 months) understands when you ask him to bring his shoe over so you can put it on, Sally (33 months) may be able to put on her socks and shoes by herself.

A toddler's way of thinking is often different from an adult's. Toddlers are just beginning to understand how things and events relate to each other.

- Toddlers think very concretely and understand words very literally. When a caregiver told Tara (24 months), "You have sharp eyes," Tara felt her eyelids and said, "No, they're not sharp."

- Toddlers can anticipate what will happen next and learn that there is order as they experience daily routines and schedules. Jeremy (28 months) knows his mommy comes to pick him up every afternoon after snack time.

- Toddlers are beginning to think about relations between things, such as in, out, under, stacking, and banging together. Chanelle (24 months) says "in" and "out" as she drives her toy car in and out of the cardboard box "garage" that a caregiver made for her.

- Toddlers are beginning to understand cause and effect. They experiment actively to see what will happen as the result of their actions. Dave (18 months) tries to see what will happen when he tips his juice over. Caregivers often find themselves helping toddlers wipe up spills.

To support infants' and toddlers' cognitive development, you must have some idea of how they think and learn. It takes careful observing to understand how very young children think. Whenever you observe, ask yourself, "What is he or she experiencing?" Try to see through the child's eyes. What might he or she be thinking and learning in a situation?

In this learning activity you will read the article "Toddlers: What to Expect." Then select two children to observe during a daily routine. Ask yourself, "What might these children be thinking?" Fill in the chart, focusing on what you observed.

Toddlers: What to Expect[1]

Which of these paragraphs best describes toddlers?

Toddlers don't sit still for a minute. They have short attention spans and are highly distractible. They always want their own way, and won't share or take turns. Toys always get lost or broken when toddlers play with them.

Toddlers are active explorers. They eagerly try new things and use materials in different ways. Toddlers want to be independent and they have a strong sense of ownership.

The first description compares toddlers with older children and looks at typical toddler behavior in negative terms. The second is a positive outlook that respects toddlers and their natural behavior.

When teachers or parents think of toddlers as miniature preschoolers, we run into problems because our expectations are not appropriate. For example, inappropriate expectations can turn toilet learning into a struggle of wills between adult and child. Meals can be chaotic because toddlers play with their food. Circle time can be a nightmare because toddlers keep wandering around or interrupting. Adult-directed activities get disrupted as toddlers choose their own ways instead of following what the teacher has in mind. Puzzles get dumped, toys are pulled off shelves and hauled to another area of the room, and verbal attempts to intervene are ignored as toddlers go about their business.

What can parents or teachers of toddlers do, either at home or in group programs, to work effectively with toddlers? Few parents have any background in child development, and many teachers have been prepared to work with older children. What are the differences between toddlers and preschoolers, and how can we make the most of these often maligned months of early childhood?

What toddlers are like

Toddlers learn with their whole bodies—not just their heads. They learn more through their hands than they do through their ears. They learn by doing, not only by just thinking. They learn by touching, mouthing, and trying out, not by being told.

Toddlers solve problems on a physical level. Watch toddlers at play for just 5 minutes and you will see them walk (which looks like wandering), climb, carry things around, drop things, and continually dump whatever they can find. These large muscle activities are not done to irritate adults—they are the legitimate activity of toddlers. Piaget calls this the sensorimotor stage of development (1952, 1954).

Toddlers can become absorbed in discovering the world around them. If you are convinced that toddlers have short attention spans, just watch them with running water and a piece of soap. Handwashing can become the main activity of the morning! Eating is another major activity, as many toddlers switch from neat to very messy in a short time. Filling and dumping are great skills to use with food or water. Of course, toddlers do put things *in* as part of the process, but they are more likely to end with dumping!

Limit group activities to eating and maybe music or a short story time.

Other toddlers are reluctant to mess around in their food once they can handle utensils well.

In addition to these primarily cognitive and physical skills, toddlers are also working on a number of socioemotional challenges. They are still developing trust in the adults who care for them, so parents and teachers need

---

Janet Gonzalez-Mena, M.A., is an instructor in the Early Childhood Program at Napa Valley College, Napa, California.

---

[1] Reprinted with permission from Janet Gonzalez-Mena, "Toddlers: What to Expect," *Young Children* (Washington, DC: National Association for the Education of Young Children, November 1986), pp. 47-51.

It takes time for the child to gain physical control, to understand what to do, and to be willing to do it.

With all of these major accomplishments emerging during toddlerhood—from approximately 14 months to 3 years of age—what, then should toddlers do all day, at home or in a group program?

Some common pitfalls

Both parents and teachers have been influenced by the push to demonstrate that children are *learning* something. Those who are unfamiliar with the remarkable natural learnings of the toddler period often feel compelled to create so-called learning activities as proof that the adult is teaching the child.

These activities often become part of a curriculum such as one I observed. For the first 45 minutes, the teacher helped children cope with separation as their parents said goodbye. The children were helped to remove their coats and hang them up, diapers were changed, and some children used the toilet. The children playing with toys argued, got frustrated, or asked for adult help. What a

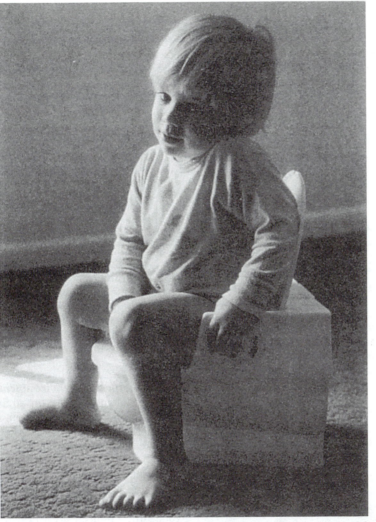

Rich Rosenkoetter

Learning to use the toilet, like all the other self-help skills, is a physical feat, as well as an intellectual and emotional one. It takes time for the child to gain physical control, to understand what to do, and to be willing to do it.

Organize routines so waiting does not consume most of the child's day.

pleasure it was to see a program responding to the variety of learnings so much a part of toddlerhood—separation and trust, self-help skills and autonomy, and problem solving through hands-on play experiences.

Just then a bell rang, and the children were herded into a group, organized, separated into smaller groups, seated at tables, and given

to work closely to help children learn how to cope with important events such as separation.

Toddlers are in Erikson's second stage—autonomy (1963). Their rapidly emerging language clearly demonstrates what it means to be autonomous: "Me do it" shows the drive for independence. "Me—mine!" indicates toddlers are beginning to see themselves as individuals with possessions. And, of course, the "NO!" toddlers are so

famous for is a further clue to their push for separateness and independence.

Some of the major accomplishments of this stage of growing independence are self-help skills such as dressing, feeding, washing, and toileting. All of these skills involve a great deal of practice, and the inevitable mishaps. Learning to use the toilet, like all the other self-help skills, is a physical feat, as well as an intellectual and emotional one.

what were termed learning activities to do. Later, the director apologized: "We were late in getting started," she explained. For her, the valuable time was the organized activity time, not the 45 minutes when toddlers were involved in taking steps toward the major accomplishments of toddlerhood!

Of course, toddlers learn from activities, just as they learn from any experience—but activities are *not* more valuable than the rest of what happens in a typical day at home or in a program. Most importantly, *activities are only valuable to the degree to which they are appropriate for the age group.*

If the activities are too advanced —perhaps requiring toddlers to sit at tables, to wait 10 minutes for their turn, or to color in the spaces of an adult's drawing—children will learn to limit and restrict themselves, to feel unsuccessful, to sense a lack of respect for themselves as individuals. An opportunity for children to explore with their senses in more creative ways will have been lost.

Sometimes traditional preschool activities can be modified for toddlers. For example, given collage materials, many toddlers will experiment by licking the glue, eating the paste, or gooping one or the other into their hair. The adult will

---

Avoid making arbitrary decisions for children, and instead help them search for constructive solutions.

---

spend more time restricting behavior than facilitating creativity, which is the purpose of making a collage.

One way to make collages appropriate for toddlers is to use Contact™ paper, sticky side out, and provide children with a number of safe objects to stick to it. A group of

12- to 24-month-olds at the Napa Valley College Child Development Center worked on a collage for several weeks as they continued to discover things to stick on the Contact™ paper left on a wall at their level. The continuing rearrangement of the collage elements showed how much more important the process is than the product at this age.

Some other activities that are easily modified are presented in Table 1.

How to fit programs to toddlers

Adults who recognize the special needs of toddlers, such as sensorimotor learning and the development of autonomy, don't just tolerate this age group—they genuinely like toddlers. What do these knowledgeable adults do, then, to create a home or group setting that fits toddlers?

1. Structure the environment (rather than depending on adult rules). Put out only as many things as you can stand to pick up when they are dumped. One teacher suspended a bucket from the ceiling filled with things just for dumping. Make sure everything is touchable (and mouthable, depending on how young the children are). Provide space and equipment for large motor activity (climbing, jumping) inside as well as outside. Include plenty of softness (a mattress for jumping, pillows for wiggling on). Supply toys that can be used in many ways, such as blocks, as well as toys that are realistic (McLoyd, 1986). Remember, toddlers who are too excited, or bored, are apt to make themselves and everyone else unhappy, so keep activities and materials at a level they can handle. Watch the children's behavior to determine when the right amount of toys are available. Their needs may change from day to day.

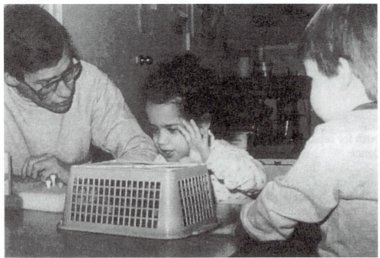

All furnishings, equipment, toys, and materials should be sturdy and safe enough to be dropped, mouthed, or climbed on. Dumping puzzles is as much fun as working time.

Subjects & Predicates

Table 1
Preschool activities that can be modified for toddlers

Preschool activity	Modified toddler activity
Easel painting	Water on chalkboards
Paint and paper	Thick soap suds with food coloring on Plexiglas™
Sponge painting	Squeeze sponges in trays with a little water on the bottom
Cooking with recipes	Cutting or mashing bananas or similar one-step food experience
Pasting tissue paper	Crumpling white tissue paper (to prevent dyes from running colors when chewed)

2. Expect toddlers to test limits. That's their job, so the more the environment sets limits, the easier it will be for you. Again, judge whether the limits are just right, rather than too strict or too lax, by observing the children's behavior. If children insist on climbing on the table, for example, perhaps another climbing structure, or large pillows, or a crawl-through tunnel is needed. Are children randomly wandering without getting involved? Maybe more staff, or more attentive staff, are needed to be anchors for children as they reach out to new activities. Or possibly more variety and some new materials need to be offered. Rotate items—even after a week or two some will have new appeal.

Be consistent and firm about the limits you set, however. Otherwise children will be confused and will continue to test limits long after toddlerhood.

3. Stay out of power struggles. Toddlers can be very stubborn so it is a waste of energy to continually butt heads with them about enforcing limits. Use choices to avoid power struggles: "You can't walk around while you eat, but you can sit in either the blue chair or the red chair." Give toddlers frequent choices, but be sure what you offer are suitable alternatives. Usually a choice between two options is sufficient.

4. Direct behavior gently, but physically. Don't depend on words alone. Prevent dangerous behavior before it occurs—hold a threatening arm before it has a chance to hit. Lead a child by the hand back to the table to finish a snack. Don't let children get in trouble and then yell at them. If you find yourself saying "I knew that was going to happen," next time, don't predict—prevent it.

Direct behavior gently, but physically. Don't depend on words alone.

5. Expect lots of sensorimotor behavior. All furnishings, equipment, toys, and materials should be sturdy and safe enough to be dropped, mouthed, or climbed on. Dumping puzzles is as much fun as working them. The sound as the pieces hit the floor seems to be music to toddler ears. You can help children see the fun of putting puzzles back together, but don't ex-pect to convince them right away that construction is more pleasurable than destruction.

6. Limit group activities to eating and maybe music or a short story time. Even then, form small groups, and expect children to leave to pursue something more exciting when they lose interest. Eventually they will want to be involved in larger and longer group activities, but toddlers are more individual doers than group listeners.

7. Share, wait, and use kind words to solve problems, but don't expect children to always follow the behavior you model. Toddlers cannot share until they first fully experience a sense of ownership. They need to see over and over again that they can trust that a favored item will not be taken away, or to find there are enough snacks for everyone so that grabbing and hoarding are not necessary. Have several of the same favorite toys.

Waiting is hard for adults and children—just remember the last time you had to wait in line! Organize routines so waiting does not consume most of the child's day. If a wait is unavoidable, keep children active with fingerplays or songs, for example, so they have something to do while they wait.

Even when toddlers lose control, adults need to maintain theirs by using words, rather than hitting or using harsh punishment, to solve problems. Choose words that respect children and support their needs, not words that ridicule or shame. For example, respond to a toileting accident with "Oh, Rosita, your clothes are all wet. They're probably uncomfortable for you, too. Let's find your dry clothes and then we'll wipe up the puddle," rather than "Look at the mess you made! Are we going to have to put you back in diapers?"

Subjects & Predicates

Toddlers cannot share until they first fully experience a sense of ownership. Have several of the same favorite toys.

8. Be gentle and help children talk through problems. Fights and struggles are bound to occur, but children will learn to solve problems with each other sooner if you do what Gerber (1979) calls *sports announcing*—"I see how much you want that, Jason"—rather than *refereeing*—"Amanda had it first, so give it to her." Avoid making arbitrary decisions for children, and instead help them search for constructive solutions.

9. Expect difficult behavior. Resistance to activities (wandering off in the middle of a song), rejection ("NO!"), and crying when they say goodbye to parents are all *good* behaviors—that's what toddlers should be doing. These behaviors show clearly that the children are in Erikson's stage of autonomy. Toddlers who are not developing well may appear depressed, have low self-esteem, seem to lack attachment to their families, or use one behavior in every situation. All toddlers won't exhibit difficult be-

haviors, but it is important to recognize such behaviors as normal and natural.

10. Define curriculum in realistic terms. An appropriate curriculum for toddlers is one that centers around
● self-care activities (such as eating, sleeping, toileting, and dressing),
● learning to cope with separation,
● making new attachments with children and adults, and
● free play in a safe and interesting environment.
All appropriate physical, cognitive, and socioemotional goals for toddlers fit easily into these activities.

11. Let toddlers be toddlers. Don't structure your curriculum around preparing toddlers for preschool by pushing them to act as if they are in a more advanced stage of development. When they have done very thoroughly what they need to do as 18-month-olds, or as

2-year-olds, or almost 3s, they will be ready to take on the tasks of a more advanced stage.

*   *   *

When we see toddlerhood as a special and distinct stage of development with its own set of tasks and behaviors, toddler's behavior becomes more understandable and manageable. Then we are not tempted to impose watered-down (or worse yet full-blown) preschool activities upon them. When we stop comparing toddlers with older children, and appreciate them for what they are, toddlers become very likable individuals. They will feel better about themselves because the adults who care for them respect them for what they should be —toddlers. YC

Select two children to observe at play or during a routine. Review the examples below, then complete the two blank forms that follow.

Observing Cognitive Development in Daily Routines
(Infant Example)

Child _Becky_   **Age** _14 months_   **Date** _September 14_

Setting _Dressing after nap_

Briefly describe what you observe:

> *Ms. Rollins is dressing Becky. She asks Becky to get her sweater. Becky sees her sweater across the table. The sleeve is within her reach. She pulls on its sleeve so she can reach it.*

What do you think this infant might be thinking?

> *Becky is thinking "means-end." She knows if she pulls on the sleeve, she will be able to get the sweater.*

Observing Cognitive Development in Daily Routines
(Toddler Example)

Child _Tony_   **Age** _27 months_   **Date** _June 8_

Briefly describe what you observe:

Because it was a warm day, the infants, toddlers, and caregivers had a picnic lunch outside. When we came in after eating lunch, Tony sat down at the table and said, "Lunch."

What do you think this infant might be thinking?

Tony has a sense of order about the day. He knows that he usually eats lunch when he comes in from play.

Observing Cognitive Development in Daily Routines

Child _____ Age _____ Date _____

Setting _____

Briefly describe what you observe:

_____
_____
_____

What do you think this infant might be thinking?

_____
_____
_____

Observing Cognitive Development in Daily Routines

Child _____ Age _____ Date _____

Setting _____

Briefly describe what you observe:

_____
_____
_____

What do you think this infant might be thinking?

_____
_____
_____

When you have completed forms for each child you observed, discuss your ideas with your trainer.

III. Promoting Thinking Skills

In this activity you will learn:

- to promote infants' and toddlers' thinking skills; and

- to use daily routines to help infants and toddlers extend their thinking.

There is so much for infants and toddlers to learn about the world around them. Yet what they learn isn't as important as how they feel about themselves as learners. For an infant or a toddler, learning and feelings go hand in hand. They need trusting, caring relationships with their caregivers to feel safe and secure enough to explore and learn. This is one of the reasons it is so important to work with young children individually or in very small groups. Being sure that each child develops a close relationship with a caregiver is one of the most important things you can do to promote cognitive development.

- **Choose moments of daily life to focus on with each child.** Talk about what you are doing together. Your participation and interest in an event make that event special for the child. Your involvement encourages young children to pay close attention to something and really think about it.

    You can help children develop the skill of using their senses by talking about how soft a diaper feels, by remarking on the sound of a door closing when you take children on a walk around the center, and by pointing out the sounds of birds chirping or a plane flying overhead.

- **While observing children, ask yourself, "What is this child thinking?"** A 9-month-old thinks and plays very differently from a 3-month-old. An 18-month-old plays very differently from the 9-month-old or from a 3-year old. Observing young children can help you figure out what kinds of games and toys help them learn.

    For example, you can help a 9-month-old learn about object permanence by covering up a ball and asking where it is. This would be meaningless to a 3-month-old. For that infant, "out of sight is out of mind"—the ball is gone from the infant's thought the moment it is covered. A 19-month-old learns about shapes by playing with balls and boxes. You can help an older toddler learn about shapes by playing sorting games.

- **Know when not to intervene and when not to interrupt their play and exploring.** Observe infants and toddlers carefully so you can decide on the best approach. Knowing when not to participate in an activity takes as much skill as knowing how and when to step in.

    As children develop, their attention spans grow. If they are constantly interrupted, they never have the chance to learn what it feels like to concentrate and focus on something by themselves.

- **Ask questions to stretch a child's thinking.** Your questions and comments should be open-ended, which means they should not have simple "yes" or "no" answers. They should make a child think about a past experience or recall something or someone that is not right there. In other words, your questions should cause children to think. Here are some examples of what caregivers might say that can help an older infant or toddler learn to think:

    - "What do you think will happen when you drop that rock into the puddle?"

    - "Why do you think that person is wearing boots?"

    - "The dog in this picture reminds me of your dog, Brandy. Why do you think she is barking?"

  Keep in mind that getting a correct response from the young child is not important. It is important to listen to what the child says and to respond in ways that encourage thinking.

- **Demonstrate that thinking is important to you.** When a child figures out how to get her ball out from under the table, you might say something like this: "You did some good thinking to figure out how to get that ball." Tell children when you are thinking about something: "I wonder if it's so cold outside that we need to wear our mittens and hats." By acknowledging and modeling thinking, you are showing that it is an important skill.

- **Use daily routines and events as opportunities for learning.** You can promote cognitive development in almost everything you do. While changing a child, play "peek-a-boo" with a clean diaper. Older infants can begin to learn the hand movements for simple songs such as "Open-Shut Them" or "Clap-Clap-Clap Your Hands." Assign each toddler a special hook to hang his or her clothes. If you hang each child's picture above his or her assigned hook, children can learn to identify their own hooks and will be encouraged to hang up their own clothes. Toddlers love to imitate adults and do adult tasks. Involve them in sponging tables and setting them for lunch. Talk about what they need to do first, second, and last.

In this learning activity, you will choose a daily routine and list five things you can do to help infants or toddlers learn to think during that routine. To help you get started, read the two examples that follow this page.

Using Daily Routines to Promote Thinking
(Infant Example)

Daily Routine: *Dressing*

List five things you can do to promote thinking skills:

1. *I can take more time dressing an infant so we can talk about what we are doing. I can enjoy our time together and make it a special, one-on-one time.*

2. *I can let infants participate as much as they can. For example, I can let mobile infants experiment with dressing themselves and let them help in whatever ways they can.*

3. *I can encourage infants to use all their senses. I can talk with infants about how their clothes feel on their skin and call attention to the sounds of snaps.*

4. *I can play "peek-a-boo" to help infants learn that people and things are still there even when they are out of sight.*

5. *I can talk about concepts such as "up" and "down" or "off" and "on" as we pull the zipper up and down or have one sock off and one sock on.*

Using Daily Routines to Promote Thinking
(Toddler Example)

Daily Routine: *Snack Time*

List five things you can do to promote thinking skills:

1. *I can take time to focus on snacks with the toddlers in my group.*

2. *I can let toddlers participate as much as they can, according to their ages and abilities. Young toddlers might help us peel bananas. Older toddlers might be ready to cook something more complex, such as pancakes.*

3. *I can encourage toddlers to use their senses as we prepare a snack and eat it. For example, we can talk about the "snap" sound that green beans make when we break them, and about their color and smell. We can watch green beans cook in a pot of boiling water. Toddlers might like to dance the way bubbles move in boiling water.*

4. *I can ask toddlers if they ever eat green beans at home, to help them think of past events.*

5. *I can talk about concepts such as "hot" and "cold," "up" and "down," and "in" and "out" as we cook and eat.*

Using Daily Routines to Promote Thinking

Daily Routine: _____

List five things you can do to promote thinking skills:

1. _____

   _____

   _____

2. _____

   _____

   _____

3. _____

   _____

   _____

4. _____

   _____

   _____

5. _____

   _____

   _____

Discuss your list with your trainer and other caregivers in your room. You may want to make lists for each daily routine and hang them to help you remember ways in which you can help infants and toddlers learn to think.

IV. Using the Physical Environment to Promote Cognitive Development

In this activity you will learn:

- to use the environment to help infants and toddlers learn new concepts and skills; and

- to select materials that invite infants and toddlers to explore and question.

How you arrange the physical environment can help you promote young children's cognitive development. Infants and toddlers use their thinking skills every day to try to understand the world around them. Your room is a very important part of a child's world. Therefore, it is important that you plan the environment carefully so it supports infants' and toddlers' cognitive development.

Here are some ways in which your physical environment can enhance infants' and toddlers' cognitive growth.

- The room should be homelike and include familiar objects that young children will want to explore, such as pots and pans, wooden spoons, plastic containers, and simple dress-up clothes such as hats, pocketbooks, and briefcases.

- The environment should reflect the children. Hanging pictures of the children and their families at child's level is a way to make sure your room reflects the children who live and play there during the day.

- The room should be organized to help children accept limits and develop a sense of order in the world.

    - Keep toys and materials that children play with on low, open shelves so older infants and toddlers can find them.

    - Pick up toys and materials during the day. It's hard to learn about order in a room that is always cluttered.

    - Organize the room so that children can begin to understand how to use different things. For example, riding toys are best in an open area; books are in the book corner near the big pillows.

- Your room can help children practice using their senses by offering them interesting things to see, touch, taste, hear, and smell.

    - Give older infants and toddlers the chance to play with water, sand, and playdough.

    - Provide bells that ring, pot lids that can be clanged together, paper that rustles when it is crumpled, and drums to bang.

- It is important to choose toys appropriate to the developmental needs of the children in your room.

  - Small rubber chewable toys are good for the youngest infants and may also be enjoyed by older infants.

  - Older infants may be ready for very simple puzzles and sorting toys, too.

Special Considerations for Toddlers

- Toddlers need safe, open spaces where they can move. Because toddlers learn using their entire bodies, "moving" and "doing" are learning activities for toddlers.

  - Give toddlers safe places to climb, jump, and run.

  - Provide challenges by planning special activities, such as an obstacle course.

- A toddler's attention span is growing. Provide space where toddlers can concentrate on activities uninterrupted even by well-meaning adults.

  - Set up tables and chairs where toddlers can work on projects such as stringing beads or simple puzzles.

  - Use very short chairs that allow a toddler's feet to rest flat on the floor while the child sits solidly on the chair seat, using the backrest; having to balance on larger chairs interrupts the toddler's concentration.

  - Provide cozy spaces where a toddler or two can look at a book.

- Include toys that are appropriate to the developmental stage of the toddlers that use them.

  - Toddlers need toys that they can push, pull, take apart, and put back together.

  - Toddlers need toys that stretch their thinking, such as wooden beads and string or simple puzzles.

Suggested Toys for Infants and Toddlers

- For **young infants:** crib toys and mobiles they can bat and kick; mirrors, soft blocks, rattles and other things that make noise when grasped; faces; plastic books; objects with different textures.

- For **mobile infants:** unbreakable mirrors, soft blocks, plastic and cardboard books, balls, stack toys, containers and small toys that cannot be swallowed, push-and-pull toys, busy boards.

- For **toddlers**: large pegboards, riding toys, puzzles with three to five pieces, more books, wagons, zipper/ buckle/ button boards, balls, cardboard cartons, stuffed animals, dolls, nesting cubes, mallet and wooden pegs, put-together play house or farm.

A complete list of appropriate toys for infants and toddlers can be found in Module 3.

In this activity you will make a toy for the children in your room, observe a child playing with your toy, and answer some questions about what the child is learning. Review the examples on the next page before making your toy.

Making Toys That Promote Cognitive Development
(Infant Example)

Child _Sally_   **Age** _5 months_   **Date** _March 12_

Setting _Infant crib_   **Toy** _Crib gym_

Briefly describe the toy you made:

I made a crib gym. I tied a piece of ribbon securely across a baby's crib. I tied a blue plastic spoon, a set of yellow plastic keys, and a lightweight wooden spoon to the ribbon.

What did the child do with the toy?

Sally smiled when she first saw the toy. She tried to hit it with her hands.

What do you think the child learned from playing with the toy?

Sally is learning how to reach out and touch something she sees.

Making Toys That Promote Cognitive Development
(Toddler Example)

Child _Reggie_   **Age** _32 months_   **Date** _March 13_

Setting _Toddler free play_   **Toy** _Feely box_

Briefly describe the toy you made:

I made a "feely box" by putting in a cardboard box some interesting objects that the toddlers knew. I made a hole in the box so the children could reach in and pull out the objects.

What did the child do with the toy?

At first, Reggie wanted to peek in the box. Then he got the idea. He reached in and felt a ball. "It's a ball!" he said. He was very excited and pulled the ball out to look at it.

What do you think the child learned from playing with the toy?

Reggie is learning what objects feel like. He is developing language by telling me the names of the objects he feels. He is learning to remember how things feel.

Now make a toy and observe how a child uses it. Then answer the questions below.

Making Toys That Promote Cognitive Development

Child _____ Age _____ Date _____

Setting _____ Toy _____

Briefly describe the toy you made:

_____

_____

_____

_____

What did the child do with the toy?

_____

_____

_____

_____

What do you think the child learned from playing with the toy?

_____

_____

_____

_____

Discuss this activity with your trainer.

V. Helping Infants and Toddlers Become Problem Solvers

In this activity you will learn:

- why it is important for infants and toddlers to develop problem-solving skills; and

- to encourage infants and toddlers to think and solve problems.

Problem solving is the process of identifying and trying out solutions for problems. Infants and toddlers develop problem-solving skills when they have many opportunities to try things and think for themselves. When caregivers provide an environment that encourages exploration and experimentation, young children are able to learn from their everyday experiences. For example, when children experiment with fitting nesting cups together or try sitting on a doll's chair, they are learning about size. When they run, climb, and crawl in and out of things, they learn about the size of their bodies in relation to things.

Why Are Problem-Solving Skills Important?

Infants and toddlers are beginning to discover who they are. They need to feel that they are competent. Helping young children learn how to solve problems is one way to ensure that they will feel good about themselves.

As they explore around them, children are learning how to think. They are learning how to learn—how to make sense of the world and how to solve problems. When a young child "learns to learn," she or he begins an ongoing pattern for life. Children who see themselves as problem solvers are likely to be curious and capable when they get older. They will probably continue to feel good about themselves and about learning throughout their lives.

What Caregivers Can Do to Encourage Problem Solving

One of the best ways you can encourage problem solving is to show children that *you* are interested in learning about the world. Show infants and toddlers how you lift a block to see if it is heavy. Squeeze and roll playdough to let them see how you use materials. Share your excitement about and pleasure in things going on in the room. Your interest and enthusiasm tell infants and toddlers that learning is important. Because they want to be like you, learning will become important to them, too.

Observe what children do so you can identify times to step back and let them try to solve their own problems. Give an infant a chance to reach a rattle on the far side of the blanket, or let a toddler retrieve a ball that has rolled under the table.

Be ready to step in, however, if a child is in danger or is getting too frustrated. An infant who is about to pull a stack of books off the counter onto his head needs help immediately. So does a toddler who begins throwing pieces of a puzzle that she can't fit. No one can learn well when under too much stress or in danger.

Engage in problem solving with infants and toddlers. When the string of a child's pull toy is stuck on a chair leg and her idea of pulling the string hasn't worked, kneel down and study the problem with her. Point out that the string is twisted on the chair leg. You may end up being the one who frees the toy, but you are giving the child the experience of how to go about solving a problem—an important lesson.

Watch children as they work to solve problems. Pause to watch children trying to pull apart pop beads or put clothes pins into a plastic milk bottle. Comment on what you see the child doing: "Wow, those beads were hard to pull apart! Now you have a bead for each hand," or "Well, look at you, fitting those big clothespins through the hole in that box! Only three more and they'll all be in the box." You are letting them know they are engaged in work that you respect.

Model problem solving by offering children opportunities to help you solve problems. For example, take a small group with you into the kitchen for more napkins, or let them help you tape the torn page of a book.

In this learning activity, you will observe children in your room so that you will recognize when they need your help to solve problems and when you should step back and let them solve their own problems. Over the next two days you will record three observations of children solving their own problems and three instances when you intervened (stepped in) to help. First read the example and then complete the blank observation form that follows.

Problem-Solving Observation
(Example)

Setting *Morning, inside*   **Age(s)** *5 to 25months*   **Date(s)** *April 12-13*

Summarize three instances in which you watched a child solve a problem. Describe the problem and how the child solved it.

1. *Malik (6 months) was just beginning to sit alone. I watched him slowly slouch over. He rolled over on his tummy and smiled.*

2. *Alicia (14 months) wanted more juice, but Ms. Tse didn't notice that her cup was empty. She waved her cup in the air, and Ms. Tse saw her.*

3. *Rachel (21 months) was eating her lunch. Ted (19 months), who was sitting next to her, reached over and grabbed a handful of her green beans. She looked at him and yelled "no!" He left her alone after that.*

Summarize three instances in which you stepped in to help a child solve a problem. Describe the problem and explain why you intervened.

1. *Julie (5 months) was rolling over. She got stuck in the sheets of the crib. She began crying. I helped her because she was upset and couldn't figure out what to do.*

2. *Charlie (16 months) was yelling. He started throwing toys. I went over and helped him stop because I was afraid he might hurt someone. I showed him how to stamp his feet to express his angry feelings.*

3. *Ojo (25 months) was trying to tie his own shoes. He wants to do things his older brother can do. I watched him try, and he was getting very frustrated. I stepped in because he was getting very upset with himself and needed help.*

Using the form below, record three observations of infants or toddlers solving their own problems and three instances in which you stepped in to help.

Problem-Solving Observation

Setting _____   Age(s) _____   Date(s) _____

Summarize three instances in which you watched a child solve a problem. Describe the problem and how the child solved it.

1. _____

_____

_____

2. _____

_____

_____

3. _____

_____

_____

Summarize three instances in which you stepped in to help a child solve a problem. Describe the problem and explain why you intervened.

1. _____

_____

_____

2. _____

_____

_____

3. _____

_____

_____

Discuss these observations with your trainer.

VI. Planning Activities That Promote Cognitive Development

In this activity you will learn:

- to select and try out appropriate activities that promote young children's cognitive development; and

- to reinforce the concepts and skills that infants and toddlers are learning in the activity.

Infants and toddlers learn to think primarily through everyday activities. This doesn't mean that there is no place for special activities to help children learn a particular skill or concept. New activities, new toys, and new experiences are enjoyable. It's also enjoyable for you to try new ideas and see how children respond.

In planning appropriate activities for infants and toddlers, keep the following guidelines in mind:

- Give infants and toddlers hands-on experiences because they learn through active use of their senses.

- Be clear in your own mind about what you think children can learn from an activity.

- Organize materials you will need ahead of time so you can focus on what the children are doing instead of running around looking for paper or crayons.

- Make the activity appropriate to the developmental stages of the children you are working with. An activity that is challenging and exciting for one child may be meaningless to a child a few months younger. Try to look at the activity through the child's eyes. Ask yourself if it makes sense and if the child will be able to learn from it.

- Plan to do an activity more than once. Learning takes time and practice. By experiencing the same activity over and over, a child really learns to understand what is happening.

- Briefly explain to children, step by step, what you are going to do.

- Choose the right time to present your activity. If you are planning a special food activity for the afternoon and an unexpected fire drill and visitor have you and the children feeling unsettled, wait until tomorrow.

5

COGNITIVE

- Be aware that what children take from an experience may be different from what you had planned. Many caregivers have been disappointed because the children responded differently to a given activity than the caregivers had anticipated. Be flexible when a walk to play on the grass turns into watching a road crew fix a hole in the road.

In this learning activity you will plan an activity to promote children's cognitive development. Review the example that follows, and complete the blank form to help you see how the activity you planned promotes cognitive development.

Promoting Cognitive Development
(Example)

Child(ren) _Any five who were interested_ **Age(s)** _10-35 months_ **Date(s)** _August 16_

Setting _Outdoors_   **Activity** _Taking a walk_

Materials needed: _A stroller and buckets_

Briefly describe your activity:

We took a short walk outside. Maria (10 months) really enjoyed herself. She laughed and babbled as she rode in the stroller. The toddlers had buckets to collect things. I talked about the leaves on the trees and the sounds of the birds and cars, the smell of the grass, and the things we collected.

What senses did the children use during this activity?

Maria saw trees, grass, and bushes. She could hear cars and birds. She touched a soft green fern. She could smell the newly cut grass. The toddlers used their whole bodies. They walked, ran, and climbed. They picked up objects and put them in their buckets.

What do you think children might learn from this activity?

They learned that it's fun to be outdoors and to explore. The toddlers learned the name for a pine cone. They learned to look carefully to find interesting things outside. Maria is learning that she likes being outside. She was smiling even though she had been cranky before we went outside.

What did you do to promote cognitive development during this activity?

I talked to them about the things we saw, heard, and smelled. I encouraged them to touch a fern and pick up objects. We talked about what they collected.

Plan and carry out an activity with the infants and toddlers you care for. Then complete this form.

Promoting Cognitive Development

Child(ren) _____   Age(s) _____   Date(s) _____

Setting _____   Activity _____

Materials needed   _____

Briefly describe your activity:

_____

_____

_____

_____

What senses did the children use during this activity?

_____

_____

_____

_____

What do you think children might learn from this activity?

_____

_____

_____

_____

What did you do to promote cognitive development during this activity?

_____

_____

_____

_____

Discuss this activity with your trainer.

Summarizing Your Progress

You have now completed all of the learning activities for this module. Whether you are an experienced caregiver or a new one, this module has probably helped you develop new skills for promoting cognitive development. Before you go on, take a few minutes to summarize what you've learned.

- Turn back to Learning Activity I, Using Your Knowledge of Infants and Toddlers to Promote Their Cognitive Development, and add to the chart specific examples of what you learned about promoting the cognitive development of infants and toddlers during the time you were working on this module. Read the sample responses on the completed chart at the end of this module.

- Next, review your responses to the pre-training assessment for this module. Write a summary of what you learned, and list the skills you developed or improved.

Your final step in this module is to complete the knowledge and competency assessments. Let your trainer know when you are ready to schedule the assessments. After you have successfully completed these assessments, you will be ready to start a new module. Congratulations on your progress so far, and good luck with your next module.

Answer Sheet: Promoting Cognitive Development

Providing Opportunities for Infants and Toddlers to Use All Their Senses to Explore the World

1. Why did Ms. Bates decide not to stop George and wipe up the cracker crumbs?

    a. She realized that a crumbled cracker wasn't a big problem.

    b. She saw George was interested in the cracker.

    c. She wanted to give George a chance to learn through all his senses.

2. What did George learn about a cracker through his senses?

    a. He learned what a cracker tastes, smells, and feels like.

    b. He learned how a cracker changes when it is crumbled.

    c. He learned the sound of the word "cracker" by hearing Ms. Bates say it several times.

Interacting with Infants and Toddlers in Ways That Help Them Develop Confidence and Curiosity

1. What was Will's way of dealing with something new?

    a. He took time to get used to something new.

    b. He watched from a distance before he moved closer to the tunnel.

2. How did Ms. Lewis encourage Will's curiosity and confidence?

    a. She offered him a ball, which he wanted to play with.

    b. She respected his reluctance to approach the tunnel.

    c. With a more adventuresome child, she demonstrated playing with balls in the tunnel.

    d. She let Will observe the play.

    e. She used a familiar routine—"peek-a-boo"—to engage Will.

Providing Opportunities for Infants and Toddlers to Develop New Concepts and Skills

1. How was Jerome's sadness about separating from his daddy related to his cognitive development?

   a. He is still learning (and isn't completely sure) that when people go away, they are going to come back.

   b. It is hard for him to imagine where his father is. It is hard for him to understand and remember *when* he will come back.

   c. When his father leaves he feels so sad that it's hard for him to remember that he has a good time in the center and that the caregivers are special people, too.

2. What things in the environment helped Jerome deal with separation?

   a. The caregiver, Mr. Jones, respected Jerome's feelings and talked with him about them.

   b. Pictures of his family on the wall, where he could easily see them, helped Jerome envision his most important people.

   c. Using a toy telephone helped Jerome feel connected to his father.

3. Why didn't Mr. Jones interrupt Jerome when he was playing "peek-a-boo?"

   a. He knew playing "peek-a-boo" was helping Jerome by letting him feel in control of someone's leaving and coming back.

   b. What Jerome was learning was more important than his coming to the table immediately for a snack.

Using Your Knowledge of Infants' and Toddlers' Development to Promote Cognitive Development

WHAT YOUNG INFANTS DO (0-8 MONTHS)	HOW CAREGIVERS CAN USE THIS INFORMATION TO PROMOTE COGNITIVE DEVELOPMENT
They visually follow and respond to objects or faces as they move.	Spend time with infants—talk with them, hold them. Let them have the opportunity to study the face of their special caregiver. Give children interesting things to see.
They hold and manipulate objects; they suck on everything.	Provide safe, soft, washable, colorful toys for children to look at and suck on so they can explore their world using every means available.
They vocalize to themselves, people, and toys.	Talk with infants. Respond to their sounds. Know when to be quiet and let children experience and enjoy making different sounds.
They begin understanding that objects or people exist even when they are out of sight.	Play "peek-a-boo" games with infants. Hide objects under a blanket and then make them reappear.
WHAT MOBILE INFANTS DO (9-17 MONTHS)	
They learn to crawl, stand up, and walk.	Provide safe and steady furniture for infants to hold on to. Place interesting things in the environment so children will want to get to them.
They begin to remember more from one day to the next.	Exchange information with parents about games and toys each child likes, so the child can play the same games at home and at the center. Take advantage of daily routines to help children develop a sense of order in the world.

WHAT MOBILE INFANTS DO (9-17 MONTHS)	HOW CAREGIVERS CAN USE THIS INFORMATION TO PROMOTE COGNITIVE DEVELOPMENT
They are able to make choices between clear alternatives.	Set up the environment so that children can make clear choices and sense order. For example, display toys clearly on low shelves—not in boxes. Offer children clear, manageable choices such as this: "Would you like to put a pear or an apple in the bag?"
They begin to solve problems on their own.	Give children the opportunity to solve some problems on their own. When you intervene, help children understand what is happening instead of immediately solving the problem yourself.
They begin to develop language.	Talk with children. Read with them. Write books about things and people they know. Become familiar with some expressions of children whose home language is different.
WHAT TODDLERS DO (18-36 MONTHS)	
They learn by helping.	Let toddlers be "partners" with you in such tasks as dressing and preparing for snack. Let them do what they can to help them feel competent and learn new skills.
They learn to talk more.	Try to extend and enrich toddlers' language. If a toddler says "ball," say "yes, that is a big red ball." Help toddlers label things, ideas, and feelings so they will be better able to use language to learn. If you don't know the child's home language, learn to speak a few familiar words and phrases.

WHAT TODDLERS DO (18-36 MONTHS)	HOW CAREGIVERS CAN USE THIS INFORMATION TO PROMOTE COGNITIVE DEVELOPMENT
They learn about concepts such as size, shape, and weight by using their bodies as they move and play with toys and things in the environment.	Give toddlers opportunities to move and to play so they can learn about size, shape, and weight.
They can concentrate for longer periods of time.	Protect toddlers from interruptions—even yours—so they can learn what it feels like to concentrate on something.
They sometimes think about actions before doing them.	Arrange the environment so it can help toddlers understand limits, make clear choices, and develop a sense of order. For example, because boxes of Bristle Blocks and pop beads are likely to be dumped, you may want to keep them on a high shelf and bring them down upon request.
They enjoy and learn through role playing and dramatic play.	Provide dolls and simple props such as hats, bags, and household objects to encourage toddlers' dramatic play.

Glossary

Classify	To put things or events in groups on the basis of what they have in common.
Closed question	A question for which there is only one right answer.
Cognitive development	Development of the expanding ability to think and reason.
Concept	An idea that combines details or several other ideas in an organized way.
Concrete	Relating to real objects.
Discriminate	To notice the differences among things.
Object permanence	Referring to the beginning of abstract thought, when a mental image is maintained of an object or person that is not within sight.
Open-ended question	A question that can be answered in many ways; one for which there isn't one right answer.
Problem-solving	The process of thinking through a problem and coming up with one or several possible solutions.
Sequencing	Putting things or events in order.

Module 6
Communication

What Is Communication and Why Is It Important?

Communication means expressing and sharing ideas, desires, and feelings with other people. Our drive to communicate is very strong, and we can recognize it in young babies. Very early on, infants learn they can communicate their needs by crying. They learn to communicate joy by smiling and cooing when they see a familiar face. By the end of their first year, most infants are saying a word or two.

As adults, we have thousands upon thousands of words to communicate with. Gestures such as a wave or a shrug are readily understood by people from the same culture. Facial expressions such as a smile or a frown communicate feelings as clearly as a pat on the back. We also communicate through images and pictures, which can represent ideas and feelings.

Although all forms of communication—gestures, facial expressions, body language, touch, pictures—are important, communication with language is the most critical. Language allows us to communicate an endless range of feelings and ideas. It enables us to interpret what others say to us. Without language, our ability to express ourselves is limited.

The use of language is crucial to a child's overall development. Cognitive development depends on a child's ever-growing ability to understand spoken or signed language and eventually to read and write in ways that others can understand. Social development, too, depends on language. The child who has difficulty expressing himself or herself well is often less able to develop friendships. And language is an important factor in emotional development. Children's self-esteem is enhanced by their growing ability to put into language how they feel—to communicate their feelings accurately to others.

The development of language is one of the major accomplishments of early childhood. In a few years a child moves from being nonverbal and able to communicate needs only through crying, to developing the ability to speak or sign and understand language. Children learn thousands of words, their meanings, and the rules for using them simply by being around caring adults who communicate with them and respond to their efforts to communicate. They are born with the urge to communicate. If we respond to their cues and show encouragement, their interest in expanding their communication skills is virtually limitless.

You can promote communication as you care for infants and toddlers throughout the day. You can talk about daily routines and experiences. The activities you plan and the materials you offer infants and toddlers can encourage them to communicate. And finally, you can help children develop listening and speaking skills through the use of storytelling, books, poems, finger plays, songs, and records.

Promoting young children's communication skills involves:

- interacting with infants and toddlers in ways that encourage them to communicate their thoughts and feelings;

- providing materials and activities that promote communication skills; and

- helping infants and toddlers develop listening and speaking skills.

Listed below are examples of how caregivers demonstrate their competence in promoting communication.

Interacting with Infants and Toddlers in Ways That Encourage Them to Communicate Their Thoughts and Feelings

Here are some examples of what caregivers can do.

- Respond to an infant's cooing sounds and imitate them. "I hear you saying 'bah, bah, bah.' That's an interesting sound."

- Encourage children to talk to each other. "It looks like Sarah's baby is sick. Why don't you ask her what's the matter?"

- Follow an infant's gaze and talk about what you both are seeing. "I see a rainbow in the water from the sprinkler, and I see a bird bathing in the sprinkler—I wonder which one you're looking at?"

- Accept a child's way of speaking while at the same time modeling correct speech. If a child says "me threw the ball," the caregiver might respond by saying, "Yes, you threw the ball all the way to the green rug."

- Help children talk about their thoughts and concerns. "You want to play with the blocks, too. Tell Andrew, 'I need some blocks.'"

- Name and talk about a child's feelings, behaviors, activities, body parts, and families to help expand the child's understanding of words. "Let me put your left arm through the sleeve. Now your sweater will keep you warm."

- Attend carefully to what children are telling you verbally and nonverbally and help them express their ideas. "Are you saying that you want to get down from my lap now?"

Providing Materials and Activities That Promote Communication Skills

Here are some examples of what caregivers can do.

- Play "peek-a-boo" or "look-away" with infants who enjoy these games.

- Use puppets to help a shy child talk. "And how are you today, Mr. Rabbit?"

- Create small activity areas where a few children can play together.

- Comment on what children are doing and experiencing. "The drum makes a loud noise." "The finger paint feels so cool and smooth."

- Comment on what infants are observing. "Hershel is crying because he doesn't feel well. Here comes his grandma to take him home until he feels better."

- Pose questions at snack or meal times to encourage children to talk. "These are really crunchy carrots. What else do we eat that is crunchy like a carrot?"

- Put out real props that encourage make-believe and dramatic play.

- Give older infants "conversation opportunities," such as seating two of them facing one another at snack or meal time.

- Make picture labels for toys and materials, and tape the labels to the shelves where those things are displayed.

- Write children's dictation and label their drawings when they go along with your idea to write. "Shall I write what you said: 'This is my mommy?' Where would you like me to write it?"

Helping Infants and Toddlers Develop Listening and Speaking Skills

Here are some examples of what caregivers can do.

- Talk often, in a normal tone of voice and using adult English, to infants as well as toddlers. Constantly using "baby talk" sends the wrong message to young children who are learning how language really works.

- Encourage children to identify pictures in a book. "Can you find the truck?"

- Encourage children to hear different sounds in their environment. "Do you hear the leaves crunching as you walk through them?"

- Make books about topics that are important to children. "I made a book about the day we cooked French toast for snack. Listen carefully to see what happens."

- Familiarize yourself with some expressions of children whose home language is different from yours. Use your knowledge to better understand what the young child is trying to communicate to you. "José, you said 'awa.' Are you thirsty? Here's some water." (Water is agua in Spanish.)

- Teach older toddlers short poems and finger plays. "Who wants to say 'Eensy Weensy Spider' with me?"

- Share your pleasure in a story as your read to individual children or small groups. "Look at that silly puppy. What's he doing now?"

- Take advantage of the different languages spoken by children's families to enrich your language environment. "Hai's sister is talking with her in Vietnamese. Let's ask them to teach us a few words."

- Recognize possible delays or impairments that might affect a child's communication, and report these to the center director so that the child can be assessed. "Ms. Taylor, I'm concerned that Trudy (24 months) isn't talking more and that many of the words she uses aren't clear. Maybe we should suggest to her parents that they have her hearing checked."

Promoting Children's Communication

The following situations show caregivers promoting the communication skills of infants and toddlers. As you read, think about what the caregivers in each scene are doing and why. Then answer the questions following each episode.

Interacting with Infants and Toddlers in Ways That Encourage Them to Communicate Their Thoughts and Feelings

Ms. Bates has just finished changing 4-month-old Eddie's diaper. She notices he is looking at the mobile hanging over the changing table. "Do you like the mobile?" she asks. She gives it a gentle tap, and it begins slowly spinning around. Eddie coos and kicks his feet. "That's pretty exciting, isn't it?" Ms. Bates says. He looks at the mobile, over to her, and back to the mobile. Ms. Bates smiles. "Ahbah," Eddie babbles. He swipes at the mobile and misses. "Do you want it to spin again?" Ms. Bates laughs. Eddie kicks his feet in the air.

1. How did Ms. Bates encourage Eddie to communicate his thoughts and feelings?

_____
_____
_____
_____

2. How did Ms. Bates let Eddie know that she was listening to him?

_____
_____
_____
_____

Providing Materials and Activities That Promote Communication Skills

"Welcome back!" says Mr. Jones as Kara (33 months), Grace (34 months), and Ms. Moore come back from their walk to the park across the street from the center. "What did you see on your walk?" "We saw a big bird!" Grace tells him. "And a bird's nest," Kara adds. "The bird was flying around and then it sat on its nest," Grace explains. "That's exciting," says Mr. Jones, smiling at the girls. "Why don't you two write about the bird you saw with Ms. Moore?" Kara and Grace get some paper and markers from the shelf and begin scribbling on their paper. "What does your story say?" Ms. Moore asks. "That's a picture of the bird," Kara says. "It says *bird*." "Do you want me to write more of your words on the paper for you?" Ms. Moore asks. "We saw a big bird," Kara dictates. "It sat on its nest in a tree," Grace adds. Ms. Moore writes down their words and reads them aloud.

1. How did Mr. Jones use a walk to promote communication skills?

_____

_____

_____

2. How did Ms. Moore promote communication skills as she helped Kara and Grace write a story?

_____

_____

_____

Helping Infants and Toddlers Develop Listening and Speaking Skills

Dora (12 months) pulls herself up from her resting mat to stand beside the toy shelf. "Bah, bah," she says and turns to look at Ms. Gonzalez sitting at the table. She smiles and says, "Hi, Dora, I thought you were still asleep." "Bah, bah," Dora repeats and stretches an arm upward toward the adult-level shelf where the balls are stored during rest time. Ms. Gonzalez follows the direction of Dora's gaze and outstretched arms. "Ball? You're awake and ready to play with the ball again?" Dora grins and makes an excited crouching motion. After getting Dora the ball, Ms. Gonzalez writes a note to her family, mentioning Dora's new word and asking them what new words they are beginning to understand at home.

1. How was Ms. Gonzalez able to understand what Dora said to her?

_____

_____

_____

2. How will Ms. Gonzalez's note to Dora's family help Dora develop listening and speaking skills?

_____

_____

_____

Compare your answers with those on the answer sheet at the end of this module. If your answers are different, discuss them with your trainer. There may be more than one good answer.

Your Own Experiences with Communication

Communication skills are central to our ability to relate to others. Our relationships with colleagues, friends, and family members depend in large part on how well we can understand and respond to what they have to say and how well they understand us.

In understanding what others have to say, we need to do three things:

- receive the message;

- interpret the message; and

- send back an appropriate response.

Many factors influence how well we understand the communications we receive from others. These factors include how we are feeling at that moment, how well we know the persons communicating with us, and how carefully we listen. For example, suppose you've had a bad morning before coming to work. You are feeling overwhelmed. Your co-worker greets you with the following statement: "This storeroom is a mess! I can't find anything in it!"

You may interpret this message as a criticism and respond defensively: "When am I supposed to find the time to deal with the storeroom? I can hardly keep up with the classroom!" Your co-worker may be surprised by your response. She might also react defensively: "Don't you think I'm just as busy as you are?"

On another day, when you are feeling more on top of things, you might interpret your co-worker's message very differently. Your response might be something like this: "You're absolutely right. We've been so busy with other things, we never seem to get to the storeroom. Maybe we can ask for a parent volunteer to help us out."

Because any message can easily be misinterpreted, it's important to clarify what we think another person really means. Questions that help clarify the message include the following:

- Are you saying that...?

- Do you mean...?

- Do I understand correctly that...?

- It sounds like you want...?

In conveying our thoughts and feelings to others, we rely on our communication skills to get our messages across accurately. We send messages verbally (using words) and nonverbally (using gestures and body language). Verbal messages can be the clearest kind of message if we say what we mean.

- "I'd like to do something about the storeroom. I can never find what I need. What do you think of the idea of asking a parent to help us out?"

- "I'd love to go to a movie tonight. What time is best for you?"

But even verbal messages can be unclear if we fail to say what we really think and want. Using the same examples, we could say:

- "What are we going to do about the storeroom?" (when we know very well what we think needs to be done).

- "What do you feel like doing tonight?" (hoping the other person will want to go to a movie but remaining unclear about our own wishes).

How do you rate your ability to communicate effectively? Check the appropriate box below.

COMMUNICATION SKILLS	MOST OF THE TIME	SOMETIMES	RARELY
I am able to state my ideas clearly.			
I am able to express my feelings in words.			
I say what I think.			
If I'm not sure what someone means, I check out what I think was said.			
I try to interpret nonverbal communication to help me better understand what someone is feeling.			

Review your answers to this brief checklist. Are there any areas that you would like to improve? As you go through this module and learn ways of helping children communicate, you may discover some strategies for improving your own communication skills.

When you have finished this overview section, you should complete the pre-training assessment. Refer to the glossary at the end of the module if you need definitions of the terms that are used.

Pre-Training Assessment

Listed below are the skills that caregivers use to promote infants' and toddlers' communication. Think about whether you do these things regularly, sometimes, or not enough. Place a check in one of the columns on the right for each skill listed. Then discuss your answers with your trainer.

SKILL	I DO THIS REGULARLY	I DO THIS SOMETIMES	I DON'T DO THIS ENOUGH
INTERACTING WITH INFANTS AND TODDLERS IN WAYS THAT ENCOURAGE THEM TO COMMUNICATE THEIR THOUGHTS AND FEELINGS 1. Being aware of children's attempts to communicate needs and feelings.			
2. Responding to young children's nonverbal communication.			
3. Serving as a language model by talking to young children.			
4. Encouraging children to try out new sounds and words.			
5. Naming objects, actions, and people and asking questions or making comments that encourage children to share ideas and feelings.			
PROVIDING MATERIALS AND ACTIVITIES THAT PROMOTE COMMUNICATION SKILLS 6. Selecting materials and equipment that promote communication skills.			

SKILL	I DO THIS REGULARLY	I DO THIS SOMETIMES	I DON'T DO THIS ENOUGH
7. Selecting and using books appropriate for the ages and interests of the children.			
8. Making books about familiar things and events that will interest and excite children.			
9. Playing games that involve children in talking and singing, such as finger plays.			
10. Providing secure and inviting places for children to play with one another.			
11. Maintaining a rich environment for children to explore and make discoveries.			
12. Providing a variety of paper and writing tools such as large crayons and fat pencils to encourage toddlers' scribbles.			
HELPING INFANTS AND TODDLERS DEVELOP LISTENING AND SPEAKING SKILLS 13. Encouraging children to notice sounds in their environment.			
14. Encouraging children to imitate sounds and repeat words.			
15. Talking with children during daily routines and activities to expand their listening skills.			

SKILL	I DO THIS REGULARLY	I DO THIS SOMETIMES	I DON'T DO THIS ENOUGH
16. Encouraging children to experiment with language.			
17. Using music and songs to extend children's listening skills.			

Review your responses, then list three to five skills you would like to improve or topics you would like to learn more about. When you finish this module, you will list examples of your new or improved knowledge and skills.

_____

_____

_____

_____

Now begin the learning activities for Module 6, Communication.

I. Using Your Knowledge of Infant and Toddler Development to Promote Communication Skills

In this activity you will learn:

- to recognize some typical behaviors of infants and toddlers that are related to communication; and

- to use what you know about infants and toddlers to promote their communication skills.

Infants begin communicating long before they can say a single word. From birth, infants tell their parents and caregivers what they need. A hungry infant may begin to cry and move his or her lips when he or she is picked up. An infant in pain may cry and hold his or her body stiffly. Soon parents and caregivers learn what an infant's different cries are saying. One cry might mean "I'm hungry" while another might mean "I'm bored; come pick me up and play with me!" By responding to infants' cries, you are teaching infants that they are effective communicators and encouraging them to continue communicating.

Within a few months most infants have learned to smile, coo, and gurgle. With these new sounds they can now communicate their interests, pleasure, and affection. When Nancy (5 months) smiles and coos at you, she is saying how happy she is to see you. By listening to what her sounds are saying and answering her, you help her learn that people take turns during conversations and that talking and listening are enjoyable.

Soon babbling begins. Infants enjoy making and listening to their own sounds. Listen and babble and talk back to infants. Play with sounds and give infants words for what you think they may be saying. Infants begin understanding words and phrases before they begin talking. For instance, Tommy (9 months) may begin clapping his hands when you say, "Pat-a-cake!"

And then the big day comes when you hear an infant's first word. It will be a word that is personally meaningful. For example, Andy, an active mobile infant, is always getting stuck as he tries climbing into, over, under, and around things. His first word was "stuck." "Ma-ma," "Da," and "Bo" (he has a cat named "Bones") were next.

Share your pleasure and excitement at first words. Your enthusiasm will encourage an infant to learn more words. Model speech in a natural way, by speaking clearly and at normal volume. As you spend your days together, talk about what you are going to do. Talk with infants even though you may not be able to understand what they are saying. Singing songs, saying rhymes, and looking at books together are activities that can help infants experience the pleasure and wonder of language and that encourage them to communicate. Because we look forward to an infant's first words, it is important to keep in mind that just as in other areas of growth, children develop language at their own pace. Some say their first words at 12 months. Others hardly speak at all until they are 2 years old. Respecting individual differences is an important part of promoting communication.

Toddlers experience an explosion of language. An 18-month-old toddler may be able to say 10 or more words. Six months later, this toddler will be saying as many as 300 words. She will say as many as 900 between her second and third birthday. While an 18-month-old may communicate the thought "I want to play with the car" by saying "car" and pointing to the red car on the shelf, a 3-year-old may say, "I want that red car."

Toddlers often have more ideas and requests to communicate than they have words to use. They are learning how to put words together in meaningful ways. Often they try to talk as fast as adults. The result can be an expressive series of different sounds called jargon. Although it can sometimes be hard to understand toddlers' jargon, their pointing and other gestures can help you understand what they are trying to tell you.

It is important to listen to toddlers and carry on conversations with them, even if you respond by asking something like this: "Are you telling me about that airplane flying over us?" Toddlers want to practice communicating with you. As you talk with them, you are showing them how important communication is.

Toddlers seem to continually ask "what's this?" by pointing or actually asking. These continual questions can become frustrating to adults. It may help to recall that toddlers are not deliberately trying your patience. Rather, they are collecting words and experience with language. Answering their questions, paying attention to their sounds, and playing with rhymes and songs are all ways in which you can foster toddler's communication.

Reading books with toddlers is another way to encourage their interest in language as well as in reading and writing. Read simple stories with pictures about things toddlers know. Good topics include eating lunch, spilling juice, getting dressed, and going shopping with mommy or daddy. You also can write your own books about things that happen in the center. Help toddlers learn that books are related to their lives. Encourage toddlers to illustrate them or to write books themselves. Their scribbles are the beginning of writing.

The chart on the next page lists some typical behaviors of infants and toddlers. Included are characteristics related to developing communication skills. The right-hand column asks you to identify ways that caregivers can use this information about child development to promote communication skills. Try to think of as many examples as you can. As you work through the module, you will learn new strategies for promoting communication, and you can add them to the child development chart. You are not expected to think of all the examples at one time. If you need help getting started, turn to the completed chart at the end of the module. By the time you complete all the learning activities, you will find that you have learned many ways to promote good communication skills for infants and toddlers.

Using Your Knowledge of Infant and Toddler Development to Promote Communication Skills

WHAT YOUNG INFANTS DO (0-8 MONTHS)	HOW CAREGIVERS CAN USE THIS INFORMATION TO PROMOTE COMMUNICATION
They communicate from birth by moving, crying, cooing, and making sounds.	
They respond to voices.	
They "talk" to themselves as well as to others, particularly people they know well.	
They make a variety of sounds—crying, coos, whimpers, and gurgles—to express feelings.	

WHAT MOBILE INFANTS DO (9-17 MONTHS)	HOW CAREGIVERS CAN USE THIS INFORMATION TO PROMOTE COMMUNICATION
They pay attention to conversations.	
They are interested in picture books.	
They use words such as "mama" and "dada."	
They know that words stand for objects.	
They may be able to say 10 or more words.	

WHAT TODDLERS DO (18-36 MONTHS)	HOW CAREGIVERS CAN USE THIS INFORMATION TO PROMOTE COMMUNICATION
Their language development is rapidly expanding.	
They understand simple directions and may follow them if they are in a cooperative mood.	
They enjoy listening to simple stories about familiar things and people.	
They gather information about the world by asking "why?" and "what's this?"	
They develop more complex pretend play.	
They make mistakes in using rules of grammar.	

WHAT TODDLERS DO (18-36 MONTHS)	HOW CAREGIVERS CAN USE THIS INFORMATION TO PROMOTE COMMUNICATION
They can hold fat crayons or pencils and make marks on paper.	
They are interested in what adults do.	

As you proceed with the rest of the learning activities, you can refer back to the chart and add examples of how you promote infants' and toddlers' communication. Discuss your responses with your trainer.

II. Understanding How Infants and Toddlers Learn to Communicate

In this activity you will learn:

- to identify the stages that children go through in learning language; and

- to assess a young child's level of language development.

Stages of Infant Language Development[1]

No one knows exactly how infants learn to talk, but we do know that most infants learn language in this basic order:

0-3 months	Infants communicate from birth. They are born knowing how to make noises. They communicate by crying, cooing, and gurgling. They listen to sounds around them and respond by kicking, being still, blinking, turning to look for the sound, laughing, or crying.
3-6 months	Infants may begin using consonant sounds that adults recognize (English-speaking families usually notice "pah, bah, dah," or "mah"). Although 5-month-old Sandy may sound like she is saying "Papa" or "Mama", she probably doesn't know the meaning of the sounds. What she is doing, though, is very important. She is learning to distinguish noises that sound similar and trying to make those noises.
6-9 months	Infants respond not only to sounds but to tones. They can tell when the person talking with them is happy or sad, encouraging or annoyed. Infants practice making new sounds as they babble to themselves. Babbling is a step toward talking. Infants try to copy the way people talk to them and how they move their mouths. They might respond to their names.
9-12 months	By the age of 1, some infants are saying a few real words—probably names of familiar things or people, such as mama, cat, ball, or bottle. Infants will begin using gestures with words, such as waving while saying "bye-bye." This shows us that they understand what they are saying.
12-18 months	Infants say one-word sentences, such as "milk" (meaning "I want some milk"). They tend to talk to themselves, making up words as they go along. They may begin speaking "jargon"; their voices may sound as if they are making complete sentences, but the sentences are made up of a mix of real words and babble.

[1]Based on Margaret Nash and Costella Tate, *Better Baby Care: A Book for Family Day Care Providers* (Washington, DC: The Children's Foundation, September 1986), pp. 40-41.

Stages of Toddler's Language Development

Between 18 and 36 months, toddlers develop the ability to express their ideas and convey their desires in words. This is a major achievement. We can look at the stages of language development in two phases.

18-24 months	During this early toddler stage, young children understand far more than they can say. By the age of 2, they may say as many as 50 words. They begin putting two words together to make a sentence and express a thought: "Mommy go" or "me do." Toddlers are great imitators and repeat what they hear. Sometimes they repeat real words, and sometimes they imitate the sounds and tones in a sing-song manner. They love nursery rhymes and songs.
24-36 months	Vocabulary expands to as many as 500 words between 2 and 3 years of age. Older toddlers use language to express their needs and desires and put words in a sequence ("coat go outside"). Toddlers can follow simple directions ("bring me the ball"). They like to play with sounds by rhyming words or changing the beginnings or ends of familiar words ("po, pay, pee, pooh"). They enjoy listening to story books and retelling simple stories.

Young children develop language at their own rates. Many factors influence how and when language develops. Some factors are individual differences present from birth. Others depend on a child's experiences with communication.

Assessing a child's language development can help you plan strategies to promote language skills. A language assessment checklist can help make the job of assessing a child's language easy.

In this learning activity you will select two children you care for and observe their language development over several days. Use the language assessment checklists to record your observations. On the following pages you will find checklists for each age group.

After you complete the assessments, share the results with another caregiver who knows these children. You will use these assessments in the following learning activity.

The checklists can be used periodically to help you observe and document the language development of the children in your program.

Language Assessment of Young Infants[2]

Child: _____ **Age:** _____ **Date:** _____

Does the young infant:

	Yes	No
1. Coo and gurgle spontaneously?	____	____
2. Respond to a familiar voice?	____	____
3. Watch you when you speak?	____	____
4. Make noises in response to sounds that you make?	____	____
5. Laugh during play?	____	____
6. Know his or her name when called?	____	____

---

[2]Adapted with permission from *Infant and Toddler Programs* by Christine Z. Cataldo, (Menlo Park, CA: Addison-Wesley Publishing Company, 1983), pp. 210-211.

Language Assessment of Mobile Infants[3]

Child: _____ Age: _____ Date: _____

Does the mobile infant:

		Yes	No
1.	Use sounds to gain attention?	____	____
2.	Understand statements such as "give it to me" or questions such as "where did it go?"	____	____
3.	Look for a person or common objects when they are named?	____	____
4.	Respond appropriately to words such as "up," "bye-bye," and "pattycake"?	____	____
5.	Stop his or her activity when you say "no," "stop," or "come here"?	____	____
6.	Use single words and gestures to indicate "mine," "see," or "more"?	____	____
7.	Label some people or things?	____	____
8.	Listen for brief periods to stories and picture books?	____	____
9.	Use two words together in "telegraphic" sentences?	____	____
10.	Carry out simple directions (for instance, getting a ball)?	____	____
11.	Answer simple questions with "yes" or "no"?	____	____
12.	Use some three-word sentences?	____	____

[3]Adapted with permission from *Infant and Toddler Programs* by Christine Z. Cataldo, (Menlo Park, CA: Addison-Wesley Publishing Company, 1983), pp. 211-212.

COMMUNICATION

Language Assessment of Toddlers[4]

Child: _____ Age: _____ Date: _____

Does the toddler:

	Yes	No
1. Display an increasing receptive and expressive vocabulary?	____	____
2. Identify many objects, people, and pictures by pointing correctly or naming?	____	____
3. Correctly follow one-step and two-step directions given in sequence?	____	____
4. Use language to express needs and desires?	____	____
5. Sometimes use language with puppets, dolls, or other props?	____	____
6. Name most significant body parts on self and others?	____	____
7. Respond to stories and explanations by listening, commenting, or retelling?	____	____
8. Ask questions such as "what's that?"	____	____
9. Enjoy language exchanges with others; initiate, respond, and maintain verbal interactions?	____	____
10. Show some understanding of simple story themes and content by responding appropriately to simple queries?	____	____
11. Experiment with language by repeating new words, numbers, or rhymes?	____	____
12. Make three- and four-word sentences?	____	____

Discuss this learning activity with your trainer.

---

[4]Adapted with permission from *Infant and Toddler Programs* by Christine Z. Cataldo, (Menlo Park, CA: Addison-Wesley Publishing Company, 1983), pp. 220-222.

III. Helping Infants and Toddlers Develop Communication Skills

In this activity you will learn:

- to recognize the importance of helping infants and toddlers develop communication skills; and

- to use various strategies and activities to promote communication skills.

Infants and toddlers develop communication skills by being around adults who respond to them and talk to them. When Sandy (4 months) cries because she is hungry and her mother nurses her, she learns she can communicate what she wants and that someone is listening to her. When Barry (17 months) points to a dish at the lunch table and you say, "That's rice," he learns that this food is called rice. When Kyle (27 months) and Leslie (32 months) are each tugging at the wagon and shouting "mine," and you intervene to suggest that they take turns pulling each other, you are helping them learn that people use language to settle disputes.

During the day at the child development center, you can use daily activities and routines to help infants and toddlers learn to communicate.

Developing a Trusting, Responsive Relationship with Each Child

Children, like most adults, are more likely to want to communicate and learn new communication skills if they know someone is listening and will respond to them. By developing trusting, responsive relationships with individual children, you encourage them to communicate.

Here are several examples of ways in which you can develop positive relationships with infants and toddlers as you spend the day together.

- Respond to crying as a form of communication. Too often, caregivers simply try to stop crying by attempting to distract a child. When John (4 months) cries, ask yourself what he might be saying, and respond accordingly.

- Take advantage of daily routines as opportunities to communicate. Talk with children in your natural tone of voice as you dress, feed, and change them. Use their names regularly. "I'm going to take off your shirt, Timmy. Then we'll put a clean one on you." "Would you like another muffin, Mary?"

- Play games in which you interact and have fun together. "Pat-a-Cake," "This Little Piggy," and "Open, Shut Them" are favorites.

- Listen to children even if you have trouble understanding what they are saying. By listening, you are telling children that what they have to communicate is important. "I'm listening, Andy. Can you show me which toy you want?"

- As children learn new words, show your excitement and pleasure. Let them know that talking is special, and encourage them to talk more.

Preparing a Physical Environment That Supports Communication

Feeling safe and comfortable encourages communication skills. As discussed in Module 3, creating a homelike environment helps infants and toddlers feel safe and promotes their learning. Talking about their parents, pets, and things they do at home can help children connect with home through language. Commenting that "your mommy told me you eat carrots at home" helps Mary (16 months) feel a link to her safe home world during lunch at the center.

Here are some examples of ways to create an environment that supports communication.

- Arrange the space so that children can spend time individually with a caregiver. Young children can easily get tired or overwhelmed by spending all their time in a group setting. Jerry (11 months) is more likely to use his first words, "Mama" or "ca" (car), when he is in a quiet space playing with his special caregiver than when he is in a group. Larry (24 months) is more likely to talk when he and Sam (28 months) are reading a story with Mr. Jones than when in a larger group.

- Have interesting things in the environment for children to see and explore. Talk about the new mobile you made from corks, the orange fish swimming in its bowl, and what sounds animals make.

- Take small group walks in and around the center to provide new experiences. A trip to the storage area for paper cups or to the office to deliver a message can be interesting—even exciting—for infants and toddlers.

- Provide lots of sensory experiences. Give young infants rattles that shake, rubber toys they can chew, and bright pictures to look at. Offer mobile infants a variety of textured surfaces to crawl and walk on and the opportunity to play with water, sand, and playdough. Offer toddlers playdough, fingerpaint, and sand. Talk about how these materials feel: mushy, soggy, drippy, gritty, and crumbly.

Serving as a Language Model

Your own use of language can promote children's communication skills. Because you are so important to infants and toddlers, they pay close attention to how you talk and communicate with them and with other adults in the room. They learn from you even when you may not be aware that you are teaching.

Here are some ways to use your own language skills to promote communication skills.

- **Name things.** As you talk about 5-month-old Jesse's red pants, the swirly lines that Erica (18 months) draws on her paper, and the giant steps that Lisa (32 months) takes as she crosses the room, you are teaching language.

- **Use your normal tone of voice.** From birth, infants are attuned to the human voice. They can grow upset when adults yell or speak angrily.

- **Use words with interesting sounds** even though the children may not be able to say them. Point out the picture of a chrysanthemum or let children taste cinnamon during a snack. Hearing words with beautiful or unusual sounds can foster interest in language.

- **Talk with children about their feelings.** Saying "I think you are sad" to Maria (5 months), "you look very happy" to Jim (16 months), and "I appreciate the way you are helping today" to Will (35 months) helps them learn that feelings have names and that people can communicate about them.

- **Play with language.** Make up rhymes and silly words. In addition to being important, language and communication can be fun. Ask Jeff (18 months) how it feels to be jumping on a "lumpy, bumpy pillow." Ask a group of toddlers, "What animal am I if I say 'moo'?"

- **Use songs and finger plays.** When young children hear songs and finger plays often enough, they will learn and use the words they hear. They can learn parts of the body while enjoying action chants such as "Head, Shoulders, Knees, and Toes." Chant or make up your own tune.

- **Display pictures.** Large, colorful pictures of familiar objects such as animals, plants, vehicles, and people give toddlers things to talk about.

- **Use books.** Read books and point to the pictures while you talk about them. Ask simple questions: "What goes 'woof, woof'?"

- **Provide puppets, dolls, and dress-up clothes.** Children will talk to puppets and dolls while they play. Props and dress-up clothes encourage toddlers to pretend, which aids speech development.

- **Be quiet sometimes.** Like adults, young children ignore constant chatter. If you are always talking, you can never be listening.

In this activity you will use the language checklists you completed on infants and toddlers to plan activities that will help them develop their language skills. After reviewing the example, plan your own activities and strategies.

Strategies for Promoting Language Development
(Infant Example)

Child _Roy_   **Age** _6 months_   **Date** _November 8_

Setting _Away from group_   **Activity** _Babbling_

What language skills do you want to help this child develop?

I want to encourage Roy to vocalize more. He watches me when I am dressing and changing him. I think he listens. But he doesn't make many sounds himself.

What strategies and activities will you try?

I am going to work on developing a special relationship with Roy. I will spend time with Roy away from the group. I wonder if he may feel overwhelmed by all the activity in the room. I will respond to his sounds and give him a turn to respond back.

What did you notice after trying these strategies and activities over a two-week period?

Roy smiles more when he sees me. I think we are developing a special relationship. Roy babbles more when we spend time alone in the pillow corner or sit in the hallway and play together. I will continue working on our relationship and be sure that Roy has time away from the large group. I will continue responding to his sounds.

Strategies for Promoting Language Development
(Toddler Example)

Child _Becky_   **Age** _30 months_   **Date** _November 10_

Setting _Toddler room_   **Activity** _Learning names_

What language skills do you want to help this child develop?

I want to help Becky learn the names of the other children in the room.

What strategies and activities will you try?

I will use children's names when I talk with Becky about what is happening in the room. I will ask her to take things to specific children. I will look at the family pictures hanging on the wall and talk with Becky about who is in the pictures.

What did you notice after trying these strategies and activities over a two-week period?

Becky knows the other children's names. When I ask her to pass the crackers to Frank, she does. I learned that Becky gets easily overwhelmed in a large group. I will be sure she has more time in small group activities so she can have more practice talking.

Strategies for Promoting Language Development

Child _____ Age _____ Date _____

Setting _____ Activity _____

What language skills do you want to help this child develop?

_____

_____

_____

_____

What strategies and activities will you try?

_____

_____

_____

_____

What did you notice after trying these strategies and activities over a two-week period?

_____

_____

_____

_____

_____

_____

Strategies for Promoting Language Development

Child _____ Age _____ Date _____

Setting _____ Activity _____

What language skills do you want to help this child develop?

_____

_____

_____

_____

What strategies and activities will you try?

_____

_____

_____

_____

What did you notice after trying these strategies and activities over a two-week period?

_____

_____

_____

_____

_____

_____

Discuss this activity with your trainer.

IV. Selecting and Using Books with Young Children

In this activity you will learn:

- to appreciate why books are an important part of a child development program;

- to choose books that are appropriate for infants and toddlers; and

- to share books with infants and toddlers.

Books are very special; they show us the familiar and allow us to "visit" new places and learn new things. They also provide tremendous pleasure. Infants and toddlers can learn to love books when they are very young. If you know how to select appropriate books and how to use them, you can prepare infants and toddlers for a lifetime of reading.

Selecting Books for Infants[5]

Until infants are about 12 months old, books are objects to be explored and handled. Later, the content of a book becomes important. Thus, if you select books that are too big and heavy for infants to manage or books with pictures and stories that are too complex, infants won't be very interested in them. Knowing what infants of different ages do with books can help you select ones that will interest them. Here are some general guidelines to help you select appropriate books for the infants in your room.

Infants under 6 months may look at books briefly but will spend most of their time exploring books—in other words, chewing, sucking, shaking, and crumpling them. Cloth and soft vinyl books with clear, large illustrations are especially good. You can introduce infants to books by singing songs and reciting nursery rhymes as you hold and care for them. They will enjoy the rhythm of the language.

Infants from 6 to 9 months begin turning the pages of books. Small "board books" with thick cardboard pages that turn easily are good for this age. Infants at this age are very interested in what they can do with paper. To save books, give them old magazines to play with; make sure that they do not eat the paper. Hold infants on your lap when you read familiar nursery rhymes. Infants at this age are usually not yet interested in the stories themselves.

Infants from 9 to 12 months begin understanding more language and are beginning to recognize objects. A book's contents will begin capturing infants' attention, especially if it is filled with pictures of familiar objects.

Infants from 12 to 18 months begin to be interested in simple stories about events and things they know. Books with simple pictures and a few words are appropriate.

---

[5]Based on Judith A. Schickedanz, *Much More Than the ABC's: The Early Stages of Reading and Writing* (Washington, DC: National Association for the Education of Young Children, 1999), pp. 12-24.

Listed below are a few examples of books that might interest the infants in your group.

- **Books without words**

    Anno, Mitsumasa, *Anno's Flea Market* and *Anno's Journey*

    Bang, Molly, *The Grey Lady* and *The Strawberry Snatcher*

    Briggs, Raymond, *Building the Snowman* and *The Snowman*

    Day, Alexandra, *Good Dog, Carl* (and other *Carl* books)

    Hoban, Tana, *Panda, Panda* and *Children's Zoo*

    Hutchins, Pat, *Changes, Changes*

    Meyer, Mercer, *A Boy, a Dog and a Friend; A Boy, a Dog and a Frog; One Frog Too Many; Frog on His Own;* and *Frog, Where Are You?*

    McCully, Emily, *First Snow; Picnic;* and *School*

    Ormerod, Jan, *Reading* and *Dad's Back*

    Turk, Hanne, *Good Night, Max; Happy Birthday, Max; Max the Art Lover;* and *Rainy Day Max*

- **Books that are good for babyhandling** (cloth, laminated pages, etc.)

    Boynton, Sandra, *The Going to Bed Book; But Not the Hippopotamus;* and others

    Bruna, Dick, *Dressing* and *Working*

    Cohen, Marsha, *Baby's Favorite Things*

    Dunn, Phoebe, *I'm a Baby*

    Greeley, V., *Zoo Animals; Pets;* and *Field Animals*

    Miller, J., *The Cow Says Moo*

    Ricklin, Neil, *Baby's Clothes; Baby's Home; Baby's Toys;* and *Mommy and Me*

Ideas for reading to infants

- Keep in mind that sharing an experience with you, not reaching the last page, is the most important thing to the infant.

- Have an infant's attention before beginning.

- Give feedback. "Yes, that's a mommy. It looks like she's playing with her baby."

- Ask simple questions such as "what's that?" Give infants time to answer. They may answer by pointing, making a sound, or saying a word. Answer the question yourself or elaborate upon it, if necessary.

Selecting Books for Toddlers[6]

Your choice of books shapes toddlers' early feelings about books and reading. It is important to select books with simple, engaging stories and pictures that are easy to identify. Knowing what toddlers do with books can help you select books that will encourage toddlers' interests.

Toddlers' language is blossoming. Because toddlers have begun making sense of the world, they enjoy stories and like identifying objects in illustrations. Here are some general guidelines to help you select books for toddlers.

- Toddlers enjoy simple stories about the world they know. Examples of good topics include spilling milk, missing mommy and daddy, going to bed, taking a bath, and sitting on the potty chair.

- Simple stories about how things work and what makes things happen may answer some of toddlers' "why" questions and give them more information about the world. Don't be surprised, though, if the "whys" keep coming. It seems that "why" is as much a way of keeping a conversation going as of getting information.

- Predictable books that are repetitive and have rhymes will delight toddlers and help them feel secure and pleased at knowing what is going to happen.

- Illustration should follow the text very closely. They can also be packed with information and action.

Listed below are a few examples of books that may interest the toddlers in your group. You can find many others in libraries or bookstores.

- **Books about daily life routines and events that toddlers know**

  Bang, Molly, *Ten, Nine, Eight*

  Brown, Margaret Wise, *Goodnight Moon*

  Burmingham, John, *The Blanket*

  Wiekland, Ilon (illustrator), *I Can Help, Too* and *See What I Can Do*

---

[6]Based on Judith A. Schickedanz, *Much More Than the ABCs: The Early Stages of Reading and Writing* (Washington, DC: National Association for the Education of Young Children, 1999), pp. 24-29.

- **Books about separation**

  Brown, Margaret Wise, *The Runaway Bunny*

  Eastman, P., *Are You My Mother?* and *Eres Tu Mi Mama?*

- **Books about beginning concepts**

  Cristini and Puricelli, *In My Garden*

  Dorling Kindersley, *My First Look at Colors*

  Hoban, Tana, *Push-Pull, Empty-Full*

  Monrad, Jean, *How Many Kisses Good Night?*

- **Books about animals**

  Carle, Eric, *The Very Hungry Caterpillar*

  Fujikawa, Gyo, *Baby Animals*

  Spier, Peter, *Gobble, Growl, Grunt*

Ideas for Reading to Toddlers

- Expect that you will be asked to read the same book again and again. Toddlers enjoy the familiar. Knowing what is going to happen next is exciting for them.

- Repeat phrases from favorite books when not reading. For example, you might repeat the "goodnights" in *Goodnight Moon* as you help toddlers get ready for their naps.

- Pause to give toddlers time to recite phrases they know and like. For example, when reading *Are You My Mother?* by P.D. Eastman you can pause to allow the children to repeat the refrain.

- Expect that an older toddler will correct you if you skip part of a well-known book or substitute words.

- Toddlers may show interest in the text. Explain that the words tell the story. Show interested toddlers words as you read.

- Older toddlers may enjoy "reading" books aloud to themselves—especially those they know well. Surprisingly, some toddlers can remember books word for word. Encourage toddlers to sometimes "read" to themselves or to a friend.

In this learning activity you will select a book that you think is appropriate for two of the children in your room and read it to each of them. Next you will answer questions about each experience. You can find many good books at the local library or in a bookstore. Begin by reading the example that follows.

A Reading Experience

(Example)

Child _Larry_   **Age** _16 months_   **Date** _September 29_

Setting _Infant free play_   **Book** _Goodnight Moon_

Briefly describe what happened when you shared a book with this child.

> _Larry came over carrying the book. He plopped it in my lap. I opened the book to the first page. He turned the pages before I read a word. I pointed to the cat in the picture. "What's that?" I asked. Larry pointed to the cat. "It's a kitty," I said. "It says meow." "Meow," said Larry. He laughed. He got up and carried the book across the room._

What do you think this child experienced as you read together?

> _I think he wanted to be with me. He likes turning the pages of a book. He enjoyed saying "meow." He likes different sounds. He really didn't want to read the whole book._

What was this activity like for you?

> _I like reading books with children. When Larry jumped up and carried the book away, I felt a little frustrated and disappointed._

If you were explaining to a new caregiver how to read a book, what would you say?

> _Don't expect to sit and read a whole book. You are helping children learn about books even though they just drop by and look at a book for a few seconds._

A Reading Experience

Child _____ Age _____ Date _____

Setting _____ Book _____

Briefly describe what happened when you shared a book with this child.

_____

_____

_____

_____

What do you think this child experienced as you read together?

_____

_____

_____

_____

What was this activity like for you?

_____

_____

_____

If you were explaining to a new caregiver how to read a book, what would you say?

_____

_____

_____

_____

A Reading Experience

Child _____   Age _____   Date _____

Setting _____   Book _____

Briefly describe what happened when you shared a book with this child.

_____

_____

_____

_____

What do you think this child experienced as you read together?

_____

_____

_____

_____

What was this activity like for you?

_____

_____

_____

_____

If you were explaining to a new caregiver how to read a book, what would you say?

_____

_____

_____

_____

V. Setting the Stage for Writing and Reading

In this activity you will learn:

- to identify the kinds of skills and understanding that build a foundation for writing and reading; and

- to create an environment that promotes development of the skills needed to write and read.

Most people agree that language development begins long before a child can speak in sentences. If you ask people when children begin to write and read, they often answer "in kindergarten." In fact, the ability to write and read has its foundation long before. Although formal attempts to teach very young children to write and read are inappropriate, caregivers can provide a rich environment that introduces infants and toddlers to written communication in appropriate ways.

The developmental process through which children become literate is referred to as emerging literacy—how children learn to use language. Young children learn to read and write through regular exposure to literacy activities in their homes and child care centers. They learn about the importance of written language when they see their parents and caregivers reading print in a variety of places—books, charts, the bulletin board—and writing—shopping lists, greeting cards, notes to each other. It takes a long time for children to make sense of language. They need to figure out for themselves: "What is the difference between drawing and writing?" "What does it mean when my caregiver uses a different tone of voice?" "What do the symbols in books have to do with the words that people say out loud?"

The Foundation for Writing

Infants and toddlers like to imitate adults. You may find mobile infants and toddlers reaching for your pencil or pen whenever you are writing near them. They are interested in the object itself as well as in what you are doing with it. They think making marks on paper is fascinating.

Making marks—scribbling—is the beginning of writing. It is a good idea to show mobile infants how to use crayons. (Young infants will end up eating them.) Large crayons will be easier for young children to hold and will not break so quickly. Provide large sheets of plain paper for them to crayon on so they can move their arms as they make creative strokes. Eventually they will make smaller, more controlled marks.

Toddlers love to scribble. By giving them the opportunity to scribble with crayons, markers, chalk, and other writing tools, you are helping them develop skills they need to write. Here are some suggestions for encouraging toddlers' scribbles.

- Provide large sheets of plain paper so they can move their arms as they make creative strokes. The large motions they will use in the beginning will eventually become smaller, more controlled marks. Within a few years, toddlers will develop into children who are able to write letters on a line.

- Don't try to control or direct toddlers' scribbling except to remind them to keep their marks on the paper.

- Scribbling follows a definite progression. Younger toddlers usually begin with a series of horizontal lines. Later vertical lines appear, then nonending circles. Observe to see how each toddler progresses.

- Comment about the lines on the paper. You might want to say, "You've made lots of blue marks" or "Those spirals fill the page." Avoid asking toddlers what they are drawing or writing. They enjoy the experience itself and are probably not trying to make a product.

Although making a scrawling line across paper may seem a long way from writing, it isn't. It's a necessary step in learning to write.

The Foundation for Reading

The most important factors influencing a child's ability to learn to read are a strong desire to read and contact with print. Children who have enjoyed listening to and looking at books from infancy will have had five years of happy experiences with reading by the time they reach kindergarten.

Infants and toddlers can learn many things about reading books:

- **Reading books is enjoyable.** Cuddling with a special adult, hearing the words, and looking at the pictures give even the youngest children good feelings about books and reading.

- **Books are related to their lives.** Sammy (12 months) may get a toy car off the shelf after seeing one in a book. Caregivers can write stories about people and events that children are familiar with so they associate books with real life.

- **What books are like.** Infants begin with the basics of what books feel and taste like and progress to knowing how to turn the pages and how the book should be held. While Jerry (4 months) chews on the corner of a book, Henry (17 months) may settle his stuffed dog on his lap and, opening the first page of a book, begin "reading" it to his special friend. Toddlers learn to turn a book so its pictures are right side up.

- **Books connect words and images.** Older infants know that the pictures and the words on a page go together. When June (18 months) sees the picture of the cricket in *The Very Quiet Cricket*, she whispers "chirp, chirp," which is what the cricket says. Gwen (32 months) moves her finger along a line with text and, if she's heard the story many times, may tell you what it says.

Creating an Environment That Promotes Writing and Reading Skills

Being in an environment where reading, books, and writing are part of daily life encourages infants and toddlers to learn about writing and reading. Here are some examples of ways the environment can promote an interest in writing and reading.

- **Make writing and reading daily activities at the center.** Sit at a low table to write a list of what to get from the storeroom so children can see you writing. Explain what you are doing. "I'm writing the words for juice and paper towels so we remember to get them in the store room."

  Point out signs as you take a walk. "That sign says 'Don't Walk,' so we'll wait until it is our turn to cross the street."

  Take children on trips to deliver a note to your director or to mail a letter. "Do you want to help me deliver this message to Mrs. Crandall?"

- **Create a book area.**

  A corner of the room is best because traffic won't be continually moving through the space. The area should be covered with soft carpeting and perhaps some pillows to make it a comfortable place to sit.

  Books need not stay only in the book area. Young children often pick up a book, look at it for a few seconds, and then carry it with them across the room where they may look at it again. This is fine. Think of a book area as the place where children can find books and where you can read with a child out of the mainstream of traffic.

  Books should be displayed clearly so children can see the covers and choose the book they want, not just the book that happens to be on top of a pile. Display books on a low shelf.

  Spend time in the book corner yourself. Your presence says clearly that books and reading are important.

- **Have comfortable chairs** where you and a child can sit and read together.

- **Involve mobile infants and toddlers in taking care of books.** Explain that books are important and that you are all going to take care of the books in your room. Model good care of books. When a book is torn, involve children in getting the tape and fixing it. You will be telling and showing them that books are valuable.

- **Make pictures part of the environment.** Some of the best books for infants and toddlers are homemade. It's easy to do. Cut familiar pictures from magazines. Choose large, colorful drawings, or photographs. Glue the pictures on sturdy cardboard and cover with clear, self-sticking plastic. Punch holes and string the pages together with a cord or ribbon. Include photographs of caregivers and infants and toddlers in the books that you make.

  Texture or "feel" books are also fun for infants and toddlers. Use cloth for the pages. Sew different fabrics on each page. Use different shapes. You might use circles, squares, and triangles. Or you might cut your fabric in the shapes of animals or flowers. Sew everything securely.

- **Provide materials and activities that encourage language and story telling.** Children will develop language skills as they play with puppets, flannel boards, dramatic play props, and people in the block area.

If you work with infants, in this learning activity you will make a picture collection and use your pictures to promote an infant's language and reading skills. If you work with toddlers, you will keep a list of all the activities you do in one week to promote the language and reading skills of toddlers. Review the examples before doing your own activities.

Begin a collection of pictures for the infants in your room. Select pictures you think will promote infants' communication skills. Here is an example of what one caregiver did.

Promoting Communication Skills
(Infant Example)

Child _Dan_   **Age** _9 months_   **Date** _February 18-28_

Setting _Book corner_

List ten pictures in your collection. Each picture should be of something that infants recognize:

1. _Dog_
2. _Baby shoes_
3. _Baby_
4. _Spoon_
5. _Banana_

6. _Flower_
7. _Cat_
8. _Cup_
9. _Father_
10. _Mother_

Briefly describe what happened when you introduced the pictures to an infant.

At first Dan (9 months) tried to eat the pictures. Then he began dumping them all on the floor and crawling over them. I know Dan likes dogs, so I showed him a picture of a dog. At first he didn't pay much attention, but then I began barking and he laughed. He looked at the picture and looked at me and tried to bark, too.

Try this activity several times over the next two weeks. Describe any changes in what the infant does.

When I bring out the container with pictures, Dan reaches in for a picture. He still may try to eat one, but he looks at them a little longer. When we look at the dog picture, he looks up at me as if waiting for me to bark—which I do. Then we laugh.

How do you think this activity is setting the stage for reading and writing?

Dan is learning to pay attention to something. He is learning that pictures are about things he knows and finds interesting.

Promoting Communication Skills

Child _____ Age _____ Date _____

Setting _____

List ten pictures in your collection. Each picture should be of something that infants recognize:

1. _____

2. _____

3. _____

4. _____

5. _____

6. _____

7. _____

8. _____

9. _____

10. _____

Briefly describe what happened when you introduced the pictures to an infant.

_____

_____

_____

_____

_____

Try this activity several times over the next two weeks. Describe any changes in what the infant does.

_____

_____

_____

_____

_____

How do you think this activity is setting the stage for reading and writing?

_____

_____

_____

_____

_____

Keep a diary of activities you introduced to help toddlers develop the skills needed for reading and writing.

Promoting Communication Skills
(Toddler Example)

Child(ren) *Jerry, Larry, Henry* **Age(s)** *24-32 months* **Date(s)** *Week of June 13-17*

Date	Activity
6/13	*I taped a large sheet of brown paper on the floor and let toddlers scribble on it.*
	I took Jerry (24 months) with me to the director's office to pick up my mail. There was a piece of junk mail I didn't want, so I gave it to him. He was very proud to get his own mail.
6/14	*I took Larry (29 months) and Henry (32 months) on a walk around the center and pointed out signs we passed. I pointed to the signs as I read signs like EXIT and Ms. Toby (the name of our director) on the door.*
	I used a flannel board with a small group of toddlers and encouraged them to tell a story using the figures.
6/15	*I let toddlers help me replace their name labels on their cubbies. As we taped up the labels, we read children's names and held the labels by each child's picture.*

COMMUNICATION

Promoting Communication Skills

Child(ren) _____   Age(s) _____   Date(s) _____

Date   Activity

_____   _____

                     _____

                     _____

                     _____

_____   _____

                     _____

                     _____

                     _____

                     _____

                     _____

                     _____

_____   _____

                     _____

                     _____

                     _____

                     _____

_____   _____

                     _____

                     _____

                     _____

                     _____

_____   _____

                     _____

                     _____

                     _____

Share and discuss what you did in this learning activity with your trainer.

Summarizing Your Progress

You have now completed all of the learning activities for this module. Whether you are an experienced caregiver or a new one, this module has probably helped you develop new skills in promoting children's communication. Before you go on, take a few minutes to summarize what you've learned.

- Turn back to Learning Activity I, Using Your Knowledge of Infant and Toddler Development to Promote Communication, and add to the chart specific examples of how you promoted the communications skills of infants and toddlers during the time you were working on this module.

- Next, review your responses to the pre-training assessment for this module. Write a summary of what you learned and list the skills you developed or improved.

_____

_____

_____

_____

_____

_____

_____

_____

_____

Your final step in this module is to complete the knowledge and competency assessments. Let your trainer know when you are ready to schedule the assessments. After you have successfully completed these assessments, you will be ready to start a new module. Congratulations on your progress so far, and good luck with your next module.

Answer Sheet: Promoting Children's Communication

Interacting with Infants and Toddlers in Ways That Encourage Them to Communicate Their Thoughts and Feelings

1. **How did Ms. Bates encourage Eddie to communicate his thoughts and feelings?**

   a. She asked him questions and talked with him even though he couldn't say anything yet.

   b. She noticed his interest in the mobile, and instead of immediately taking him off the changing table, she gave him time to watch the mobile and communicate about it.

2. **How did Ms. Bates let Eddie know that she was listening to him?**

   a. She took time to follow Eddie's gaze up at the mobile even though he didn't say any words.

   b. She gave words for what she thought he might be saying.

   c. She tapped the mobile and talked about it when she noticed he was interested in it.

Providing Materials and Activities That Promote Communication Skills

1. **How did Mr. Jones use a walk to promote communication skills?**

   a. He asked Kara and Grace what they saw on their walk.

   b. He suggested that they write a story about their walk.

2. **How did Ms. Moore promote communication skills as she helped Grace and Kara write a story?**

   a. She encouraged them to "write" in their own ways even though they couldn't write letters yet.

   b. She wrote the words that the girls dictated to her.

   c. She read the girls' words aloud to them.

Helping Infants and Toddlers Develop Listening and Speaking Skills

1. **How was Ms. Gonzalez able to understand what Dora said to her?**

    a.   Dora got her attention by saying "bah, bah."

    b.   She observed Dora stretching her arm toward the shelf.

    c.   She observed Dora gazing up at the shelf.

    d.   Ms. Gonzalez knew what is kept on the shelf.

    e.   Dora must have had fun with the ball earlier, because Ms. Gonzalez asked her, "Play with the ball again?"

    f.   Ms. Gonzalez asked Dora, "Ball?" When Dora got excited, Ms. Gonzalez knew that was what Dora wanted.

2. **How will Ms. Gonzalez's note to Dora's family help Dora develop listening and speaking skills?**

    a.   Dora's family will probably let her know they're happy she's learning to talk and to ask for what she needs or wants.

    b.   Dora's family might encourage her to play ball to give her a chance to practice her new word.

    c.   Dora's family might encourage her to say other words that begin with the "b" sound—"bath," "baby," "bye-bye," and so on.

    d.   Dora's family might observe her gestures and listen more carefully to figure out other words that she begins to use to ask for things.

    e.   Dora's family will know that Ms. Gonzalez is interested in what new words Dora is beginning to use at home, and they are likely to share her words with Ms. Gonzalez.

    f.   Dora's family will feel like partners with Ms. Gonzalez in Dora's language development.

Using Your Knowledge of Infant and Toddler Development to Promote Communication Skills

WHAT YOUNG INFANTS DO (0-8 MONTHS)	HOW CAREGIVERS CAN USE THIS INFORMATION TO PROMOTE COMMUNICATION
They communicate from birth by moving, crying, cooing, and making sounds.	Try to understand what different movements and cries mean and respond appropriately to help infants learn that their communications can lead to responses. Make interesting sounds, and sing to encourage them to practice listening.
They respond to voices.	Talk with infants as you care for them. Tell infants what you are doing, and pause to give them time to respond so they can experience what a conversation feels like.
They "talk" to themselves as well as to others, particularly people they know well.	Respond to infants' babbling and cooing. Be sure each infant has a special caregiver. Having someone special to "talk" with encourages infants to communicate more.
They make a variety of sounds—crying, coos, whimpers, and gurgles—to express feelings.	Respond to infants' sounds. Talk with infants—especially during caregiving routines. Tell infants ahead of time what is going to happen. Even though they don't understand all the words you say, they will be learning that people communicate about things they do together.
WHAT MOBILE INFANTS DO (9-17 MONTHS)	
They pay attention to conversations.	Include infants in conversations. Show respect by not talking about infants when they are present.
They are interested in picture books.	Read books with infants. Write simple books for infants about things and people they know to help them see that books are related to their lives. Share your interest and enthusiasm about books with infants.

WHAT MOBILE INFANTS DO (9-17 MONTHS)	HOW CAREGIVERS CAN USE THIS INFORMATION TO PROMOTE COMMUNICATION
They use words such as "mama" and "dada."	Encourage infants to say words by sharing your excitement and pleasure when they say a word. When a child's home language is different from yours, arrange for an adult who speaks that language to spend some time with you. Learning a few words of a child's home language will help you build a trusting relationship with that child.
They know that words stand for objects.	Name and talk about things in the room and outdoors to help expand infants' vocabulary.
They may be able to say 10 or more words.	Talk with infants. Expand on what they say to model complete sentences. For example, when an infant points to a truck on the counter and says "truck," ask, "Do you want the truck?"
WHAT TODDLERS DO (18-36 MONTHS)	
Their language development is rapidly expanding.	Encourage toddlers' language by talking with them even though you don't understand everything they are saying. Encourage toddlers to talk with each other.
They understand simple directions and may follow them if they are in a cooperative mood.	Help toddlers practice following verbal directions by giving them simple directions to follow. For example, say, "Will you get your coat, please?" or "Put the paintbrush in the can." Understand that toddlers may or may not follow your directions.
They enjoy listening to simple stories about familiar things and people.	Read with toddlers. Set up a "reading nook" with simple books about things toddlers know. Write books with toddlers about things that happen at the center.
They gather information about the world by asking "why?" and "what's this?"	Offer simple stories about how things work or what makes things happen. Talk with toddlers about what you are doing together.

COMMUNICATION

WHAT TODDLERS DO (18-36 MONTHS)	HOW CAREGIVERS CAN USE THIS INFORMATION TO PROMOTE COMMUNICATION
They gather information about the world by asking "why?" and "what's this?"	Offer simple stories about how things work or what makes things happen. Talk with toddlers about what you are doing together.
They develop more complex pretend play.	Provide an area where older toddlers can play without being interrupted. Provide props such as a doll crib, a stroller, plates, and spoons to extend their play with dolls. You will be helping them learn to order and extend their thinking, which is necessary for communicating.
They make mistakes in using rules of grammar.	Accept toddlers' way of speaking to encourage them to talk more. Serve as a model by speaking clearly and correctly.
They can hold fat crayons or pencils and make marks on paper.	Encourage toddlers' interest in writing. Talk to them about writing that you do—making lists and so on. Provide a variety of paper and "writing implements" they can use to scribble.
They are interested in what adults do.	Encourage toddlers' interest in reading and writing. For example, point out that that you are reading the recipe when you cook together and that you are writing a list of supplies so you can remember what to get from the kitchen.

Glossary

Communication	The act of expressing and sharing ideas, desires, and feelings.
Emerging literacy	The developmental process through which children become literate, including speaking, reading, and writing.
Language	A system of words or signs and rules for use in self-expression and reading.
Nonverbal communication	The act of conveying feelings or ideas without using language.
Reading skills	Visual and perceptual skills needed to read, including recognizing differences and similarities and following sequences in the direction of the written language (English uses a left-to-right sequence).